SHADOW GOVERNMENT:

What Obama Doesn't Want You to Know About His Czars

By
Scott Wheeler and Peter Leitner

Capitol Media Group, LLC
344 Maple Avenue West #375
Vienna, Virginia 22186

ISBN 0615368964   978-0-615-36896-2

Printed in the United States of America on acid-free
paper that meets the American National Standards
Institute Z39-48 Standard.

Special Thanks to Oleg Atbashian for cover design, research, editing and writing and to Andy Madden for research and writing

Table of Contents

Afpak Czar — Richard Holbrooke

Official title:	Special Representative for Afghanistan and Pakistan
Official responsibilities:	To coordinate U.S. efforts in Afghanistan and Pakistan
Reports to:	Secretary of State
Senate confirmation:	None
Salary:	Information unavailable
Ideology / political affiliation:	Longtime partisan Democrat, with his only higher allegiance lying with himself and his personal legend

President Obama and Secretary of State Hillary Clinton have decided to attach one of the world's most delicate regions, Afghanistan and Pakistan, or Afpak as they call it, to quite possibly the country's most volatile diplomat: Slobodan Milosevic's favorite American,[1] Richard Holbrooke. The move is a political stroke akin to tying a Fabergé egg to the rear bumper of an El Camino.

Holbrooke is difficult to work with, distrusted in the region he is being sent to negotiate with, brash, seemingly corrupt, and shamelessly egotistical, which apparently in this administration qualifies him to serve in a loosely defined, freshly created position, with questionable checks on his power and few identifiable goals to be held to achieving.

Who Is Richard Holbrooke?

A fixture of the Democrats' foreign policy establishment, Holbrooke has 45 years of experience in putting wrong-headed foreign policy ideas into practice, from appeasing North Vietnamese politburo members at the pointless Paris peace talks to the current negotiations with leaders of Iran and the Taliban, which are likely to bring predictably similar results.

Born in April 1941 in New York City, Richard Holbrooke earned a B.A. from Brown University in 1962. During the Vietnam War, he served as a staff assistant at the U.S. Embassy in Saigon, which qualified him to join President Johnson's team of Vietnam experts in the White House. Successfully climbing the career ladder, Holbrooke later helped to undermine the war effort by drafting a volume of the infamous "Pentagon Papers." It happened when Defense Department officials, tasked with compiling a classified history of U.S. involvement in Vietnam, assigned the actual writing to left-wing opponents of the war, such as Holbrooke. In 1971, this "secret history" emerged into public view. Describing the Vietnam War as unwinnable, it had a harsh, demoralizing effect on the country.

Holbrooke's subsequent career easily fits into election cycles. With Democrats losing the White House to Nixon in 1972, he moved on to spread his ideology as managing editor of *Foreign Policy* magazine. Four years later, he was reactivated as national security coordinator for Jimmy Carter's 1976 presidential campaign, later becoming Carter's one-term assistant secretary of state for East Asian and Pacific affairs.

After Reagan's landslide victory in 1980, Holbrooke spent three long Republican terms at Lehman Brothers, while also managing his own Washington-based consulting firm, Public Strategies. In 1988, he made a futile attempt to regain relevancy as policy adviser in Al Gore's failed presidential bid, but success had to wait until the next cycle. In 1992, he became campaign adviser to Bill Clinton, who later appointed Holbrooke to important positions inside the State Department. The high point of Holbrooke's career was his role as the architect of the 1995 Dayton Peace Accords, which put an end to Yugoslavia by splitting it into several independent nations. Toward the end of Clinton's presidency, Holbrooke also became U.S. ambassador to the United Nations, replacing Bill Richardson.

Another loss of the White House to the Republicans meant another exile in the private sector for Holbrooke. This time he joined the board of directors of American International Group. During this period, 2001 to 2008, AIG engaged in wildly speculative credit-default insurance schemes that threatened to topple the entire American financial system. Some believe that had Democrat John Kerry won the presidential election in 2004, Holbrooke most likely would have been his choice for secretary of state.

In 2007, continuing with his wrong-headed approach to foreign policy, Holbrooke called for "a new strategy in Iraq," advocating "a careful, phased redeployment of U.S. troops." It was the exact opposite of the subsequent victorious troop surge that achieved the overall objective of establishing a unified, democratic, self-governing and self-sustaining Iraq that became our ally in the war on terrorism. Today, on Holbrooke's advice, President Obama has declared an end to the war on terror and assigned Holbrooke to negotiate with terrorists in Afghanistan.

A History of Corruption

One of the first steps Holbrooke took as a czar was to denounce Afghan President and American ally Hamid Karzai's government as a failure, in large part because of "massive, officially sanctioned corruption."[2] In fairness to Holbrooke, this is a topic he knows something about. In 1998, Bill Clinton nominated Holbrooke, then the vice chairman of Credit Suisse First Boston, as America's United Nations ambassador, but he was not confirmed for over a year, as the process was retarded by Republican allegations that he did favors for Credit Suisse while still employed by the government,[3] as well as a federal ethics inquiry into his inappropriate contact with embassies. Holbrooke denied any wrongdoing and, like any other innocent man, agreed to pay the Justice Department $5,000 to settle the charges and end the investigation.[4]

In 2008, Holbrooke surfaced as one of the high-ranking public officials to have received a cut-rate loan as a part of the Countrywide VIP Program scandal. These so-called Friends of Angelo's (a reference to the Countrywide CEO at the time, Angelo

3

Mozilo) received preferential treatment in what appeared to be an effort by Countrywide to buy influence.[5] Holbrooke, his wife, and his son all received special loans through this ruse.[6]

To add an extra tier to the hypocrisy, Holbrooke also happened to be on the board of directors at AIG when the company voted to dish out at least $165 million in bonuses[7] to traders in the Financial Products Division, a group of people who played a key role in creating the current economic disaster.[8] Obama has been fighting to block these bonuses, calling them an unjustifiable "outrage," an issue that is not simply about economics but "about our fundamental values." Obama railed on behalf of small-business owners, proclaiming, "And all they ask is that everyone, from Main Street to Wall Street to Washington, play by the same rules. That is an ethic that we have to demand."[9] Apparently, in the Obama administration, demanding this ethic, which is pertinent to our fundamental values, does not preclude you from naming one of the men directly responsible for said affront to basic decency to a position of immense power in a very ethically ambiguous part of the world.

Volatile Egotism

Holbrooke's greed manifests itself not only in monetary transactions. In fact, what he seems to be most hungry for is reputation. Many have bemoaned his constant pleas for attention from the news media.[10] A maniacal egotist, the man actually employs a personal archivist[11] and often alienates the people he works with,[12] which could be seen as a major problem for a negotiator. It also seems that it would be a negative for someone who is working in a brand-new and undefined capacity where there is no pre-existing vertical structure. Or someone who is going to be working side by side with another strong personality in Gen. David Petraeus. Petraeus has become accustomed to being the most powerful American in the region and may not appreciate Holbrooke's histrionics intruding into his domain.[13]

Holbrooke's old pal Hillary Clinton admits that he sometimes must be "brought down to earth and reined in."[14] His style can be described as pyrotechnical, which could have some very harmful consequences in what is commonly referred to as the most problematic region on the planet. Even friends describe him as "the diplomatic equivalent of a hydrogen bomb."[15]

Questionable Company

While he supported his buddy Hillary Clinton during the primaries, Holbrooke was careful to keep paths open should Obama win the nomination. He had two close friends in the Obama camp, both of whom were exiled from the team, surely because of their tact and habits of not doing anything a presidential candidate would have to disassociate himself from.[16] And the fact that Clinton now occupies the secretary of state position that Holbrooke has been so often considered for could pose problems. Holbrooke's history indicates that his selfish ambition prevents him from being able to work successfully under those close to him. Early in his career, Holbrooke worked in the U.S. Foreign Service in Vietnam with Anthony Lake, and he says that the two were best friends. He went so far as to name one of his sons Anthony. So when Lake was named national security adviser under Bill Clinton while Holbrooke was left out of the administration, Holbrooke did what any good friend would do: He allowed jealousy and tension to percolate into animosity until the friendship was over.[17] So there is little reason to expect that things should go smoothly as Holbrooke now reports directly to the woman he mentored. After advising her on policy for so long, it seems unlikely that he will be happy taking a subordinate position to her now. Holbrooke also signed the papers recommending that M. Larry Lawrence, who served as U.S. ambassador to Switzerland, be buried in Arlington Cemetery. Lawrence had made fraudulent claims to being injured on a Merchant Marine ship during World War II, and when the claims were discovered to be false, his body was exhumed and removed from the cemetery.[18]

An Undefined Role

When dealing with someone as potentially problematic as
Holbrooke, it would seem important to try to keep him in line by
giving him a defined job, with specific goals, within an established
chain of command. Obama and Clinton, on the other hand, have
decided it would be a better bet to create a brand-new role for
Holbrooke, so there is no precedent for what powers he possesses
and what checks exist on those powers. People appointed to
similar positions are generally classified as envoys, which puts
them within the framework of the State Department, while
Holbrooke was given the title of representative, giving him extra
negotiating power and making it difficult to discern what exactly
falls under his jurisdiction. It is not clear whether he or the
traditional State Department overseers now control the U.S.
Embassies in Afghanistan and Pakistan. His position seems to
overlap with pre-existing parts of the State Department, but he is
reporting directly to the president, through Secretary Clinton.[19]
This seems to be either an unnatural extension of presidential
authority or a wild man acting without proper supervision.

As undefined as his responsibilities are, there is even less
delineation as to what he is expected to accomplish. For a man
who never shies away from publicity, Holbrooke is exceptionally
vague when describing what exactly he is setting out to achieve.
He is bold enough to create his own think tank on Afghanistan
that recommends that the United States declare an end (a
surrender?) to the "war on terror" and begin negotiating with
members of the Taliban,[20] yet he will not spell out what will
constitute progress in the region beyond "we'll know it when we
see it."[21]

Bad Reputation

On top of everything else, Holbrooke is already on poor terms
with most of the region he has just been assigned to. In addition to

his attacks on Karzai, Holbrooke has opened fire on U.S. Ambassador to Afghanistan William Wood, by likening him to Saddam Hussein's genocidal cousin Ali Hassan Majid. And the new U.S. message has not impressed Kabul.[22]

Additionally, his negotiating style and the region may be ill matched. In the Balkans, his main weapon to pressure Milosevic was the threat of bombings and military assault, threats that carry little weight in this region. The culture is not conducive to the typical U.S. diplomacy that Holbrooke practices, and there has been very little ground given on the key issues by any side.[23]

Holbrooke's credibility as a negotiator may have taken a hit in the eyes of those he will be negotiating with, as his claim to fame, the Dayton Peace Accords, has been tarnished by allegations from former Bosnian Serb leader Radovan Karadzic. Karadzic maintained that Holbrooke promised that he would not be tried for any war crimes if he would "become invisible long enough for the Dayton agreement to be implemented in full." Holbrooke vehemently denied these claims, and while it is hard to simply take Karadzic at his word, it is not unreasonable to think that the allegations will raise doubts in the minds of the Taliban members that he is negotiating with in Afpak.[24]

— *Rick Rush*

---

[1] "Richard C. Holbrooke," Who Runs GOV, <http://www.whorunsgov.com/Profiles/Richard_C._Holbrooke>
[2] Paul Richter, "Appointment of Holbrooke Unnerves South Asia," Feb. 2, 2009, *Los Angeles Times*, <http://articles.latimes.com/2009/feb/02/world/fg-holbrooke2>
[3] "Richard C. Holbrooke," Who Runs GOV, <http://www.whorunsgov.com/Profiles/Richard_C._Holbrooke>.
[4] Phillip Shenon, "Senate Confirms U.N. Appointment After 14 Months," *The New York Times*, Aug. 6, 1999
[5] Lisa Myers and Amna Nawaz, "Feds Probe Countrywide's 'VIP' program," Oct. 30, 2008, *Deep Background: NBC News Investigates*, <http://deepbackground.msnbc.msn.com/archive/2008/10/30/161387 7.aspx>

[6] Marc Gunther, "It's the Directors, Stupid," March 22, 2009, Marc Gunther, <http://www.marcgunther.com/2009/03/22/its-the-directors-stupid/>

[7] Ibid.

[8] "Obama Tries to Stop AIG Bonuses: 'How Do They Justify This Outrage?' " CNNPolitics.com, <http://www.cnn.com/2009/POLITICS/03/16/AIG.bonuses/index.html>

[9] Ibid.

[10] Jodi Kantor, "Back on World Stage, a Larger-Than-Life Holbrooke," Feb. 7, 2009, *The New York Times*, <http://www.nytimes.com/2009/02/08/us/politics/08holbrooke.html?_r=2>

[11] Ibid.

[12] "Richard C. Holbrooke," Who Runs GOV, <http://www.whorunsgov.com/Profiles/Richard_C._Holbrooke>

[13] Paul Richter, "Appointment of Holbrooke Unnerves South Asia," Feb. 2, 2009. *Los Angeles Times*, <http://articles.latimes.com/2009/feb/02/world/fg-holbrooke2>

[14] Jodi Kantor, "Back on World Stage, a Larger-Than-Life Holbrooke," Feb. 7, 2009, *The New York Times*, <http://www.nytimes.com/2009/02/08/us/politics/08holbrooke.html?_r=2>

[15] Ibid.

[16] "Richard C. Holbrooke," Who Runs GOV, <http://www.whorunsgov.com/Profiles/Richard_C._Holbrooke>

[17] Ibid.

[18] Gerry Braun, "Former Ambassador Who Faked War Record Reburied in San Diego," Arlington National Cemetery Website, <http://www.arlingtoncemetery.net/abuse34.htm>

[19] Jodi Kantor, "Back on World Stage, a Larger-Than-Life Holbrooke," Feb. 7, 2009, *The New York Times*, <http://www.nytimes.com/2009/02/08/us/politics/08holbrooke.html?_r=2>

[20] Ibid.

[21] "Richard C. Holbrooke," Who Runs GOV, <http://www.whorunsgov.com/Profiles/Richard_C._Holbrooke>

[22] Paul Richter, "Appointment of Holbrooke Unnerves South Asia," Feb. 2, 2009. *Los Angeles Times*, <http://articles.latimes.com/2009/feb/02/world/fg-holbrooke2>

[23] Ibid.

[24][24] Nic Robertson, " Karadzic Details 'Deal' With U.S. to Vanish," CNN.com/Europe, <http://www.cnn.com/2008/WORLD/europe/08/01/karadzictrial/index.html>

AIDS Czar — Jeffrey Crowley

Official title:	Director of the Office of National AIDS Policy
Salary / Direct cost to taxpayers:	$102,000
Responsibilities:	Coordinating AIDS policy both internationally and domestically
Reports to:	President Obama, Director of the Domestic Policy Council Melody Barnes
Senate confirmation:	None
Relation to Obama:	None prior to appointment
Ideology / political affiliation:	Liberal, former gay rights activist and advocate of free health care for people living with AIDS[1]

Who Is the AIDS Czar?

Jeffrey Crowley, M.P.H., is one of the very few of Obama's appointees who will occupy a familiar position: the AIDS czar. Bill Clinton first created this position in 1993, and it has been occupied on a fairly regular basis ever since. Crowley is now serving as the director of the Office of National AIDS Policy, a post that had been vacant for the past two years.

Crowley, who is openly gay, has been in the AIDS business for years, working his way up the ranks of the National Association of People with AIDS, from public policy intern in 1994 to deputy executive director for programs from 1997 to 2000. For the past nine years, Crowley has been working as a senior researcher at Georgetown University's Institute for Health Care Research and Policy. He holds a bachelor's degree in chemistry from Kalamazoo College and a master's in public health from Johns Hopkins University. The White House press release names "Medicaid policy; including Medicaid prescription drug policies; Medicare policy; and consumer education and training" as his areas of expertise[2].

The gay community has lauded 43-year-old Crowley's appointment. In fact, the Gay and Lesbian Leadership Institute's Presidential Appointments Project — described as a "talent bank for openly LGBT professionals seeking appointed positions in the next presidential administration"[3] — even recommended him for the job[4].

— *Lucy Leitner*

[1] Davids, Julie. "New AIDS Czar, Noted Medicaid Geek, Widely Praised by Advocates." Weblog entry. AIDS Connect: Your Chicago HIV/AIDS Community. Feb. 26, 2009. Aug. 31, 2009 <http://www.aidsconnect.net/?q=content/blog/new-aids-czar-noted-medicaid-geek-widely-praised-advocates>.
[2] Ibid.
[3] *Gay and Lesbian Leadership Institute*. The Gay and Lesbian Leadership Institute. Aug. 31, 2009 <http://www.glli.org/presidential>.
[4] "Obama Names Gay Man to Lead Office of National AIDS Policy." GayPolitics.com. Feb. 26, 2009. Gay and Lesbian Victory Fund and Leadership Institute. Aug. 31, 2009 <http://www.gaypolitics.com/2009/02/26/obama-names-gay-man-to-lead-office-of-national-aids-policy/>.

Auto Recovery Czar–Ed Montgomery

Official title:	Director of Recovery for Auto Communities and Workers
Official responsibilities:	Support the auto industry with government resources[1]
Reports to:	Economic Advisor Larry Summers, Secretary of Labor Hilda Solis
Senate confirmation:	None
Salary:	Information unavailable
Ideology / political affiliation:	Liberal, former ACORN board member, on academic advisory committee for Soros-funded Center for American Progress (CAP)[2]

Who Is the Auto Recovery Czar?

Pittsburgh native and economist Ed Montgomery has spent much of his career in academia. He has taught at Carnegie Mellon University, Michigan State University and the University of Maryland. He completed the apparent prerequisite to an Obama czarship by serving in the Clinton administration. Under Clinton, he was the chief economist in the Labor Department and the principal representative to the Council of Economic Advisors.[3] He specializes in job training and local development.[4]

What is the problem?

Montgomery has some serious damage to clean up. The auto industry shed over 400,000 jobs over 2008 and 2009, leaving towns built on the industry in total devastation.[5] His work will be targeted at the "Rust Belt," the former industrial powerhouse region centered in Michigan, Ohio and Indiana. Michigan, the worst hit of all had an unemployment rate of 14.9% in January 2010, the worst rate in America.[6] Flint, Michigan, once a centerpiece of General Motors, is now down to 7,500 GM jobs.[7] And the auto jobs are not coming back.

What are they planning to do about it?

The government is planning a drastic overhaul that even the administration admits will cause even more job loss.[8] So they threw a czar at it. Obama announced Montgomery as follows:

> I'm designating a new Director of Recovery for Auto Communities and Workers to cut through the red tape and ensure that the full resources of our federal government are leveraged to assist the workers, communities, and regions that rely on our auto industry. Edward Montgomery, a former Deputy Labor Secretary, has agreed to serve in this role.
>
> And together with Labor Secretary Solis and my Auto Task Force, Ed will help provide support to auto workers and their families, and open up opportunity to manufacturing communities in Michigan and Ohio and Indiana and every other state that relies on the auto industry.
>
> They will have a strong advocate in Ed. He will direct a comprehensive effort that will help lift up the hardest-hit areas by using the unprecedented levels of funding available in our Recovery Act and throughout our government to create new manufacturing jobs and new businesses where they're needed most -- in your communities. And he will also lead an effort to identify new initiatives we may need to help support your communities going forward.[9]

Basically, all of that just means that the government is dumping a lot of its stimulus money on this problem, and Montgomery is going to decide where it lands. It also seems he will be spending quite a bit of time trying to get people to use programs that already exist. The Workforce Investment Act, a retraining program Montgomery helped create, is getting an extra $1.25 billion to help dislocated workers, and states can apply for grant money. The government aims to create jobs relating to technology and energy, while Montgomery will try to entice defense, research and green industries to the region. The stimulus program calls for major infrastructure projects to create more jobs as well.

Montgomery is also taking on an ambassador-esque role. He is supposed to be spending time in the Rust Belt and return to Washington to speak the workers' minds.[10]

What has he been doing?

Montgomery has certainly been making his appearances. He attending a meeting in Flint and toured a GM plant there. He heard the community leaders' opinions and watched workers on an assembly line.[11] He has also attended a workshop in Detroit on how to apply for federal grants and other financial assistance.[12] He has also announced some very expensive projects, including $25 million in stimulus funds to retrain ex-auto workers[13] and $10.3 million from the Environmental Protection Agency for brownfield cleanup.[14] Whether using a czar to heighten the profile of these efforts actually helps anyone other than the administration is another question.

Why do we need an auto recovery czar?

As with many czarships, it is easy to question the need for an auto recovery czar. He is dealing with issues regarding unemployment and labor, which one would assume would fall under the Secretary of Labor's jurisdiction. Obama's hand-picked Secretary of Labor, Hilda Solis, was recently named among Obama's 5 worst secretaries by U.S. News & World Report.[15] Perhaps she is simply incapable of handling her responsibilities and needs some assistance. If this is the case, one could point out the fact that Obama may be better served to replace his secretary than to pay a second bureaucrat to do a single job. Obama's insistence on using unconfirmed czars for such tasks suggests a concerted effort to avoid congressional oversight. But really, the main function of the Auto Recovery Czar seems to be public relations. Montgomery's title is a blatant attempt to tell the communities that have been affected by the turmoil in the auto industry that Obama cares about them, whether or not the czar actually accomplishes anything. Robert Scott, a senior international economist at the Economic Policy Institute says that Montgomery's appointment is "a symbol more than anything else that he cares about the people being displaced."[16] So, Obama seems to be attempting to prove to factory employees in the Rust Belt that he cares about creating jobs for them by spending government funds to create a job for the University of Maryland's Dean of economics. I'm sure they are all relieved.

— *Rick Rush*

---

[1] "List of Obama's Czars." Premiere Radio Networks, Inc. Aug. 21, 2009. Apr. 8, 2010 <http://www.glennbeck.com/content/articles/article/198/29391/>.

[2] "Ed Montgomery Curriculum Vitae." Docstop.com. 2010. Apr. 8, 2010 <http://www.docstoc.com/docs/12411202/Ed-Montgomery-Curriculum-Vitae/>.

[3] "Edward B. Montgomery," Who Runs GOV, <http://www.whorunsgov.com/Profiles/Edward_B._Montgomery>

[4] Tami Luhby, "Obama taps czar to help autoworkers," Mar. 31, 2009, CNNmoney.com, <http://money.cnn.com/2009/03/30/news/economy/recovery_director/index.htm>.

[5] Ibid.

[6] "Unemployment Rate," Google.com, 2010, <http://www.google.com/publicdata?ds=usunemployment&met=unemployment_rate&idim=state:ST260000&dl=en&hl=en&q=michigan+unemployment+rate>.

[7] "Auto recovery czar Ed Montgomery tours Flint General Motors plant," May 8, 2009, The Flint Journal, <http://www.mlive.com/business/mid-michigan/index.ssf/2009/05/auto_recovery_czar_ed_montgome.html>

[8] Tami Luhby, "Obama taps czar to help autoworkers," Mar. 31, 2009, CNNmoney.com, <http://money.cnn.com/2009/03/30/news/economy/recovery_director/index.htm>

[9] "Transcript: Obama's Announcement on the Auto Industry," Mar. 30, 2009, New York Times, <http://www.nytimes.com/2009/03/30/us/politics/30obama-text.html?pagewanted=1&_r=2>.

[10] Tami Luhby, "Obama taps czar to help autoworkers," Mar. 31, 2009, CNNmoney.com, <http://money.cnn.com/2009/03/30/news/economy/recovery_director/index.htm>.

[11] "Auto recovery czar Ed Montgomery tours Flint General Motors plant," May 8, 2009, The Flint Journal, <http://www.mlive.com/business/mid-michigan/index.ssf/2009/05/auto_recovery_czar_ed_montgome.html>.

[12] Kathie Kroll, "Ed Montgomery, auto recovery czar, asked to help auto suppliers," May 26, 2009, Cleveland Ohio Business News, <http://www.cleveland.com/business/index.ssf/2009/05/ed_montgomery_auto_recovery_cz.html>.

[13] "New Car Czar Promises $25 Million to Retrain Auto Workers," Jul. 17, 2009, Employment Spectator. <http://www.employmentspectator.com/2009/07/new-car-czar-promises-25-million-to-retrain-auto-workers/>

[14] "Auto recovery czar Ed Montgomery tours Flint General Motors plant," May 8, 2009, The Flint Journal, <http://www.mlive.com/business/mid-michigan/index.ssf/2009/05/auto_recovery_czar_ed_montgome.html>

[15] Paul Bedard, "Washington Whispers," Mar. 12, 2010, U.S. News Weekly.

[16] Tami Luhby, "Obama taps czar to help autoworkers," Mar. 31, 2009, CNNmoney.com, <http://money.cnn.com/2009/03/30/news/economy/recovery_director/index.htm>.

Bailout Czar — Neel Kashkari

Official title:	Assistant Secretary of the Treasury for Financial Stability
Salary / Direct cost to taxpayers:	$139,600-191,300[1]
Responsibilities:	Overseeing the spending of $700 billion in bailout funds
Reports to:	Hank Paulson, Tim Geithner
Senate confirmation:	Yes[2]
Relation to Obama:	Already held the position when Obama entered office
Ideology / political affiliation:	Republican

Recent bailout czar, one of the few holdovers from the Bush administration left his $700-billion wallet in D.C. for a life of chopping wood near his cabin in California. As *The Washington Post* reported in December 2009, "Congress savaged him. Wall Street Journal editorials doubted him. His hometown buddies urged him to use the money to buy the Cleveland Browns and fire the coaches. His wife spoke to him so rarely, she described them as 'dead to each other.' He lost sleep, gained weight and saw a close adviser, Don Hammond, suffer a heart attack at his Treasury desk."

So he left, putting his belongings in storage to pursue a simple life and what he called "Washington detox," an existence that consisted of building a shed, losing the 20 pounds he put on in DC and walking his dogs.[3] It sounds so literary, like a classic, big city breakdown or the beginning of a Stephen King novel. Herb Allison replaced him over the summer when the job proved too much for the 35-year-old who had faced constant criticism for his age, lack of experience and even that his name could easily be mispronounced as "Cash & Carry."

In early 2010, *Associated Press* reported that Kashkari had taken a job at Pimco (Pacific Investment Management Company), a formidable bond investment corporation in Newport Beach, CA that is closely linked to the Treasury Department and its Secretary Timothy Geithner.[4]

Though he was only six years out of business school, 35-year-old Neel Kashkari was granted the power to hand out all the federal bailout money. As the Treasury Department's assistant secretary for financial stability, he was not confirmed by the Senate when given his $700 billion wallet.

Who Is the Bailout Czar?

What is known about Kashkari is that he began his career as an engineer at TRW, a NASA contractor, but colleagues felt that he wanted a more glamorous life than science could afford[5]. He enrolled at the University of Pennsylvania, and while on track to receive his M.B.A., he interned at Goldman Sachs. After graduation, he went to work for the investment giant and, soon after, made his way to Washington, D.C. With his relatively short career so far, and much of it spent in the drastically different area of engineering, many worried that Kashkari was not prepared to save the nation from a financial shambles.

A 35-Year-Old With Extraordinarily Little Experience

Kashkari has only been in the financial business since 2002, when he joined the high-powered investment firm Goldman Sachs. It was there that he met CEO Henry Paulson, who would bring his young protégé to Washington in 2006 when he was sworn in as treasury secretary[6]. Succeeding his seeming mentor will be a formidable task as a *Time Magazine* survey lists Paulson as one of the top 25 people blamed by Americans for the current economic disaster[7]. Kashkari's ties to Goldman Sachs have also been controversial, as the mega-firm has strong influence in Washington. With headlines like "Political Interference Seen in Bank Bailout Decisions,"[8] the *Wall Street Journal* and other publications have become increasingly suspicious of preferential treatment given to certain banks during the massive bailout.

Goldman Sachs as a Paragon of Virtue: What Planet Are You From?

"Both Treasury Secretary Henry Paulson and his key advisor, Neel Kashkari, formerly held top jobs at Goldman Sachs, and it seems clear that their highly controversial and, to economic historians, bafflingly unorthodox bailout plan serves Wall Street's interests — particularly those of their former employer — far more than the American public's," wrote Eamonn Fingleton in the October 2008 issue of *The American Conservative*[9]. Last fall, when Kashkari was given the job of overseeing the then less comprehensive bailout plan under the Bush administration, liberal bloggers railed against it, calling his appointment "repugnantly crony" and "brazenly corrupt."[10] And now, with his even larger wallet, conservatives too may take objection to the self-described "free market Republican" colluding with the Obama administration to expand government control over private banks.

Gee, I Haven't Been Indicted Yet

Lawmakers in Washington and journalists alike have questioned the ties between the Treasury Department and Goldman Sachs since the government bailed out American International Group Inc. — the firm that subsequently gave $13 billion of its $180 billion to Goldman — while it let Goldman competitor Lehman Brothers collapse[11]. Journalists have also noticed the ever-expanding gap in profits between Goldman Sachs and its remaining competition. While Goldman boasted over $3 billion in profits, other banks border on bankruptcy[12].

"Even if the Obama administration and the Fed were to declare with one voice that banks such as Goldman were on their own, no one would believe it," read an editorial in the *Wall Street Journal* in July.

There has also been concern over how the firm has spent its bailout money. As reported in an October issue of the U.K. paper *The Daily Mail*, Goldman was still putting aside billions of taxpayer dollars for salaries and year-end bonuses. The exorbitant amount of money being disbursed to the investment firm's employees would effectively reward the bankers who created this financial maelstrom in the first place[13]. By allotting so much federal money to Goldman Sachs—jokingly referred to in the press as "Golden Sacks"—Paulson and Kashkari have effectively rewarded their former employer for failing. By letting other banks plummet into bankruptcy, they have eradicated most of the competition. A *Washington Times* investigation also found a correlation between banks that have spent significant amounts of money lobbying the White House and firms that have received substantial amounts of federal bailout money[14].

Members of Congress have also grown concerned that Goldman is exploiting its taxpayer-financed status to engage in risky banking practices and have even written a letter to Federal Reserve Chairman Ben Bernanke to ask why the government is allowing this behavior to persist[15].

Bailout Program and Corruption: More to Follow

The bailout has also been under fire from federal investigators who are looking into corruption of government money recipients in the hasty plan that is becoming increasingly complex and more expensive. The Obama administration has expanded the original $750 billion plan to 12 programs that will use up to $3 trillion in federal funds. The decision to buy "bundled loans in the form of mortgage-backed securities from investment markets"[16] has been seen as an exceptionally ripe opportunity for buyer conspiracies to extort kickbacks. The government, hence the taxpayer, would be taking all the risks.

George Will also noted in a March column that the original intent of using the bailout money to purchase toxic assets had not been met, although the "capricious and increasingly anti-constitutional government"[17] had already burned through $325 billion. "Such political malfeasance is pertinent to the financial meltdown as the administration, desperately seeking confidence, tries to stabilize the economy by vastly enlarging government's role in it," Will wrote, emphasizing one of the other major concerns that seem to accompany every decision Obama has made: the continuously expanding federal government.

Denizens of Back Alleys and Secret Meetings

The bailout program has also been criticized for a lack of transparency and the president's seeming refusal to honor his promise to keep citizens apprised of what is happening with their tax dollars. "The public wants to know what the Treasury is doing," read an April editorial in the *Washington Times*. "To be fair, it's possible that Mr. Obama has no idea either."[18]

During the federal investigation into where exactly these billions of dollars were being spent, Kashkari has refused investigators' requests for documents detailing how bailed-out banks have been spending the government money. The bailout czar has been repeatedly criticized for brisk, ambiguous answers to important questions about what is being done to fix this melted economy.

"Kashkari's impatient tone comes amid a growing desire for openness about how the government agencies, including the Treasury, are handling billions of taxpayer dollars being used to prop up Wall Street," *New York Post* writers Kaja Whitehouse and Mark Decambre wrote in their critique of Kashkari's rushed question-and-answer session with hundreds of financial execs[19].

Again . . . Who Is the Bailout Czar?

With so little known about the bailout czar and his unwillingness to supply the public with information about where he is emptying his massive wallet, it is difficult to tell where Neel Kashkari ends and Barack Obama begins. "Working at Goldman Sachs doesn't qualify you for doing this job," said the former director of research at the Federal Reserve Bank of Atlanta, Robert Eisenbris[20].[21]

— *Lucy Leitner*

---

[1] Rainey, Michael. "So How Much Is Bailout Czar Neel Kashkari Getting Paid?" AOL Money & Finance. Oct. 31, 2008. Apr. 8, 2010. <http://www.bloggingstocks.com/2008/10/31/so-how-much-is-bailout-czar-neel-kashkari-getting-paid/>.

[2] Christie, Rebecca. "U.S. Treasury's Kashkari to Lead Bank Bailout Office (Update1)." Bloomberg.com. Oct. 6, 2008. Apr. 12, 2010 <http://www.bloomberg.com/apps/news?sid=ak5RqnboIhG0&pid=20601103>.

[3] Blumenfeld, Laura. "The $700 billion man; Neel Kashkari left his position as federal bailout chief for an off-the-map existence. 'Washington detox,' he calls it." *The Washington Post* Dec. 6, 2009: A1.

[4] "Pimco hires former TARP chief Kashkari." Washington Post.com Dec. 7, 2009. March 24, 2010 <http://www.washingtonpost.com/wp-dyn/content/article/2009/12/07/AR2009120704444.html>.

[5] "Kashkari Faces Major Task as 'Bailout Czar.' " USA Today.com Oct. 11, 2008. Aug. 27, 2009 <http://www.usatoday.com/money/economy/2008-10-11-bailout-czar_N.htm>.

[6] Ibid.

[7] "25 People to Blame for the Financial Crisis." Time.com. Aug. 27, 2009 <http://www.time.com/time/specials/packages/article/0,28804,1877351_1878509,00.html>

[8] Paletta, Damian and David Enrich. "Political Interference Seen in Bank Bailout Decisions." *The Wall Street Journal* Jan. 22, 2009.

[9] Fingleton, Eamonn. "Street Sweeping." *The American Conservative*. Oct. 20, 2008.

[10] Watson, Paul Joseph. "Fox Guarding the Henhouse: Ex-Goldman Sachs Exec to Oversee Bailout." Weblog Entry. Alex Jones' Prison Planet Oct. 7, 2009. Aug. 29, 2009 <http://www.prisonplanet.com/fox-guarding-the-henhouse-ex-goldman-sachs-exec-to-oversee-bailout.html>.

[11] Solomon, Deborah. "Geithner Says No Tilt to Goldman." *The Wall Street Journal* August 22, 2009.

[12] "A Tale of Two Bailouts." *The Wall Street Journal* July 16, 2009: p. A13.

[13] Duke, Simon. "Goldman Sachs Ready to Hand Out £7bn Salary and Bonus Package… After It's £6bn Bail-Out." October 30, 2008. August 29, 2009 <http://www.dailymail.co.uk/news/worldnews/article-1081624/Goldman-Sachs-ready-hand-7BILLION-salary-bonus-package--6bn-bail-out.html>.

[14] Haberkorn, Jennifer. "Bailout Recipients Also Major Lobbyists." *The Washington Times* January 23, 2009.

[15] Grim, Ryan. "Goldman Sachs: Gambling With Your Money?" HuffingtonPost.com July 27, 2009. August 29, 2009 <http://www.huffingtonpost.com/2009/07/27/goldman-sachs-gambling-wi_n_245566.html>.

[16] Vartabedian, Ralph and Tom Hamburger. "20 Criminal Bailout Probes (for Starters); The U.S. Bank Rescue Plan Is Ripe for Fraud, Its Overseer Reports." *Los Angeles Times* April 21, 2009, Home Edition: p. A1.

[17] Will, George F. "The Toxic Assets We Elected." *The Washington Post* March 24, 2009: p. A13.

[18] "Obama's Code of Secrecy; Government Is Hiding Billions in TARP Fraud." *The Washington Times* April 15, 2009: p. A18.

[19] Whitehouse, Kaja and Mark Decambre. "Answers, Please! Kashkari Angers Troubled Financial Execs." NY Post.com November 11, 2008. August 27, 2009 <http://www.nypost.com/seven/11112008/business/answers__please__138094.htm>.

[20] Waldie, Paul. "It's Very Complicated." Truth Out.org October 7, 2009. August 27, 2009 <http://www.truthout.org/100708B>.

Border Czar – Alan Bersin

Official title:	DHS Assistant Secretary for International Affairs and Special Representative for Border Affairs
Official responsibilities:	Improving relationships with DHS partners at home and abroad, leading efforts to reduce violence along the Southwest border
Reports to:	Secretary of Homeland Security
Senate confirmation:	None
Salary:	Information unavailable
Ideology / political affiliation:	Long-standing Democrat, with the occasional opportunistic nod of the head to conservatives when it serves to further his own career

As *Time Magazine* points out, "In certain circles in [San Diego], Bersin is a verb. Bersin is a punch line. Bersin is the boogeyman."[1] Obama's new border czar has built up quite the reputation in the city where he has spent most of the past 20 years of his career.

Bersin held essentially the same job under President Bill Clinton as Attorney General Janet Reno's special representative on border issues from 1995 through 1998. Today, as part of Obama's efforts to hark back to the high economic times of the 1990s, the White House felt the need to reappoint yet another one of Clinton's former underlings to solve the same problem he proved incapable of solving then.

Who Is Alan Bersin?

Alan Bersin was born in 1946 in Brooklyn, N.Y., where he grew up attending public and Hebrew schools. He later attended Harvard, Oxford, and Yale, which helped him to establish a network of connections that proved useful in propelling his otherwise lackluster and incompetent career. Upon graduating in 1973, he briefly worked at the Los Angeles Police Commission, moving on to join a Los Angeles law firm. Apparently failing at private practice, in 1992 Bersin quit the firm and moved to San Diego to teach at the USD School of Law. That didn't seem to work out well for him either because the same year Bersin went into politics on behalf of the Clinton-Gore presidential campaign. Shortly afterward, he was handsomely rewarded with the position of U.S. attorney for San Diego, despite the lack of required experience and qualifications. Later, he also became Janet Reno's border czar.

Following a host of incompetent administrative decisions, in 1998, Bersin abandoned that position and made another radical turn in career, using his connections to secure the post of superintendent of San Diego Public Schools — once again, despite the obvious lack of experience and qualifications. In this new role, Bersin quickly gained the notoriety of a bull-headed bureaucrat whose aptitude for confrontation was rivaled only by his ineptitude in everything else. That, however, didn't prevent him from becoming secretary of education for California in 2005, which he abandoned a year later for the position of chairman of the San Diego Regional Airport Authority, which he held until 2009.

WhoRunsGov.com, a Democrat-friendly Washington Post Co. publication, notes that "Bersin has always known some of the right people. He attended Harvard University at the same time as Vice President Al Gore, and met President Bill Clinton at Oxford University, where they were both Rhodes scholars. He then went to Yale Law School with Clinton and met Hillary Rodham Clinton. His wife, Lisa Foster, is prominent in San Diego social and political circles. Bersin knew Homeland Security Secretary Janet Napolitano because they were both federal prosecutors in the Clinton administration along the U.S.-Mexico border."[2]

Bull-Headed

Bersin is also known for somehow acquiring jobs for which he is entirely unqualified. In 1993, he was recommended by California Democratic Sen. Barbara Boxer and nominated by President Clinton as U.S. attorney for San Diego despite the fact that he had no prosecutorial experience and virtually no criminal-law background.[3] After three years as Clinton's "border czar," Bersin changed directions by accepting an offer as superintendent of the

San Diego Unified School District despite having no previous experience in education[4] and never even having sent his own children to public schools.[5]

Finding oneself unprepared for such an important role, someone else might at least seek advice from those more experienced in the field. Not Bersin. As *Time Magazine* puts it, his "seven-year term as San Diego education superintendent—at the time one of the longest in the nation—was notable for the vehement opposition it drew from teacher unions and school board members." He eventually admitted, "There were mistakes made. There were dozens and even hundreds of mistakes made."[6] That might seem like a good reason to start listening to those around him, but the effect it had on Bersin was quite the opposite. As he himself said, "I am now so used to being vilified and having our initiatives mischaracterized or maligned that I have recently found myself failing to listen seriously to my opponents"[7]—a claim fully backed up by his detractors. In the words of a San Diego elementary school teacher who worked under him, "Alan Bersin is a dictator who never took the opinion of the classroom teacher."[8]

His baseless obstinacy looked much like the neurotic defensiveness representative of all incompetent hacks. It revealed a man whose mind was closed to advice from people with greater qualifications and knowledge. This makes Bersin unlikely to have close cooperation with border governors who, in the words of his former Mexican counterpart, are "the ones who best understand the reality. The fundamental vision must come from the region."[9] Bersin admits he will need willing partners in order to succeed[10]—but is he fit to be a willing partner himself?

Unlike Bersin's scandal-ridden tenure at the school system, in this case, the federal government doesn't yet have a pre-existing group of knowledgeable people in place for him to ignore. At the time of Bersin's appointment, Obama had not even named an ambassador to Mexico; nor had Mexico found anyone to replace its own equivalent of the border czar after the previous one had resigned, citing a lack of support from the Mexican government. There isn't much in the way of standing border patrols either.[11] Finally Bersin has the opportunity to claim greater experience than his co-workers—which, come to think of it, makes him even less likely to listen to their advice.

Two-Faced

For someone so intent on getting his own way, it is surprisingly hard to pin down what Bersin really stands for. That is, if he indeed stands for anything beyond political opportunism.

Since 1999, he has given more than $50,000 to political campaigns, almost exclusively to Democrats. In the 2008 election cycle, he donated nearly $40,000, the maximum possible, to both Hillary Rodham Clinton and Barack Obama, as well as $28,500 to the Democratic National Committee.[12]

However, working in conservative San Diego County, Bersin has learned to cloak himself in a conservative veneer, causing some Democrats to question whether he is truly a liberal.[13] At the same time, conservatives see him as an opportunist and a shameful illustration of how effectively Democrats can exploit illegal immigration for their own advancement.[14]

Alan Bersin long ago learned that double talk and political flip-flopping are indispensable tools when it comes to satisfying detractors and advancing his career. His first tenure as the border czar began with a promise to focus on drug smugglers and human traffickers instead of "economic migrants."[15] But when he took office, Bersin prosecuted so many minor immigrant violators that the sheer quantity overloaded the justice system, causing much criticism and many complaints from immigration lawyers and criminal defense attorneys.

In another flip, Bersin once took a lot of credit for building a border fence in the course of 1994's Operation Gatekeeper,[16] but today he is rejecting the notion, saying that "building 2,000 miles of fence I don't think is on the table."[17] In other words, he was willing to build enough of a fence to garner favor among Republicans, but he would not support a move large enough to have a real impact, lest he alienated Democrats.

Past Failure

Operation Gatekeeper has proven to be something of a nightmare in border politics. While building a local fence did stop border crossing directly into San Diego, it essentially pushed the illegal trail farther east into the Arizona desert. Crossing the desert resulted in a dramatic increase in immigrant deaths, hurting America's relations with Mexico without effectively slowing illegal immigration.[18] Bersin's claim that at the end of his first reign border arrests were at an 18-year low[19] doesn't hold water because his overbearing focus on San Diego caused him to neglect vast areas to the east where most crossings went undetected. Latino activists have stated that Bersin represents death.[20] The ability to create a perfect confluence of ineffectiveness and offensiveness seems to be Bersin's main qualification and his only accomplishment at any job he has ever held at taxpayers' expense.

Added Power

Consistent with its policies of rewarding failure and punishing success, the Obama administration has not only reinstalled Bersin in the position where he had failed before; it has also given him more clout. Someone in the White House must believe that the performance of a bull-headed incompetent hack can be improved by giving him more power to abuse.

Reporting directly to Homeland Security Secretary Janet Napolitano, Bersin finds himself even higher on the totem pole than he ever was under Clinton.[21] According to Bersin, "The difference is not so much in the role, but rather in the authority that attaches to this position that was not present 13 years ago."[22]

Bersin did little to solve the border enforcement issue then, and illegal immigration remains a serious chronic problem. Since that time, the stakes have gone up, adding escalated drug trafficking and cartel violence into the bargain.[23] The liberal wayback machine has now moved Bersin back to square one, to face the same opportunity he once wasted, only with more authority and opposite an even more dangerous situation. What could possibly go wrong?

— Rick Rush

---

[1] Gilbert Cruz, "Alan Bersin: Obama's 'Border Czar,' " April 16, 2009, Time.com, <http://www.time.com/time/nation/article/0,8599,1891573,00.html>

[2] WhoRunsGov.com, "Alan D. Bersin," 2009, http://www.whorunsgov.com/Profiles/Alan_D._Bersin

[3] Valerie Alvord, "Visiting USD Professor Selected for U.S. Attorney," *San Diego Union-Tribune*, Oct. 22, 1993

[4] Valerie Alvord, "Bersin Has Friends, and Foes, in High Places," *San Diego Union-Tribune*, March 9, 1998

[5] Gilbert Cruz, "Alan Bersin: Obama's 'Border Czar,' " April 16, 2009, Time.com, <http://www.time.com/time/nation/article/0,8599,1891573,00.html>

[6] Ibid.

[7] Ibid.

[8] Ibid.

[9] Sandra Dibble, "Bersin to Focus on Violence in 2nd Tour as Border Czar," April 16, 2009, Sign On San Diego, <http://www3.signonsandiego.com/stories/2009/apr/16/1n16bersin235118-bersin-focus-violence-2nd-tour-bo/>

[10] Alex Kingsbury, "Obama's Border Czar Alan Bersin Is Taking On Drug Gangs and Illegal Immigrants," May 4, 2009, *U.S.News & World Report,* <http://www.usnews.com/articles/news/national/2009/05/04/obamas-border-czar-alan-bersin-is-taking-on-drug-gangs-and-illegal-immigrants.html>

[11] Ibid.

[12] Center for Responsive Politics http://www.opensecrets.org/indivs/search.php?name=Bersin,+Alan&state=&zip=&employ=&cand=&all=Y&sort=N&capcode=f6g22&submit=Submit

[13] Ruben Navarrette, "Which Alan Bersin Will Show Up as Czar?" April 17, 2009, Dallas News.com,
<http://www.dallasnews.com/sharedcontent/dws/dn/opinion/viewpoints/stories/DN-navarrette_20edi.State.Edition1.2ca2bc9.html>
[14] Ibid.
[15] "List of Obama's Czars," Aug. 21, 2009. Glenn Beck.com,
<http://www.glennbeck.com/content/articles/article/198/29391/>
[16] Ruben Navarrette, "Which Alan Bersin Will Show Up as Czar?" April 17, 2009, Dallas News.com,
<http://www.dallasnews.com/sharedcontent/dws/dn/opinion/viewpoints/stories/DN-navarrette_20edi.State.Edition1.2ca2bc9.html>
[17] Sandra Dibble, "Bersin to Focus on Violence in 2nd Tour as Border Czar," April 16, 2009, Sign On San Diego,
<http://www3.signonsandiego.com/stories/2009/apr/16/1n16bersin235118-bersin-focus-violence-2nd-tour-bo/>
[18] Gilbert Cruz, "Alan Bersin: Obama's 'Border Czar,' " April 16, 2009, Time.com, <http://www.time.com/time/nation/article/0,8599,1891573,00.html>
[19] "List of Obama's Czars," Aug. 21, 2009. Glenn Beck.com,
<http://www.glennbeck.com/content/articles/article/198/29391/>
[20] Gilbert Cruz, "Alan Bersin: Obama's 'Border Czar,' " April 16, 2009, Time.com, <http://www.time.com/time/nation/article/0,8599,1891573,00.html>
[21] Ruben Navarrette, "Which Alan Bersin Will Show Up as Czar?" April 17, 2009, Dallas News.com,
<http://www.dallasnews.com/sharedcontent/dws/dn/opinion/viewpoints/stories/DN-navarrette_20edi.State.Edition1.2ca2bc9.html>
[22] Dolia Estevez, "Border Duty in an Era of Shared Responsibility," Poder360, <http://www.poder360.com/article_detail.php?id_article=2406>
[23] Ruben Navarrette, "Which Alan Bersin Will Show Up as Czar?" April 17, 2009, Dallas News.com,
<http://www.dallasnews.com/sharedcontent/dws/dn/opinion/viewpoints/stories/DN-navarrette_20edi.State.Edition1.2ca2bc9.html>

Car Czar — Ron Bloom

Official title:	Head of the Auto Task Force
Salary / Direct cost to taxpayers:	Unknown
Responsibilities:	Monitoring government investment in private car companies
Reports to:	Treasury Secretary Timothy Geithner and National Economic Council head Larry Summers
Senate confirmation:	None
Relation to Obama:	Worked for SEIU and United Steel Workers Union before accepting cabinet position[1]
Ideology / political affiliation:	"Free Market is Nonsense"

New car czar Ron Bloom has no experience in the auto industry. But who really is qualified to oversee the unprecedented government ownership of the largest American industries? Anyone besides Stalin?

Socialist Takeover of U.S. Auto Industry

"Already the socialism that has arrived in this country since January 20 is terrifying, especially in the automobile industry," said Ben Stein when he discussed Bloom's appointment on the *Glenn Beck* program in July.

Obama's government-financed restructuring of the United States auto industry has been compared to that of Soviet Cold War-era Communist economics and recalls Joseph Stalin's Five-Year-Plans, that necessitated far-reaching government involvement into what should have been independent industry. And what better way to evoke Russian totalitarianism than by naming a czar? Ron Bloom is one of the newest inductions into Obama's czarist oligarchy bent on government control of consumerism. He will function as the monitor of the government's substantial investment into companies like GM, of which the feds own 60 percent, and Chrysler. Obama's federally mandated resuscitation of the auto industry mirrors the stress that Stalin put on manufacturers after

World War I, and the closure of so many dealerships is much like the punishment meted out to factories that failed to produce under the notorious Communist regime.

In October 2009, videos surfaced of a keynote speech that Bloom delivered in February 2008, in which he praised Mao Zedong and trashed the free market. As per car czar Ron Bloom,

> Generally speaking, we get the joke. We know that the free market is nonsense. We know that the whole point is to game the system, to beat the market or at least find someone who will pay you a lot of money, 'cause they're convinced that there is a free lunch.

> We know this is largely about power, that it's an adults only no limit game. We kind of agree with Mao that political power comes largely from the barrel of a gun. And we get it that if you want a friend you should get a dog.[2]

Bloom Behind Moves to Close Thousands of Car Dealerships

Thousands of Chrysler and GM dealerships around the country have been and are being closed around the country, cutting around 200,000 jobs in the process. In July, the House of Representatives approved a bill that would stop the planned closures of the dealerships, but Bloom urged the Senate to vote against the plan, veritably using his opinion to attempt to override the vote of the 435 elected members of the House of Representatives[3]. Newspaper articles from the immediate aftermath of the new czar's address quote dissenting voices of both Democratic and Republican representatives. In addition to the staggering number of jobs lost by the closures, many of the owners of the defunct dealerships have filed for personal bankruptcy[4].

"I don't believe that companies should be allowed to take taxpayer funds for a bailout and then leave local dealers and their customers to fend for themselves with no real notice and no real help. It's just plain wrong," said Sen. John D. Rockefeller IV, a West Virginia Democrat, in June[5].

Ignores Congress and the American People

Not only has the new car czar been willing to override the opinion of Congress to further Obama's agenda; he has also compromised the desires of the American people. The plan to create environmentally "clean" cars is a top priority of the Obama administration. However, because GM's electric car has been deemed too costly to be a commercially successful product in the near future, the government seems to pushing its new auto industry to slash SUV production and manufacture compact, more fuel-efficient cars[6]. The major problem is that surveys and sales indicate that Americans do not want smaller cars[7]. They want big cars that will protect them in case of a collision and four-wheel drive that will prevent skidding off icy roads. And families of six cannot cram into a Toyota Prius no matter how much they are told it will help the environment. Government control of industry production and forcing public consumption of certain merchandise defeat the very purpose of capitalism.

The government is GM's "largest shareholder, customer, tax collector, regulator, partner in determining employees' compensation, protector of dealers, and pension guarantor," writes Pulitzer Prize-winning author George Will on Townhall.com. Government representatives, including Bloom, have continually denied having any control over General Motors' operations, even though they are the majority shareholder in the company and what were once decisions made by corporate officials are now subject to federal oversight. Referencing Obama's removal of GM's CEO and forced merger between Chrysler and Fiat, he indicts the president's creation of new automotive products and "imposing fuel economy requirements that will control size, weight, passenger capacity, and safety."[8]

Part of the American way of life is freedom of choice. How can one party be pro-choice about abortion but against choice when it comes to cars?

The president of the American Policy Center, Tom Deweese, likens the proposed plethora of cheap compact cars with which Washington hopes to fill American highways to the Yugo disaster of the 1980s. "Small, affordable, and easy on gas — the perfect modern car for our current economic and environmental crisis that the Obama administration is hell-bent on perpetuating, regardless of economic or scientific fact," wrote Deweese in "The Coming Communist-American Auto Industry," which has been published on a number of conservative blogs and websites[9]. Once again, Soviet imagery, long anathema in the American socio-political realm, is at the forefront.

"We now have government-controlled industry dictated by those who do everything through political agenda. They have a vision, and it looks a lot like the Yugo," Deweese concluded.

Zero Experience — Only a Political Agenda

And Ron Bloom, labor leader, is at the helm of this unprecedented government interference into the private sector. With no real experience in the auto industry, Bloom, 53, is the successor of the even less qualified Steven Rattner — who left his post amidst an SEC investigation into his private equity firm. Bloom is a former investment banker who made his name working with the United Steelworkers union. Though he has helped to resolve labor conflicts, he is vastly unprepared for the job of tackling the flailing automotive industry, a far more complex operation than the manufacturing of steel[10].

"He has no experience in the auto industry. I mean, it's amazing. There are millions of people in this country with experience in the automobile business — they're not getting anything," Stein said.

Though former co-workers in the steel industry have attested to Bloom's ability to relate to the low-level worker[11], his abandoning of the thousands who work in dealerships seems to contradict any professed compassion for blue-collar employees. He has a history of streamlining businesses by trimming fat and making mergers. This conjures the idea of a high-powered "efficiency expert" brought into struggling businesses to fire seemingly expendable employees while collecting a six-figure salary.

Several columnists have also expressed worries that labor unions are one of the many problems plaguing the industry.

"Will he be saving the industry or helping the unions perpetuate its woes?" asked J. P. Freire and David Freddoso in the *Washington Examiner*. "So far, the Obama administration's 'bankruptcy negotiation' technique has amounted to strong-arming and ruining the reputations of senior creditors who resist being written out in favor of unions. With the choice of Bloom, it is more obvious that the unions now sit on both sides of the negotiating table."[12]

Touts Dentist Chair Bargaining — Something Is Seriously Wrong Here

The following quote from Bloom himself attests to his management style: "Let me give you some advice. First, we are big believers in dentist chair bargaining. For those of you not familiar with this approach, it is inspired by the story of the man who walks into his dentist's office, grabs the dentist by the balls, and says, 'Now, let's not hurt each other.' We do have a lot to lose, and we and everyone else knows it. But what you need to understand is that we are willing to lose it."

— *Lucy Leitner*

[1] Pickert, Kate. "Ron Bloom, Obama's Car Non-Czar." Time Magazine. Feb. 18, 2009. Apr. 8, 2010. <http://www.time.com/time/nation/article/0,8599,1880228,00.html>.

[2] "Obama's Czar Ron Bloom Agrees With Mao - address at Investor Conf part3" [Video]. (2008). Retrieved 5 March 2010 from http://www.youtube.com/watch?v=RCvQ8BSUv-g.

[3] "Obama Auto Task Force Warns Against House Plan to Restore Dealerships." AP Wire July 21, 2009.

[4] Bunkley, Nick. "Obama Auto Advisor Tells Lawmakers Not to Undo Dealer Closings." The New York Times July 22, 2009, Late Edition: p. B3.

[5] Whoriskey, Peter and Kendra Marr. "Senators Blast Automakers Over Dealer Closings; GM, Chrysler Defend Massive Shutdowns." The Washington Post June 4, 2009, Suburban Edition: p. A15.

[6] Feulner, Ed. "CEObama, The Car Czar; Federal Money Put Feds in the Driver's Seat." The Washington Times April 9, 2009: p. A17.

[7] "North American Consumers Still Prefer Large, Luxury Vehicles." The Auto Channel August 12, 2009. August 26, 2009 < http://theautochannel.com/news/2009/08/12/474036.html>.

[8] Will, George. "Have We Got a Deal For You." Townhall.com June 7, 2009. August 25, 2009 < http://townhall.com/columnists/GeorgeWill/2009/06/07/have_we_got_a_deal_for_you>.

[9] Deweese, Tom. "The Coming Communist-American Auto Industry." Canada Free Press.com May 27, 2009. August 26, 2009 < http://www.canadafreepress.com/index.php/article/11418>.

[10] Carty, Sharon Silke. "Task force exec can see all sides; Bloom has experience with management, labor and Wall Street." USA Today March 19, 2009, First Edition: p. 7A.

[11] Thomas, Ken and Tom Krisher. "Obama's Auto Advisor Has Wall Street, Labor Ties." ABCnews.go.com February 16, 2009. August 26, 2009 http://abcnews.go.com/Business/wireStory?id=6891263.

[12] Freire, J.P. and David Freddoso. "New Car Czar is Union Man." Washington Examiner.com July 13, 2009. August 25, 2009 http://www.washingtonexaminer.com/opinion/blogs/beltway-confidential/A-czar-too-far-50674082.html.

Central Region Czar — Dennis Ross

Official title:	Special Assistant to the President and Senior Director for the Central Region, National Security Council
Official responsibilities:	His area of responsibility encompasses the Middle East, the Gulf, Afghanistan, Pakistan, and South Asia.
Reports to:	National Security Adviser and the President
Senate confirmation:	No
Salary:	Unknown[1]
Ideology / political affiliation:	Conservative, national security oriented

Who Is He?

Dennis Ross holds the rank of ambassador and has played a leading role in shaping U.S. involvement in the Middle East peace process and in dealing directly with the parties in negotiations. He was this country's point man on the peace process in the Clinton administration. He was instrumental in assisting Israelis and Palestinians in reaching the 1995 Interim Agreement; he also successfully brokered the Hebron Accord in 1997, facilitated the Israel-Jordan peace treaty, and intensively worked to bring Israel and Syria together. A scholar and diplomat with more than two decades of experience in Soviet and Middle East policy, Ambassador Ross worked closely with Secretaries of State James Baker, Warren Christopher, and Madeleine Albright.

Prior to his service as special Middle East coordinator under President Clinton, Ross served as director of the State Department's Policy Planning office in the George H. W. Bush administration. In that position, he played a prominent role in developing U.S. policy toward the former Soviet Union and the unification of Germany and its integration into NATO. In addition, he was instrumental in arms control negotiations and the development of the Gulf War coalition. He served as director of Near East and South Asian affairs on the National Security Council staff during the Reagan administration and as deputy director of the Pentagon's Office of Net Assessment. Ross was also a director and distinguished fellow at the Washington Institute for Near East Policy. He is a 1970 graduate of UCLA.

A Genuine Man of Principle and Accomplishment — How Did He Get in Here?

Dennis Ross is a remarkable man who must have wandered down the wrong road and found himself as one of the few bright honest lights in an administration that is noted for the absence of both. But then again, he also worked in the Clinton administration, thus proving that he is uniquely capable of holding his nose while faithfully protecting U.S. equities in the ever-treacherous Middle East.

Ross is uniquely qualified to fill the role of special assistant to the president and senior director for the central region (which encompasses the Middle East, the Gulf, Afghanistan, Pakistan, and South Asia). He has the temperament and intellectual tools to tackle the most difficult tasks set before him. He is obviously not afraid of challenges as he chose the Sisyphean task of trying to bring peace to the Middle East. Over the years, he had to deal with the likes of Yasser Arafat, whom Abba Eban once famously characterized as someone who "never missed an opportunity to miss an opportunity."

Yet throughout the many disappointments, lost opportunities, and deadly politics of Middle East negotiations, Ross excelled in upholding American values, objectives, and hopes for a general reconciliation and lasting peace.

Is He Being Used?

The Obama administration may be serious about enlisting Ross's considerable experience and talents in an honest effort to reach an equitable settlement. Some suspect, however, that President Obama may be using the trust and good faith inherent in Ambassador Ross's presence as political cover for behind-the-scenes efforts to bring disproportionate pressure upon Israel in an attempt to pressure it into unacceptable unilateral concessions to its hostile neighbors.

Certainly the mission Ross has been given is Quixotic at best. Without argument, he has the most difficult portfolio in the diplomatic and national security realm: the Middle East, the Gulf, Afghanistan, Pakistan, and South Asia. Compounding his challenges is the fact that he must deal with the likes of Richard Holbrooke — Obama's so-called Afpak czar. Attempting to rein in that monumental ego may pose the greatest challenge of all.

Now Ross is Being Vilified by the Obama White House

Unfortunately, the past few months have seen Ross become increasingly marginalized by the Obama Administration in direct proportion to its increasingly anti-Israel policies. The Obama White House has gone so far as to begin a whispering campaign aimed at raising doubt as to Ross' loyalties to the United States due to his opposition to the obvious pro-Arab tilt and increasingly strident anti-Israel rhetoric.

---

[1] "List of Obama's Czars." Premiere Radio Networks, Inc. Aug. 21, 2009. Apr. 8, 2010
<http://www.glennbeck.com/content/articles/article/198/29391/>.

Climate Czar — Todd Stern

Official title:	Special Envoy for Climate Change
Salary:	Information unavailable
Responsibilities:	Develop international policies and strategies to reduce greenhouse gas emissions and combat global warming and climate change
Reports to:	Secretary of State Hillary Clinton
Senate confirmation:	None
Relation to Obama:	Financial supporter since 2004
Ideology / political affiliation:	Democrat / Environmentalist

Would you like to see the global warming charlatan Al Gore installed, without any Senate confirmation hearing, to a powerful government position of a Climate Czar, from which he could easily destroy national economy and squander American wealth in the name of his alarmist fantasies, while enriching special interest groups and fulfilling the international Left long-held dream of cutting America down to size? Probably not. But what if he had a different name while pursuing the same activist agenda? What if he lacked Al Gore's goofy appearance, easily recognizable in thousands of editorial cartoons over the years, while holding the same harebrained beliefs? Would such a Climate Czar be more acceptable to the American people?

Meet Todd Stern - Special Envoy for Climate Change, or Climate Czar for short - a panic-stricken global warming fanatic who once used to holler the-end-is-near rants on leftist websites in the following fashion: "Evaporation and rainfall are increasing; glaciers are retreating; sea ice is shrinking; sea level is rising; permafrost is melting; wildfires are increasing; storm and flood damage is soaring. The canary in the coal mine is singing for all she's worth."[1] Well, today Stern is in a position to write memos to the president.

But is Stern's newly created position even necessary? Germany's Leipzig Institute of Marine Science has forecasted no additional global warming over the next decade in their policy paper *Nature*.[2]

In an article originally published in *The Washington Times,* Patrick Michaels, a Senior Fellow in Environmental Studies at the Cato Institute wrote, "Science no longer provides justification for any rush to pass drastic global warming legislation."[3]

Who is our Climate Czar?

Just like his alter ego Al Gore, the "global warming expert" Todd Stern has no scientific background - he is a lawyer with a Bachelor of Arts from Dartmouth and a law degree from Harvard.[4] But the unwavering ideological loyalty while grooming Al Gore's favorite hobby-horse helped Stern, a native Chicagoan, to make a quick career within the Clinton Administration. Serving Bill Clinton as the head of Initiatives on Global Climate Change (1997-1999), Stern was a senior negotiator at the Kyoto Protocol parley in 1997.[5] He later served the Clinton Administration as an advisor to the Secretary of the Treasury from 1999 to 2001.[6]

Stern's meteoric rise as an ideological commissar on the taxpayer's dime came to a halt when Al Gore lost presidential election to George W. Bush. Resentful Stern spent the Bush years in exile at John Podesta's Center for American Progress (a far-left think tank funded in part by liberal financier George Soros), as did other flotsam of the sunken Clinton apparatus, many of whom have now become high-ranking Obama Administration officials, including several Czars mentioned in this book. At the Center, Stern served as a Senior Fellow with the focus on perpetuating the mythology of global warming.[7]

In that capacity, he has been writing incessant hysterical calls for the American government and the rest of the world to uphold economy-crippling policies aimed at curbing greenhouse gases,[8] sign the Kyoto Protocol he helped to negotiate,[9] introduce a cap and tax system,[10] mandate unrealistic fuel efficiency standards of 60 miles per gallon for all vehicles,[11] and replace all incandescent light bulbs with compact florescent bulbs.[12]

Based on questionable at best and very controversial science, these far-left utopian proposals come with a hefty price tag to the American taxpayers, American industries, and the American economy. If left unchecked, Stern's ideological agenda could have a devastating impact on our economy and the way we carry out our daily routines.

Sharply Reducing Emissions Unilaterally

President Obama has said he wants to sharply reduce greenhouse gas emissions, which bogus "experts" like Al Gore and Todd Stern allege are responsible for global warming, rising sea levels, and "increasingly unpredictable weather patterns."[13] Todd Stern has now been charged with accomplishing this goal. He is currently working to fulfill Obama's promise to reduce U.S. carbon emissions to 1990 levels by 2020 and to further reduce emissions by 80 percent of current levels by 2050.[14] In March 2009, during United Nations climate talks in Bonn, Germany, Stern confirmed that these emission reductions are "a core priority for the President both at the domestic and international level."[15]

The main issue on Stern's front burner is how to coerce foreign governments into supporting a global climate change pact that can be agreed upon by the United Nations in December 2009. According to *The Washington Post*, he has a parade of foreign officials passing through his office in this effort to reach an agreement[16]. Do these efforts have any merit? *Washington Post* writer, George Will, mocked the global climate change pact in an April 2009 column.

> Reducing carbon emissions supposedly will reverse warming, which is allegedly occurring even though, according to statistics published by the World Meteorological Organization, there has not been a warmer year on record than 1998. Regarding the reversing, the U.N. Framework Convention on Climate Change has many ambitions, as outlined in a working group's 16-page "information note" to "facilitate discussions." For example:

"Tariffs can be lowered to grant special preference to climate-friendly goods, or they can be maintained at high levels to discourage trade in GHG- [greenhouse gas-] intensive goods and services." The working group says protectionism "in the service of climate change objectives" might virtuously "shelter domestic producers of climate-friendly goods." Furthermore, using "border carbon adjustment," a nation might virtuously "impose costs on imports equivalent to that [sic] faced by domestic producers" operating under a carbon tax. Or a nation with a cap-and-trade regime regulating carbon emissions by domestic manufacturers might require foreign manufacturers "to buy offsets at the border equal to that [sic] which the producer would have been forced to purchase had the good been produced domestically." Cynics will see only potential for mischief by governments, including the U.S. government, using such measures to give a green patina to protectionism. [17]

When it comes to climate change initiatives, Todd Stern has downed the Kool Aid and is busy making a new batch to share with the American public. He has written extensively on global warming and greenhouse emissions. In a 2007 paper he co-wrote with William Antholis of the Brookings Institute, he laid out a climate strategy for the next president of the United States. Now he is that president's Climate Czar.

[The President's] first mission must be to implement a serious, mandatory climate program at home, not only because the United States is a dominant producer of heat-trapping greenhouse gases, but also because it will have no international credibility unless and until it acts decisively at home. At the same time, the president should pursue a layered diplomacy centered on a core group of major emitters; active engagement with key bilateral partners, especially China; and the multilateral UN Framework Convention on Climate Change (UNFCCC). [18]

Steve Moore, Senior Economics writer and Editorial Board member of the *Wall Street Journal* has this to say about Stern's agenda: "to act unilaterally to reduce planetary greenhouse gases is the height of feel-good folly."[19]

Lisa Jackson, Administrator of the Environmental Protection Agency, responded to a question from Senator James Inhofe (R-OK) during a 2009 climate change legislation hearing, by stating that unilateral limits on carbon dioxide emissions "would not impact CO2 levels." [20] Additionally, a recent Massachusetts Institute of Technology (MIT) study has concluded that "the different U.S. policies have relatively small effects on the CO2 concentration if other regions do not follow the U.S. lead."[21]

Indeed, these unilateral measures may not have any impact on the atmosphere, but their impact on U.S. economy would be devastating. Scrambling to comply with the regulations, American companies would be put at a competitive disadvantage in the global economy, while taxpayers would carry the burden of compliance expenses that industries would inevitably pass on to the consumers. In addition, according to a basic economic law, any policy that raises operation costs will ultimately lead to job losses.

Environment vs. the Economy

A zealous proponent of a unilateral carbon reduction program, Todd Stern has written at length on the subject,[22] asserting that a national limit on carbon emissions would lead to their gradual reduction worldwide,[23] while completely disregarding the disastrous economic cost of this arbitrary measure to the American people.

Confronted with the reality that a carbon reduction program would be expensive and a hard sell to American taxpayers, Stern didn't as much as pause to rethink his position. Instead, he focused his efforts on designing a more attractive wrapper for his poisonous product. In a 2007 paper published in the *Washington*

Quarterly he noted why a cap and trade scheme would be more politically feasible than a pure carbon tax that would have had the same impact.

> A carbon tax would accomplish much the same thing [as a cap and trade system] with less administrative complexity. Cap and trade, however, more clearly sets an emissions limit and would be more politically appealing both because raising taxes is always difficult.[24]

In plain language that means "Let's dupe American consumers with a wag-the-dog marketing fraud and sell them a seductive packaging without letting them know what the product is and how much it would cost them over the years."

On June 25, 2009, the U.S. House of Representatives passed HR 2454, more commonly referred to as the *Waxman-Markey* Cap and Trade bill[25]. Stern has called the legislation the "centerpiece of the President's domestic program" and described it as "extremely far-reaching and ambitious legislation."[26]

Stern failed to mention that this far-reaching and ambitious centerpiece comes with a hefty price tag, described as one of the largest tax increases in the history of the world.[27] According to an MIT study, the legislation could cost the average household more than $3,900 per year[28] and the Heritage Foundation has estimated job losses due to the legislation to average 1,145,000 at any given time from 2012-2035."[29]

Kyoto revisited in Bonn and Copenhagen

Today Todd Stern is applying a similar marketing strategy while negotiating with foreign leaders a legally binding Cap-and-Trade-like scheme at the international level. The attractive packaging only mentions that emission reduction policies are aimed at decreased consumption, while the unseen product inside is ultimately intended to downsize the global economy.

The Heritage Foundation's Center for Data Analysis found that an emissions reduction bill being debated in the U.S. Senate in the spring of 2008 (S. 2191) would be tantamount to economic self-mutilation. "In just the first two decades.... The estimated aggregate losses to Gross Domestic Product (GDP), adjusted for inflation, [would be] $4.8 trillion." If the US signs onto a legally binding emissions reduction agreement, we would de facto give other countries the control to shrink our economy.

The original Kyoto Protocol, which our Climate Czar helped to negotiate and never stopped advocating for, was never ratified by the U.S. in large part because of the economic concerns it raised.[30] An *Investors Business Daily* Editorial detailed the true impact of the Kyoto Protocol as follows:

> This is the hidden truth about Kyoto: It isn't greenhouse gases the U.N. wants to control. It's big, successful capitalist economies like America's that it wants to rein in. (The world's fastest-growing polluters, India and China, are exempt.) The U.N. itself estimates that reducing global warming would require a permanent hit of at least 1.5% of world GDP — or roughly $1 trillion a year for decades to come.[31]

Another reason for the Kyoto Protocol's demise was the unlevel playing field it created by failing to apply the same restrictions to many "undeveloped countries," such as, the oil-rich United Arab Emirates.[32] In a 2007 paper, Stern wrote:

> [The] Kyoto accord also exempted developing countries from making commitments. This action was appropriate in light of the industrialized world's much greater historic responsibility for producing emissions and its much greater wealth.[33]

According to Marc Morano, former climate researcher and speechwriter for the U.S. Senate Environment and Public Works Committee Chairman Sen. James Inhofe (R-OK) and executive editor of the eco-news center ClimateDepot.com "The sooner we can eliminate the UN from climate and energy policy, the better off energy distribution and the developing world's poor will become. The world needs energy initiatives, not anti-energy initiatives, and as we go forward, the less the United Nations has to do with climate and energy, the better. After all, passing a "scientifically meaningless" climate bill that does not impact global temperatures or CO2 levels is hardly worth spending a moments time worrying about. If we did actually face a man-made climate catastrophe and the "solutions" of the UN and Congress were our only hope, we would all be DOOMED!"

Despite the scientific data that shows there is no need for this type of regulation and the dire economic forecasts of its harmful results, the Obama Administration has called on Stern to negotiate a politically viable new climate agreement that can avoid the pitfalls and ultimate fate of the Kyoto Protocol.[34]

To this end, Stern is now hammering out a deal with the United Nations Framework Convention on Climate Change (UNFCCC) to implement a global version of Cap and Trade that would replace the Kyoto Protocol. The UNFCCC is meeting again in Copenhagen, Denmark in December 2009, and Stern hopes to have a plan in place by then that can be agreed upon.[35]

It is highly dubious, however, to anticipate any acceptable or affordable agreement coming out of these negotiations. While Stern and the Obama Administration have expressed the need and desire to have all countries involved in any emissions reduction program, that outcome is unlikely. This is how Charles Krauthammer described India's rejection of a binding emissions agreement on Fox News' Special Report:

> [I]n the context of India, it makes no sense at all. Our logic is that we say to the Indians, "yes, for the last 100 years, we have polluted the atmosphere in order to attain a high level of standard of living and become rich. And our demand is that you at the beginning of your development with hundreds of millions still in poverty,

stop all this, give up the idea of using cheap fuels as we
did, and stay poor." Now, that is a hell of an argument.
It makes no sense at all.[36]

And if other countries will not allow a climate agreement to put
their economies at risk over questionable science claims, why
should the U.S.?

But Todd Stern and the Obama Administration have already
demonstrated through their push for Cap and Trade legislation
and CAFE standards that the cost to the American taxpayer and
harm to the American economy are no obstacle for advancing
their ideological agenda. For example, the recent increase in fuel
efficiency (CAFE) standards alone is estimated to cost the
American consumers more than $1,300 per new vehicle if they
choose to downsize their ride; it will be much more if they keep
the size of the vehicle they currently own.[37]

Acting as the Administration's key negotiator on global
environmental policies, Stern has the ability to change the way we
live our lives on a daily basis. He has the power to alter the type of
cars we drive, the light bulbs we use, price we pay at the pump
and the cost of our electricity bill each month. The proposals that
he is in charge of negotiating are so vast in scope that everything
from our Gross Domestic Product, to our employment rates, to
our tax rates could be significantly impacted by his actions.

It is futile to warn social engineering "experts" like Todd Stern of
the consequences of their willful blindness of to real-life economic
laws. They are used to not be held responsible for their actions,
conveniently blaming the failures of their policies on the "evils" of
capitalism. There is little doubt, should Todd Stern's utopian
dream become a reality, the resulting economic hardships will be
once again blamed on free enterprise, accompanied by calls to
restrain the free markets even further. As before, the sympathetic
left-leaning media will eagerly amplify these calls while
protecting the real culprits from any meaningful criticism.

As all self-righteous demagogues of his stripe, Todd Stern avoids serious debate by declaring that "the time for denial, delay and dispute is over" - something he asserted at a news conference announcing his appointment.[38] Which is the same as telling American taxpayers, "I win, you lose."

American taxpayers have no one to count on in this fight except the power of their own votes in the next elections.

---

[1] Center for American Progress website, "Global Warming Goes to the Movies" by Todd Stern, May 28, 2004 - http://www.americanprogress.org/issues/2004/05/b83975.html

[2] Cato Institute, "Global Warming Myth" by Patrick J. Michaels, May 16, 2008.

[3] Cato Institute, "Global Warming Myth" by Patrick J. Michaels, May 16, 2008.

[4] The Dartmouth, "Stern '73 to be climate-change envoy" by Anna Perret, January 27, 2009.

[5] *Time*, "Climate Change Envoy Todd Stern" by Frances Romero, January 26, 2009.

[6] The Glen Beck Show, "List of Obama's Czars", August 17, 2009.

[7] Center for American Progress Website - http://www.americanprogress.org/events/2009/06/china.html

[8] The Glen Beck Show, "List of Obama's Czars", August 17, 2009.

[9] *Time*, "Climate Change Envoy Todd Stern" by Frances Romero, January 26, 2009.

[10] *The Washington Quarterly*, "A Changing Climate: The Road Ahead for the United States by Todd Stern and William Antholis, The Center for Strategic and International Studies and MIT, Winter 2007, p. 178

[11] Center for American Progress, "Capturing the Energy Opportunity: Creating a Low-Carbon Economy" By John Podesta, Kit Batten and Todd Stern, November 27, 2007 - http://www.americanprogress.org/issues/2007/11/energy_chapter.ht ml

[12] Center for American Progress, "Capturing the Energy Opportunity: Creating a Low-Carbon Economy" By John Podesta, Kit Batten and Todd Stern, November 27, 2007 - http://www.americanprogress.org/issues/2007/11/energy_chapter.ht ml

[13] Foxnews.com, "US hopes to avoid repeat of Kyoto Protocol" by By VANESSA GERA, Associated Press Writer, March 27, 2009.

[14] Foxnews.com, "US hopes to avoid repeat of Kyoto Protocol" by By VANESSA GERA, Associated Press Writer, March 27, 2009.

[15] Foxnews.com, "US hopes to avoid repeat of Kyoto Protocol" by By VANESSA GERA, Associated Press Writer, March 27, 2009.

[16] *The Washington Post*, "Top Emissions Negotiator an Expert on Political Climate, Too" by Juliet Eilperin, April 15, 2009.

[17] *The Washington Post*, "Climate Changes Dim Bulbs"by George Will April 2, 2009

[18] *The Washington Quarterly*, "A Changing Climate: The Road Ahead for the United States by Todd Stern and William Antholis, The Center for Strategic and International Studies and MIT, Winter 2007, p. 175-176

[19] *The End of Prosperity: How Higher Taxes Will Doom the Economy* by Arthur Laffer, Steve Moore and Peter Tanous, Threshold Editions, October 2008

[20] *Investor's Business Daily,* "Climate Of Control" by Investor's Business Daily, July 14, 2009.

[21] *Investor's Business Daily,* "Climate Of Control" by Investor's Business Daily, July 14, 2009.

[22] *The Washington Quarterly*, "A Changing Climate: The Road Ahead for the United States by Todd Stern and William Antholis, The Center for Strategic and International Studies and MIT, Winter 2007, p. 178

[23] *Wall Street Journal*, "The Cap and Tax Fiction", June 26, 2009. P. A 12

[24] *The Washington Quarterly,* "A Changing Climate: The Road Ahead for the United States by Todd Stern and William Antholis, The Center for Strategic and International Studies and MIT, Winter 2007, p. 178

[25] http://clerk.house.gov/evs/2009/roll477.xml

[26] Press Briefing of the U.S. Delegation UNFCCC Climate Change Talks, Bonn, Germany, March 29, 2009 - http://germany.usembassy.gov/events/2009/mar-29-stern/

[27] *Human Events*, "Congress Must Defeat Clean Energy and Security Act", May 5, 2009.

[28] *The Weekly Standard,* "Fuzzy Math" by John McCormack, April 22, 2009.

[29] Testimony before the Senate Republican Conference, The Economic Impact of the Waxman-Markey Cap-and-Trade Bill by Ben Lieberman, Senior Policy Analyst for Energy and Environment in the Thomas A. Roe Institute for Economic Policy Studies at The Heritage Foundation, June 22, 2009.

---

[30] *National Review Online,* "Kyoto by Another Name" by Marlo Lewis, June 16, 2004.
[31] *Investors Business Daily,* "Greens Spell Progress R-e-c-e-s-s-i-o-n" by *Investors Business Daily, November 18, 2008.*
[32] *News Busters,* "AP Writer: Bush 'Rejected' Kyoto Treaty, Though Senate Never Ratified" by Tom Blummer, January 16, 2007.
[33] *The Washington Quarterly,* "A Changing Climate: The Road Ahead for the United States by Todd Stern and William Antholis, The Center for Strategic and International Studies and MIT, Winter 2007, p. 179
[34] Foxnews.com, "US hopes to avoid repeat of Kyoto Protocol" by By VANESSA GERA, Associated Press Writer, March 27, 2009.
[35] *Washington Post* "Top Emissions Negotiator an Expert on Political Climate, Too" by By Juliet Eilperin, April 15, 2009
[36] Foxnews.com "Special Report' Panel on Paying for Health Care Reform", July 21 2009. -
http://www.foxnews.com/story/0,2933,534253,00.html
[37] *Car and Driver,* "Obama's CAFE Fuel Economy Standards to Create Fleet of Tiny, Expensive Vehicles - Car News" by Steve Siler and Mike Dushane May 2009.
[38] Washington Post, "Stern Appointed Climate Change Envoy," January 26, 2009

Copyright Czar – Victoria Espinel

Official title:	Intellectual Property Enforcement Coordinator
Salary / Direct cost to taxpayers:	Unknown
Responsibilities:	Fighting IP infringement
Reports to:	President
Senate confirmation:	Yes
Relation to Obama:	Member of Obama 2008 Economic Globalization and Trade (EGT) policy committee. Hosted "Globalization" fundraiser for Obama for America – 2008.
Ideology / political affiliation:	Democrat[1]

Victoria Espinel has the resume necessary to make her a great fit for the United States' first-ever copyright czar position. She has a JD from Georgetown University Law School and experience teaching intellectual property law at a collegiate level. However, critics worry that she may be little more than a sycophantic puppet for struggling record companies. The Pro-IP Act, passed during the Bush administration — was a piece of highly controversial legislation that created the office that Espinel now occupies that has been called, at best, unnecessary and, at worst, draconian.

President Bush signed the Pro IP Act (Prioritizing Resources and Organization for Intellectual Property Act of 2008) into law in October 2008. The bill created the copyright czar position to patrol counterfeit products entering the US market that are unsafe to citizens (an issue that undoubtedly needs to be resolved to protect consumers) and the illegal use of intellectual property. The legislation was called "dangerous and unnecessary"[2] as it called for much harsher penalties for people caught engaging in such hardcore criminal activities as downloading music. William Patry, the senior copyright lawyer for Google referred to the law as the most "outrageously gluttonous IP bill ever introduced in the US" and conveyed his disapproval of the "unslakable lust for more and more rights, longer terms of protection, draconian criminal provisions and civil damages that bear no resemblance to the damages suffered."[3] Critics have called the bill unnecessary as the courts already assess outlandish fines to song downloaders. Commonly cited is the absurd case of Jammie Thomas, a Native American mother of four who was fined almost $2 million for downloading twenty-four songs when she became the first defendant to refuse to settle out of court.

The law also calls for more seizure provisions. In *Heretical Ideas Magazine,* IP attorney, Tom Traina gives the hypothetical of a small business streams music — the vast majority or all of which is legally obtained — in the office through one computer. "However, under the law as it's written, the business could have lost its entire computer infrastructure as a result... Not only that, but the entire computer infrastructure could have been seized *even if all the music was legal* — all that would be necessary is the *accusation* of infringement."[4] Many have opined that the punishments are far greater than the crimes and that normal citizens will wind up paying excessive fines to floundering record companies that industry critics say are operating on an outdated business model.

Instead of keeping up with the information age, in which more and more products are becoming available on line for direct download, recording companies are still trying to sell a physical product at high prices. Why would a college student clutter an already tiny dorm room with CDs when he can just download the songs directly to his hard drive? Critics have viewed the record companies' litigious attitudes as a means to shut down their on line competition and collect fines from unwitting criminals to support an obsolete business model.

And unfortunately, it was these very companies that pushed for the Pro-IP Act in the first place. Advocates of more lenient intellectual property laws worry that Espinel will be a mere puppet for the struggling recording industry. In an open letter to President Obama, the United States Pirate Party (a group that condemns illegal downloading, but advocates the creation of a new solution that will stop criminalizing average Americans), the group writes, "We especially hope that President Obama will not continue to fall under the sway of corporations who'd rather preserve dying business models than create real change."[5] As Mike Masnick writes on TechDirt.com that the position of copyright czar is "the entertainment industry's personal representative in the White House, in charge of "coordinating" (i.e., "driving") strategy on making sure that the entertainment industry's obsolete business model is always protected directly by the White House."[6]

And critics worry that Victoria Espinel may be just the puppet that the industries need. She has advised several congressional committees on intellectual property issues, including the House Ways and Means, House Judiciary, Senate Judiciary and Senate Finance. She is also the president and founder of Bridging the Innovation Divide, a non-profit that empowers Americans to create. A lawyer who most recently served as a Visiting Assistant Professor at the George Mason University School of Law, Espinel also worked in the United States Trade Representative's office as an assistant trade representative for intellectual property and innovation.[7] Her history at the USTR has worried critics that admonish the group for operating secretly to enforce stricter IP laws.

Pro IP detractors have also criticized the placement of the copyright czar's department within the Office of Management and Budget as opposed to the more appropriate Office of Science and Technology Policy. Masnick notes that by putting Espinel in the budget office, it keeps her away from the tech-savvy staff that truly understands how the Internet has changed the recording industry and is far more apt to pursue innovative in copyright law.[8]

Copyleftists — the term applied to those for freer copyright privileges — are also concerned about how such excessive fines will stifle creativity in an age in which artists are constantly referencing previous works. As attorney John Melber writes in *The Huffington Post*,

> In a period when, thanks to digital technology, anyone can make a film or cut an album, this outdated policy has several bad consequences. First, it suppresses a new form of cultural expression. Imagine how much culture would have been lost in the last century had authors, playwrights and commentators needed to seek permission (let alone pay) every time they wanted to quote someone else's writing. Second, given our retrograde copyright policy, the cultural expression that happens anyway (The Legendary K.O. and the millions of other video mashups on YouTube) is at best of dubious legal standing, and at worst a crime. Finally, because this kind of expression is illegal under current copyright laws, we have simply criminalized an enormous segment of the population.
>
> It's worth remembering that, despite the alarmist claims of the content industry, copyright was not created to prop up giant media companies or pad the trust funds of celebrities' heirs. The Founding Fathers were wary of an overzealous copyright policy because they understood what Congress has long since forgotten: that there are significant economic and social costs to granting "too much" copyright. This is because granting someone a copyright is essentially giving that person a monopoly over his or her creation. Since we generally disfavor monopolies, for obvious reasons, the original principle behind our country's copyright policy was to grant only the minimal monopoly necessary to induce the maximum cultural creation. But today, we have something closer to the inverse: maximum monopolies functioning as corporate welfare for the content industry while severely curtailing individual artistic creation.
>
> As the chief US trade negotiator for intellectual property, Espinel has had plenty of opportunity to think about copyright from the content industry's perspective, which is probably why Hollywood and the RIAA are so pleased with her appointment. I hope she disappoints them by pushing

for a return to a copyright policy that truly fosters
creativity.[9]

Espinel has already drawn criticism for her intentions with the
position that she professed in her confirmation hearing in early
November 2009, in which she focused on her goal to protect jobs
that depend on intellectual property. As per Espinel, "If I am
confirmed as the United States Intellectual Property Enforcement
Coordinator, I will work side by side with agencies, Congress,
stakeholders and the public to ensure that jobs that depend on
intellectual property are not compromised by others'
unwillingness to respect and enforce the rule of law." However, as
Masnick writes, "But intellectual property law is not about
'protecting jobs,' it's about encouraging innovation. Innovation
can be disruptive. Jobs can get shifted around. Protecting jobs is
not encouraging innovation. It's the opposite."[10]

Extreme copyright enforcement makes normal people—often
teenagers and college students[11]—into criminals and stifles
technological innovation and the freedom to share files over the
Internet. Hopefully Espinel will not use her position to act as a
shill for the record companies in yet another way that the Obama
administration has fused business and government.

— *Lucy Leitner*

---

[1] "United States Senate Committee on the Judiciary Questionnaire For
Victoria Espinel." United States Senate. Oct. 7, 2009. Apr. 8, 2009
<http://judiciary.senate.gov/nominations/111thCongressExecutiveNo
minations/upload/Espinel-Public-Questionnaire.pdf>.
[2] Bangeman, Eric. "Pro-IP Act is Dangerous and Unnecessary, Say
Industry Groups." Ars Technica. 2 Feb. 2008. 2 March 2010 <
http://arstechnica.com/tech-policy/news/2008/02/white-paper-pro-
ip-acts-damage-increases-are-dangerous.ars>.
[3] Anderson, Nate. "House Committee Hears the Cons of the Pro-IP Act."
Ars Technica. 13 Dec. 2007. 2 March 2010 < http://arstechnica.com/tech-

policy/news/2007/12/house-committee-hears-the-cons-of-the-pro-ip-act.ars>.

4 Traina, Tom. "Meet the Copyright Czar." Heretical Ideas. 22 Oct. 2008. 2 March 2010 < http://www.hereticalideas.com/2008/10/meet-the-copyright-czar/>.

5 "Obama's Copyright Problem." [Weblog Entry.] United States Pirate Party. 26 Jan. 2010. (http://www.pirate-party.us/content/obamas-copyright-problem). 2 March 2010.

6 Masnick, Mike. "IP Czar Won't Be in the Most Sensible Place Because Industry Doesn't Like It?" Tech Dirt. 4 Sept. 2009. 2 March 2010 <http://www.techdirt.com/articles/20090902/1559226084.shtml>.

7 "President Obama Announces Key Administration Post." Music Industry News Network. MusicDish, LLC. 7 March 2010 < http://www.mi2n.com/press.php3?press_nb=123485>.

8 Masnick, Mike. "Obama Finally Appoints IP Czar… Puts it in the Wrong Department." Tech Dirt. 25 Sept. 2009. 2 March 2010 < http://www.techdirt.com/articles/20090925/1549476326.shtml>.

9 Melber, Jonathan. "A Remix Manifesto for Our New Copyright Czar." The Huffington Post. 30 Sept. 2009. 2 March 2010 < http://www.huffingtonpost.com/jonathan-melber/a-remix-manifesto-for-our_b_305064.html>.

10 Masnick, Mike. "IP Czar Focused on Protecting Jobs, Not Promoting Progress?" Tech Dirt. 6 Nov. 2009. 2 March 2010 < http://www.techdirt.com/articles/20091106/0214196822.shtml>.

11 Lavoie, Denise. "Joel Tennenbaum: Record Companies Try to Gag Student, Stop From Promoting Illegal Downloads." The Huffington Post. 7 Dec. 2009. 7 March 2010 <http://www.huffingtonpost.com/2009/12/07/joel-tenenbaum-record-lab_n_383295.html>.

Cybersecurity Czar— Howard A. Schmidt

Official title:	Director of the White House Office of Cybersecurity
Salary / Direct cost to taxpayers:	Unknown
Responsibilities:	Protecting U.S. government from cyberthreats / crime
Reports to:	Deputy National Security Adviser John O. Brennan
Senate confirmation:	No[1]
Relation to Obama:	No previous relationship with Obama
Ideology / political affiliation:	Unknown

Prying Into the Private Realm of the Internet

For months, the cybersecurity czar position was vacant, almost like it was a doomed post that had a higher turnover rate than being a drummer for Spinal Tap. Finally, in December 2009, Howard A. Schmidt agreed to take the job to advise the president to shut down the Internet. It is a job that nobody seems to want to take and many journalists and government officials do not want to exist.

Rod Beckstrom didn't want it: He left in March, citing bureaucratic power grabs. Melissa Hathaway left in August, noting a lack of empowerment to manage the task with which she had been charged. Though never named a czar, Mischel Kwan— director of the United States Computer Readiness Team— resigned from her post for feeling similarly helpless in waging the war against cybercrime.[2]

> "While the organizational and political problems are all too real, it is also obvious that taking the cybersecurity czar job is a lose-lose situation. That is because whoever takes on this role will be charged with completely protecting federal systems from dangerous intrusions— a task that is virtually impossible in today's

interconnected world," wrote tech consultant Ara Trembly[3].

Paul Kurtz, a cybersecurity consultant, turned down the offer to fill the czar position in February[4], as have Tom Davis (former Virginia representative to Congress), Gen. Harry D. Radeuge Jr. (former director of the Defense Information Systems Agency), Scott Charney (Microsoft executive), and John W. Thompson (Symantec chairman)[5]. Experts have noted that the position is extremely difficult to fill both because of the lack of qualified applicants and because it is a job that is virtually impossible to perform with any degree of effectuality.

"The position as set up is designed more for bureaucracy and empire building, not driving change for the better of cybersecurity," said John Pescatore, an analyst with IT research and advisory firm Gartner Inc[6]. He has also argued that cybersecurity does not start with government control over the Internet but with the use of policy to rid the system of vulnerabilities to attack[7].

"Signing on to fight the war against cybercrime is one thing. Signing up to fulfill a politician's unrealistic expectations is another, because any failure — and who really knows what constitutes failure here? — will be pinned to the chest of the unfortunate individual who takes the czar's post," Trembly wrote.

And that man is Howard A. Schmidt, an air force veteran and 11-year Chandler, Arizona police officer who made the switch from law enforcement to cybersecurity quite by accident. Involved in a narcotics bust, Schmidt maneuvered through the password protection on the drug dealer's computer to find spreadsheets listing criminal activities. Capitalizing on his aptitude for computer crimes, he specialized in this type of case and rejoined the Air Force, after graduating from the University of Pheonix in 1994, as head of computer crime and information warfare. He departed in 1997 to become chief security officer at Microsoft, a job he kept for five years. After a brief stint aiding in the draft of then-President George W. Bush's post-9/11 cybersecurity plan, Schmidt returned to the private sector as the chief information security officer for eBay. Two years later, he became CEO and president of Information Security Forum, a nonprofit cybersecurity firm. Though most of his ideas were ignored during the Bush administration, Schmidt returns to the White House in a more powerful post that permits him to advise the president to shut down the Internet.[8]

Why Give Obama the Power to Shut Down the Internet?

A controversial bill introduced in March by Democratic Sen. John D. Rockefeller IV of West Virginia and Republican Sen. Olympia J. Snowe of Maine, with input from the White House, called for the creation of a cybersecurity czar who would have the power to advise the president to shut down the Internet if a cyberthreat is perceived. The bill also pushes to give the czar a home in the creation of the Office of the National Cybersecurity Adviser[9]. This would essentially set up an entirely new government enterprise composed of officials chosen by the president and his appointed czar. And the Department of Homeland Security, with its history in dealing with cybersecurity issues, would be left out of the loop. However, the most objectionable stipulation in the bill is that it gives the federal government the unprecedented power to regulate the private sector.

"The Senate Commerce Committee wants to hand control of the Internet over to the Obama White House. Increased government intervention isn't the answer to the nation's cybersecurity policy," read a *Washington Times* editorial[10].

"The Iranian and Chinese governments are known for controlling the Internet use of their citizens. This could not happen in the U.S., could it? The Senate is considering such a bill to create control of the U.S. cyberspace," wrote Denise Clay for *Huliq News*.[11]

Civil liberties watchdog groups have been especially attentive to the bill's provision to allow the government to probe into whatever is included in the undefined phrase "critical infrastructure," which experts argue could extend to mean banks, telecommunications, and Internet service providers.

"The language is vague and open ended," said Leslie Harris, president of the Center for Democracy and Technology. "If you read broadly and the Internet falls under this, it could be devastating to both innovation and civil liberties."[12]

"I think it's reasonable for critical infrastructure and government contractors, but if it extends into general business, it's doomed to failure," said Rick Mogull, founder of security consultancy Securosis.[13]

Experts have also voiced concern over the clause for a single standard for cybersecurity that the whole Internet would have to operate under, stating that this would leave everyone open to threats to security if the one standard were infiltrated.[14] Overall, the plan to federalize the Internet and to give Obama the right to declare a cyberemergency is unprecedented and has been met with overwhelmingly negative opinions.

Although the new bill gives authority to pry into private activity, those who have occupied the position of cybersecurity czar have felt powerless to implement real change. One commonly cited problem with the job is that the czar will report to both the National Economic Council and the National Security Council, creating an administrative mess and turf wars among the various offices.[15] This lends a certain ambiguity to the position: Will the czar be combating cybercrime or acting as a liaison between government agencies? Authorities within the White House promise that they have eliminated the problem by instructing Schmidt to report directly to National Security Adviser John O. Brennan. However, he must still collaborate with National Economic Council Director Lawrence H. Summers, because the director insists that cybersecurity is directly related to economic security. Sources also say that he will have direct access to Obama.[16] There has also been some concern that the cybersecurity czar position will do little but replicate the work of the technology triad of Aneesh Chopra, Vivek Kundra, and Jeffrey Zients. On Federal News Radio, Lurita Doan worried about the costs associated with creating a new office in this troubled economy:

> Last week, President Obama informed American citizens that the money had run out and the government was now in deficit spending. So, it is mystifying why he would waste federal money creating a duplicative office, with redundant, ill-defined responsibilities[17].

The actual duties of the cybersecurity czar are a mystery that Doan argues should be "clearly delineated, and the president should explain why he thinks these duties can't be performed by any of the various existing members of his cabinet."

There's a Czar for That

With Hathaway's departure, many had voiced the opinion that she should not be replaced, that Obama should ditch the idea of allotting federal money to create a new post that no one wants to fill. The formation of the new office would extend the federal government's reach even further into the private sector and give the president the unprecedented power to shut down the Internet, yet it would still leave the appointed czar feeling completely ineffectual.

But overall, Schmidt's appointment has been met with approval. A veteran of both the private sector and the government, pundits have almost unanimously approved of Obama's choice for whatever this job may be.

According to a video message from Schmidt, directly following his appointment, his goals are to create a comprehensive plan to secure networks in order to guarantee an organized response to future cyber threats, to strengthen partnerships (both domestically and abroad) between the public and private sectors, promote the development of security technologies and raise awareness in protection against cybercrime.[18] Schmidt has begun drafting a plan for cybersecurity that he presented declassified aspects of the Comprehensive National Cybersecurity Initiative (CNCI) at the RSA event in San Francisco in early March 2010.

> "The CNCI is a twelve-part initiative that covers several key aspects of digital security, including the cloak-and-dagger counterintelligence stuff. Its overall intent, revealed for the first time since its inception in 2008, is to be the first line of defense against immediate cyberattacks, to defend against every possible kind of attack, and to work to improve future cybersecurity," wrote journalist Kit Eaton, covering the event for *Fast Company*.[19]

Schmidt's 40 years of experience in various security capacities and his proactive attitude have left most critics optimistic about the future of U.S. protection from cyber attacks. However, the loosely defined position and bureaucracy surrounding it still cast a dubious shadow over what appears to be an otherwise capable man.

The constant criticism, the Big Brother imagery associated with government control of the Internet, and the notion of helplessness espoused by former post occupants put a blemish on Obama's apparent mantra: "There's a czar for that."

— *Lucy Leitner*

---

[1] Nakashima, Ellen and Wilgoren, Debby. "Obama Names Howard Schmidt as Cybersecurity Coordinator." *The Washington Post*. Dec. 22,

2009. Apr. 8, 2010 <http://www.washingtonpost.com/wp-dyn/content/article/2009/12/22/AR2009122201429.html>.

[2] "Another U.S. Cybersecurity Official Resigns." *Techweb* Aug. 10, 2009.

[3] Trembly, Ara. "White House Cyber-Security Czar: The Job No One Wants." *Insurance Networking News* Aug. 13, 2009. Insurance Networking News and SourceMedia Inc. Aug. 27, 2009 <http://www.insurancenetworking.com/news/insurance_cyber_security_Obama_White_House_risk_data_security-12834-1.html>.

[4] Greenburg, Andy. "Obama's Unwilling Cyber Czars." Forbes.com July 20, 2009. Aug. 30, 2009 <http://www.forbes.com/2009/07/20/cybersecurity-obama-economy-technology-security-cybersecurity.html>.

[5] Kamen, Al. "White House Still Has a Vacancy for a Lesser Czar." *The Washington Post* July 29, 2009, Suburban Edition: p. A15.

[6] Vijayan, Jaikumar. "Pressure on Obama to Move Fast on Cybersecurity Appointment." *Computer World* Aug. 4, 2009. Aug. 30, 2009 <http://www.computerworld.com/s/article/9136246/Pressure_on_Obama_to_move_fast_on_cybersecurity_appointment>.

[7] "Obama Should Scrap Cybersecurity Czar, Analyst Says." Techweb May 28, 2009.

[8] "Howard A. Schmidt." WhoRunsGov. The Washington Post. 2 March 2010. < http://www.whorunsgov.com/Profiles/Howard_A._Schmidt>.

[9] Warrick, Joby and Walter Pincus. "Senate Legislation Would Federalize Cybersecurity." *The Washington Post* April 1, 2009, Met 2 Edition: p. A4.

[10] "White House Control of the Internet; More Government Intervention Won't Mean Better Cybersecurity." *The Washington Times* Aug. 30, 2009: p. B2.

[11] Clay, Denise. "Senate Cybersecurity Act of 2009 Could Shut Down the Internet." *Huliq News* Aug. 29, 2009. Aug. 30, 2009, <http://www.huliq.com/7504/85556/senate-cybersecurity-act-2009-could-shut-down-internet>.

[12] Greenberg, Andy. "The Senate's Cyber Lightning Rod." Forbes.com April 1, 2009. Aug. 30, 2009 <http://www.forbes.com/2009/04/01/cybersecurity-government-google-technology-security-cybersecurity.html>.

[13] Brenner, Bill. "Federalizing Cybersecurity: Necessary or Nitwitted?" CSOonline.com April 1, 2009. Aug. 30, 2009 <http://www.csoonline.com/article/487745/Federalizing_Cybersecurity_Necessary_or_Nitwitted_>.

[14] Clay, Denise. "Senate Cybersecurity Act of 2009 Could Shut Down the Internet." *Huliq News* Aug. 29, 2009. Aug. 30, 2009, <http://www.huliq.com/7504/85556/senate-cybersecurity-act-2009-could-shut-down-internet>.

[15] Kamen, Al. "White House Still Has a Vacancy for a Lesser Czar." *The Washington Post* July 29, 2009, Suburban Edition: p. A15.

[16] Nakashima, Ellen. "Obama to Name Howard Schmidt as Cybersecurity Coordinator." *The Washington Post.* 22 Dec. 2009: A4.

[17] Doan, Lurita. "Is This Czar Really Necessary?" Federal News Radio June 2, 2009. Aug. 27, 2009 <http://www.federalnewsradio.com/?nid=104&sid=1686811>.

[18] Mimiso, Michael S. "Howard Schmidt Named Cybersecurity Coordinator." SecuritySearch 21 Dec. 2009. 4 March 2010 < http://searchsecurity.techtarget.com/news/article/0,289142,sid14_gci1377518,00.html>.

[19] Eaton, Kit. "U.S. Cybers Security Czar Comes out of the Shadows to Reveal Defense Plans." Fast Company 4 March 2010. 4 March 2010 < http://www.fastcompany.com/1570414/us-cyber-security-tzar-howard-schmidt-rsa-cnci-web-attacks>.

Disinformation Czar – Linda Douglass

Official title:	Director of Communications for the White House Office of Health Reform
Salary / Direct cost to taxpayers:	Salary not listed in White House employee salary chart[1]
Responsibilities:	Silencing "disinformation" about Obama's health care plan
Reports to:	Health Care Czar Nancy-Ann DeParle
Senate confirmation:	None
Relation to Obama:	Admired him since they met while she was covering the Senate in 2005 for ABC, advised him on his campaign in 2007, husband donated to his presidential run.
Ideology / political affiliation:	Democrat. Left journalism to be part of "hope and change."

Former Journalist Becomes ObamaCare Mouthpiece

Commonly referred to as Obama's Minister of Propaganda[2], a flack[3], a shill[4], a "snitch czarina"[5] and even Joseph Goebbels[6], Linda Douglass represents the fallibility of journalistic integrity. A respected television journalist for over thirty years, Douglass's switch from objective reporting to the highest, most controversial PR position in the country is in the least a breach of ethics and at most puts her objectivity in the past three decades of her career in doubt.

She began a long career in journalism in 1973 when she served as a researcher at a TV station in Los Angeles and was promoted to a political editor in two years later. In 1981, she became an L.A. correspondent for CBS, serving as the network's lead campaign reporter in the 1984 presidential race. After serving as KCBS-TV's political editor and evening news co-anchor, she moved to Washington, DC in 1993.[7]

Douglass has a long association with powerful members of the Democratic Party, including a friendship with Clinton-Gore campaign chair Mickey Kantor. In the early-1990s, when she was covering Washington, DC for CBS, she and her husband, attorney and democratic fundraiser John Phillips, became close friends with Bill Clinton-appointed Justice Department official Webb Hubbell and his wife Suzy. The couples vacationed together to the Greek islands and when Hubbell (who had previously come under fire for his membership to an all-white country club[8]) was indicted for cheating his clients and tax fraud, Douglass and Phillips stood by his side. Phillips was even associated with a foundation that agreed to pay the disgraced government official $45,000 to write an article. They finally abandoned their friend when the full extent of his corruption was exposed and were never suspected of any criminal activity.[9]

Now Douglass finds herself on the other side; she can maintain close friendships with politicians and be partisan herself, but she also has shut the journalistic eye that searches for the truth behind loaded statements from PR professionals. As Byron York writes in the The Washington Examiner, "She's free to be partisan — no recusals necessary — but she's squandering the credibility she built earlier in her career. You can be the most polished communicator in the world, but you can't make a convincing argument if you have nothing to say." Chief political correspondent York also wonders how she can simply ignore what a few years ago was part of her job to question.

After serving as lead reporter on the 1994 Clinton heath plan coverage, she left CBS in 1998 for ABC where she covered the Clinton impeachment and the presidential campaigns of 2000. In December 2000, ABC named her Capitol Hill correspondent and was charged with covering the aftermath of September 11 and the Enron scandal in 2002. She retired from journalism in 2006 for a fellowship at Harvard where she offered Obama campaign advice in 2007. After writing about the election for the National Journal, she became a senior strategist and spokeswoman for Obama's campaign in May 2008.[10] And she has been there ever since, ridding herself of the journalistic obligation to report truth to become a mere mouthpiece for the president and his controversial health care initiative. But her admiration of Obama began when she was still with ABC, covering the Senate for the network in 2005. As *The Washington Post* quoted, "I'd come home and say, 'This guy is really impressive. He's got an unusually clam demeanor. He's very smart and strikes me as someone with good judgment.'"[11]

She is one of fourteen (as of February 2, 2010 when *Washington Post* film critic Desson Thomson made the far less controversial decision to become a speechwriter for Ambassador Louis Susman)[12] journalists to leave their professions to join the Obama White House as speechwriters or other positions in the communications capacity. While there is a precedent for this behavior (Ron Nesson in the 1970s to serve Gerald Ford), the fact that fourteen journalists have passed through what is being called the "revolving door" is excessive. As Jim Rutenberg wrote in the *New York Times*, "An unusual number of journalists from prominent, mainstream organizations started new government jobs in January, providing new kindling to the debate over whether Mr. Obama is receiving unusually favorable treatment in the news media... They are for the most part, more traditional journalists from organizations that strive to approach the news with objectivity."[13]

This rash of press defectors sets a dangerous precedent for the credibility of what conservatives already suspect to be a dubious political media. It exposes a degree of truth in the long-standing conspiracy theories of right-leaning pundits that were always relegated to the realm of paranoia. As Politico's Ben Smith writes in response to Douglass's original switch to campaign strategist, "It's a home run of a data point for anyone who thinks the press is in the tank for Obama."[14] Marc Ambinder, political blogger for atlantic.com wrote, "To conservative media critics, the divide between the press corps and modern political liberalism is fairly narrow, and easy to jump over, and Douglass's decision will reconfirm their sense that bias pervades newsrooms."[15]

Douglass's former employer ABC came under fire in June, 2009 from the Congressional Media Fairness Caucus that accused the network of a breach of ethics when it ran a four-program marathon about health with Obama. In a letter to ABC News president David Westin, the Caucus wrote,

> The manner in which news programming is being presented – at the White House with the President and First Lady without opposition – is unprofessional and contrary to the journalistic code of ethics to present news fairly and independently. This is not a Presidential news conference open to all news media. This is an exclusive arrangement from which the President and his viewpoint stand to gain. It's as if ABC News is providing in-kind free advertising for President Obama.[16]

Conservative blogger Pamela Geller also questions Douglass's numerous ties to news media. Sarcastically, she asks on her Atlas Shrugs Video blog, "You think she like uses her old contacts at all? No, they have too much integrity for that."[17]

In August 2009, Douglass came under fire from conservatives when the White House released a statement on its official website. The video post featured Douglass warning Americans of all the "disinformation that's out there about health-insurance reform." She further accuses ObamaCare opponents of fear mongering and that "they're taking sentences and phrases out of context, and they're cobbling them together to leave a VERY false impression." The video montage to which she is referring is entitled "SHOCK UNCOVERED," in which Obama states, "I happen to be a proponent of a single payer, universal health care program. That is what I would like to see." Bloggers and pundits rebutted immediately, noting that although Douglass accused the makers of the video (that also shows Obama stating, "I don't think we're going to be able to eliminate employer coverage immediately. There's going to be, potentially, some transition process: I can envision a decade out, or 15 years out, or 20 years out.") of taking his statements out of context and "cobbling them together," she offers no proof that the video was fake.[18]

In a follow-up interview with Howard Kurtz on CNN, she vehemently denied the President's support of the single-payer system, stating, "This was a bunch of clips that were taken out of context with a headline that said the president wants to eliminate private insurance. Well that is the absolute opposite of what he's talking about." Kurtz then observed that some of the clips from the video in which Obama endorses his plan for universal health care were dated from before he was president. He then asked if Obama's views have changed since he was a senator, to which Douglass responds, "He didn't have a different position when he was a senator."[19] Needless to say, the interview became fodder for conservative blogs and websites.

But what caused the biggest backlash against the disinformation czar was the following statement posted below the her video on the White House blog;

> There is a lot of disinformation about health insurance reform out there, spanning from control of personal finances to end of life care. These rumors often travel just below the surface via chain emails or through casual conversation. Since we can't keep track of all of them here at the White House, we're asking for your help. If you get an email or see something on the web about health insurance reform that seems fishy, send it to flag@whitehouse.gov.

Fringe bloggers and the mainstream media read the solicitation as a Goebbels-like call for citizens to report others. Others analyzed the legal issues with Douglass's request. Erick Erickson cited 5 U.S.C. § 552a that states that government agencies shall "maintain no record describing how any individual exercises rights guaranteed by the First Amendment unless expressly authorized by statute or by the individual about whom the record is maintained or unless pertinent to and within the scope of an authorized law enforcement activity." Erickson goes on to state,

> The White House may take the position that certain of its offices aren't subject to the Privacy Act, but most Presidents instruct their staffs to comply. This will be a the first significant time the White House has ignored the Privacy Act and may open President Obama up to litigation.[20]

As Dorothy Rabinowitz writes in the *Wall Street Journal*, "Neither has she [Douglass] seemed to entertain any second thoughts about the tenor of a message enlisting the public in a program reeking of a White House effort to set Americans against one another — the good Americans protecting the president's health-care program from the bad Americans fighting it and undermining truth and goodness."[21]

Describing perpetrators of such heretical activity, Douglass declares contemptuously, "There are people out there with a computer and a lot of free time."

If Douglass hasn't realized, media is changing. With the rise of the Internet, mainstream media outlets are fading and every facet of journalism — from sports to politics — is being taken over by grassroots bloggers who put everyone from sports heroes to 15-minute famers to politicians on trial. The people with too much time and a computer are the new face of journalism, espousing viewpoints that even the now corporately owned "alternative" weeklies are too dependent on advertising to publish. Bloggers find niches to independently use their first amendment rights and, of course, the health care debacle is the hot item.

As a professional journalist, it can only be assumed that Douglass studied both ethics and media law in preparation for her career. How did she so quickly bypass the ethical dilemma of switching from questioning those in power to simply regurgitating what they've said? It is one thing to root for the home team when covering a sports beat in a local paper, but quite another to become a highly paid spokesperson for the ever-expanding federal government. And did she somehow miss a class discussion on the first amendment? Some apologists liken her switch from journalism to PR to a film critic's switch to screenwriting. Both know the criticism that they would face from their former peers — whose jobs are to deconstruct what is happening — but there is a massive difference in the effects of writing a film and preaching the stance of a controversial president.

Maybe instead of uttering empty, inane phrases such as, "One thing we learned during the campaign was if you give people all the facts, they will become better informed,"[22] Douglass should return to her journalistic roots and she'd learn that there is come credence to the concerns that so many of her countrymen and women are expressing.

The Honeymoon period is over. Americans are starting to question the Jesus of the campaign trail. And disciples like Linda Douglass, who Rabinowitz describes as having "the air of a person consigned to service in a holy order,"[23] should get used to it.

— Lucy Leitner

----

[1] Malkin, Michelle. "Health care czar's office calls for Internet snitch brigade." [Weblog entry]. Michelle Malkin LLC. Aug. 4, 2009. Apr. 8, 2010 < http://michellemalkin.com/2009/08/04/health-care-czars-office-calls-for-internet-snitch-brigade/>.
[2] "Linda Douglass, Obama Minister of Propaganda, Hung Out to Dry." The Rush Limbaugh Show. Rush Limbaugh. 10 Aug. 2009.
[3] Kurtz, Howard. "As Obama Aid, Reporter Dons Flack Jacket." *The Washington Post*. 16 June 2008: C1.
[4] Whitlock, Scott. "Ex-Journalist Linda Douglass Returns to ABC to Shill for Obama." [Weblog entry.] NewsBusters. Media Research Center. 4

June 2008. (http://newsbusters.org/blogs/scott-whitlock/2008/06/04/ex-journalist-linda-douglass-returns-abc-shill-obama). 2 March 2010.

5 Crocker, David P. "Linda Douglass: White House Snitch Czarina." [Weblog entry.] Behind Blue Lines. 5 Aug. 2009. (http://www.behindbluelines.com/2009/08/05/linda-douglass-white-house-snitch-czarina/). 2 March 2010.

6 Linkins, Jason. "Red State's Erick Erickson Defends Controversial Twitter Posts on 'Colbert Report.'" The Huffington Post 5 Jan. 2010. 3 March 2010 <http://www.huffingtonpost.com/2010/01/05/redstates-erick-erickson_n_411660.html>.

7 "Linda Douglass." WhoRunsGov. 2009. The Washington Post. 2 March 2010 < http://www.whorunsgov.com/Profiles/Linda_Douglass>.

8 Johnston, David. "Justice Post Nominee Says He Has Quit Golf Club." *The New York Times*. 20 May 1993: A16.

9 York, Byron. "The Empty Words of a Journalist Turned Flack." *The Washington Examiner*. 7 Aug. 2009.

10 "Linda Douglass." WhoRunsGov. 2009. The Washington Post. 2 March 2010 < http://www.whorunsgov.com/Profiles/Linda_Douglass>.

11 Kurtz, Howard. "As Obama Aid, Reporter Dons Flack Jacket." *The Washington Post*. 16 June, 2008: C1.

12 Baker, Brent. "Washington Post's Thomson the 14th Journalist to Join Obama Administration." [Weblog entry.] NewsBusters. Media Research Center. 2 Feb. 2010. (http://newsbusters.org/blogs/brent-baker/2010/02/03/washington-posts-thomson-14th-journalist-join-obama-administration). 3 March 2010.

13 Rutenberg, Jim. "Ex-Journalists' New Jobs Fuel Debate on Favoritism." *The New York Times*. 3 Feb. 2009: A17.

14 Smith, Ben. "National Journal's Douglass Joins the Obama Campaign." [Weblog entry.] Capitol News Company, LLC. 21 May 2008. (http://www.politico.com/blogs/bensmith/0508/National_Journals_Douglass_joins_the_Obama_campaign.html). 3 March 2010.

15 Ambinder, Marc. "Linda Douglass's Decision: Beginning a Debate." *Atlantic*. 21 May 2008.

16 "Congressional Media Fairness Caucus Letter to ABC News." Docstoc 2010. Docstoc. 3 March 2010 < http://www.docstoc.com/docs/7625138/Congressional-Media-Fairness-Caucus-Letter-To-ABC-News>.

17 Geller, Pamela. "Atlas Vlogs Linda Douglass, Obama's Newest Minister of Propaganda." [Weblog entry.] Atlas Shrugs. 10 Aug. 2009.

(http://atlasshrugs2000.typepad.com/atlas_shrugs/2009/08/atlas-vlogs-linda-douglass-obamas-newest-minister-of-propaganda.html). 3 March 2010.

[18] Douglass, Linda. "Facts Are Stubborn Things." [Weblog entry.] The White House. 4 Aug. 2009. (http://www.whitehouse.gov/blog/Facts-Are-Stubborn-Things/). 3 March 2010.

[19] "Protesters Disrupt Health Care Town Halls." Reliable Sources. Howard Kurtz. CNN. 9 Aug. 2009.

[20] Erickson, Erick. "White House Actions May Be Unlawful." [Weblog entry.] Red State. Eagle Publishing, Inc. 5 August 2009. (http://www.redstate.com/erick/2009/08/05/white-house-actions-might-be-illegal/). 3 March 2010.

[21] Rabinowitz, Dorothy. "Obama's Tone-Deaf Health Campaign." *The Wall Street Journal*. 10 Aug. 2009: A17.

[22] "Protesters Disrupt Health Care Town Halls." Reliable Sources. Howard Kurtz. CNN. 9 Aug. 2009.

[23] Rabinowitz, Dorothy. "Obama's Tone-Deaf Health Campaign." *The Wall Street Journal*. 10 Aug. 2009: A17.

Diversity Czar — Mark Lloyd

Official title:	Chief Diversity Officer at the Federal Communications Commission (FCC), Associate General Counsel
Official responsibilities:	Work to ensure communications field is competitive and generates widespread opportunities for women, minorities
Reports to:	FCC Chairman
Senate confirmation:	None
Salary:	Information unavailable
Ideology / political affiliation:	Virulently anti-capitalist and racially fixated left-wing activist, admirer of Hugo Chavez's model of silencing the free media

It appears that Hugo Chavez's Marxist revolution is something to be admired in the Obama Administration. Almost one year after radical activist Mark Lloyd publicly stated his fascination with Chavez's "incredible revolution" and the way the Venezuelan dictator took over the media and silenced free speech, President Obama installed him as the Diversity Czar at the Federal Communications Commission (FCC), giving this disciple of Saul Alinsky full power to act on his totalitarian fantasies in controlling speech on the radio.

Lloyd has long been on a crusade to destroy conservative talk radio and to drive talk show hosts like Rush Limbaugh, Mark Levin, Sean Hannity, Glenn Beck, and hundreds of others off the air through a myriad of regulations and fees hiding behind the guise of "diversity." On July 29, 2009, his zeal was rewarded in the form of a powerful position as the Chief Diversity Officer at the FCC.[1] The choice of Mark Lloyd to fill this newly created post[2] sheds enough light on the Obama Administration's true intentions in the field of "media diversity" to qualify the entire affair as a backdoor attempt to reinstate the Fairness Doctrine.

Who is Our Diversity Czar?

As most left-wing activists of his caliber do, Mark Lloyd maintains a presentable façade of a communications attorney with experience of a broadcast journalist, including work at NBC and CNN,[3] an adjunct professor Georgetown University, a visiting scholar at the Massachusetts Institute of Technology (MIT),[4] senior fellow at the Center for American Progress (a far left think tank funded in part by liberal financier George Soros[5]), and most recently as Vice President for Strategic Initiatives at the Leadership Conference on Civil Rights[6], where he oversaw this left-wing coalition's media and communications initiatives.[7]

But throughout this seemingly spectacular career within the free-market capitalist establishment, Mark Lloyd has always been and still remains what some describe as virulently anti-capitalist, almost myopically racially fixated and exuberantly pro-regulation left-wing activist specializing in ways to censor conservative media outlets,[8] who has written extensively on ways to combat conservative talk radio through FCC regulations and licensing fees.[9]

Return of the Fairness Doctrine?

The Fairness Doctrine is a former FCC regulation that required broadcasters to carry a certain level of opposing political viewpoints. The FCC overturned the regulation in 1987 after it determined that it restricted journalistic freedom.[10]

If Lloyd is claiming that he is not in favor of or pushing for reinstatement of the Fairness Doctrine,[11] it is only because his mind is fixed on something even worse. In an August 14, 2009 letter to FCC Chairman Genachowski, U.S. Senator Charles Grassley's (R-IA) raised his concerns over Lloyd's appointment and asked for a commitment that the FCC would not bring back the Fairness Doctrine or impose new similar restrictions. Below is an excerpt from Senator Grassley's letter:

On July 29, 2009, you announced the appointment of
Mark Lloyd as Associate General Counsel and Chief
Diversity Officer for the Federal Communications
Commission (FCC). I write today to express my concerns
with this appointment...

Simply put, I strongly disagree with Mr. Lloyd. I do not
believe that more regulation, more taxes or fines, or
increased government intervention in the commercial
radio market will serve the public interest or further the
goals of diversifying the marketplace. I am concerned
that despite his statements that the Fairness Doctrine is
unnecessary, Mr. Lloyd supports a backdoor method of
furthering the goals of the Fairness Doctrine by other
means. Accordingly, I ask that you clarify and reaffirm
your commitment to me to oppose any reincarnation of
the Fairness Doctrine. Further, I ask you to affirmatively
state that you will not pursue an agenda that includes
any new restrictions, fines, fees, or licensing
requirements on commercial radio that would
effectively create a backdoor Fairness Doctrine. I
appreciate your prompt reply regarding this important
matter.

Senator Grassley's concern has plenty of merit when you analyze
Lloyds past writings on talk radio. In his 2006, book title *Prologue
to a Farce: Communications and Democracy in America*, Lloyd calls for
the FCC to impose licensing fees on private broadcasting
companies equal to their total operating costs which would be
passed along to fund public broadcasting outlets. [12] This 100%
operating cost tax is Lloyd's ludicrous scheme to rev up the
Corporation for Public Broadcasting (CPB) while driving private
broadcasters off the airways.

Government Controlling the Airwaves

In this excerpt from *Prologue to a Farce*, Lloyd calls for more FCC
regulations and lays out a funding system that would crush

private broadcasters and skew the spectrum market toward public broadcasters.

> The Corporation for Public Broadcasting (CPB) must be reformed along democratic lines and funded on a substantial level. The CPB board should be elected, eight members representing eight regions of the country...
>
> Federal and regional broadcast operations and local stations should be funded at levels commensurate with or above those spending levels at which commercial operations are funded. This funding should come from license fees charged to commercial broadcasters. Funding should not come from congressional appropriations. Sponsorship should be prohibited at all public broadcasters."
>
> Local public broadcasters and regional and national communications operations should be required to encourage and broadcast diverse views and programs. These programs should include coverage of all local, state and federal government meetings, as well as daily news and public issues programming. In addition, educational programs for children and adults, and diverse independent personal and cultural expression should be encouraged. Local radio and television public broadcasters should be required to work closely with local libraries, community centers, cable public access operations [...to] train and educate citizens how to use and interpret media.
>
> [S]pectrum allocations should be established that create clear preferences for public broadcasters ensuring that regional local and communities are well served.
>
> 3. The FCC should be fully funded with regulatory fees from broadcast, cable, satellite and telecommunications companies. The FCC should be staffed at regional offices, matching those CPB regions at levels sufficient to monitor and enforce communication regulation. Clear federal regulations over commercial broadcast and cable

programs regarding political advertising and
commentary, educational programs for children, the
number of commercials, ratings and information about
programs before they are broadcast, and accessibility of
services to the disabled should be established and
widely promoted.[13] "

Going Beyond the Fairness Doctrine

In 2007, while working at the Center for American Progress, Lloyd
co-wrote a report titled "The Structural Imbalance of Political Talk
Radio." The report analyzed conservative talk radio's dominance
over what the report refers to as "progressive" talk radio, while
completely and disingenuously ignoring the fact that talk radio is
the only conservative alternative to Left-dominated television,
newspapers, entertainment, and education establishments. But
Lloyd is not the kind of a researcher who allows facts to stand in
the way of a politically favorable conclusion fabricated with a
deliberately false methodology. According to Lloyd's report, each
day the airwaves are filled with 90 percent more conservative talk
than "progressive" talk.[14]

The report concluded:[15]

> [T]he gap between conservative and progressive
> talk radio is the result of multiple structural
> problems in the U.S. regulatory system,
> particularly the complete breakdown of the
> public trustee concept of broadcast, the
> elimination of clear public interest requirements
> for broadcasting, and the relaxation of
> ownership rules including the requirement of
> local participation in management.

Apparently, in Lloyd's left-leaning universe, the free market and
consumer choice have no bearing on what radio audiences listen
to or what broadcasters choose to provide.

The report conclusion went further to state that "Ownership diversity is perhaps the single most important variable contributing to the structural imbalance based on the data.... stations owned by women, minorities, or local owners are statistically less likely to air conservative hosts or shows." If this data were true it certainly explains the left's continual push for diversity in media ownership.

The report developed three suggestions to combat the conservative dominance:

> 1. Restore local and national caps on the ownership of commercial radio stations.
> 2. Ensure greater local accountability over radio licensing.
> 3. Require commercial owners who fail to abide by enforceable public interest obligations to pay a fee to support public broadcasting.[16]

Many credit the repeal of the Fairness Doctrine for the rise of talk radio. While Diversity Czar Lloyd and President Obama claim they have no intention of pursuing a reinstatement of the Doctrine,[17] implementing recommendations like these would have the same - if not more - damaging impact.[18]

In an article Lloyd wrote while at the Center for American Progress titled "Media Maneuvers: Why the Rush to Waive Cross-Ownership Bans," he implores liberals to emulate the strategy used by President Franklin Delano Roosevelt in challenging conservative talk show hosts and station owners. Lloyd wrote: FDR understood what he was up against. He understood not only how to use media effectively, but also the importance of media ownership and the rules that determined media ownership.[19]

In a paper titled "Forget the Fairness Doctrine," Mark Lloyd argued the point that the Fairness Doctrine would not go far enough and that additional regulations need to be implemented:[20]

> [W]e call for ownership rules that we think will create
> greater local diversity of programming, news, and
> commentary. And we call for more localism by putting
> teeth into the licensing rules. But we do not call for a
> return to the Fairness Doctrine.
>
> Despite what we thought was fairly stark evidence of
> conservative bias, despite clear proposals to address that
> bias, Rush Limbaugh and other distortionists insisted
> that we were calling for a "return" of the Fairness
> Doctrine. But as we wrote, "simply reinstating the
> Fairness Doctrine will do little to address the gap
> between conservative and progressive talk unless the
> underlying elements of the public trustee doctrine are
> enforced, in particular, the requirements of local
> accountability and the reasonable airing of important
> matters."

Although Lloyd, President Obama, and other Democrat leaders
claim that they are not pursuing the re-implementation of the
Fairness doctrine, their actions speak louder than words. There
was a reason why opponents to conservative radio and television
created the position of a Diversity Czar and installed Frank Lloyd
at the FCC. Under the guise of "diversity," this admirer of Marxist
dictators is prepared to implement policies that go far beyond the
reach of the Fairness Doctrine.

Hooray for Hugo Chavez and Government Controlled Airwaves

On August 26, 2009, the Glenn Beck show on the Fox News
Channel aired a clip of our Diversity Czar Mark Lloyd lauding
Hugo Chavez and his control of the media.

Mark Lloyd speaking at the 2008 National Conference for Media
Reform on June 7, 2008:

...and social change, in Venezuela with Chavez, really
an incredible revolution – a democratic revolution – to
begin to put in place saying that we're going to have
impact on the people of Venezuela...the property
owners and the folks who were then controlling the
media in Venezuela rebelled – work frankly with folks
here in the U.S. government – worked to oust him and
came back...and had another revolution, and Chavez
then started to take the media very seriously in this
country[21]

Seton Motley of the Media Research Council, a guest on Glenn
Beck, further explained Lloyds disturbing comments. Lloyd
described the communist revolution in Venezuela as "incredible"
and noted that Hugo Chavez almost lost the revolution because of
big property owners revolting and because of help from the U.S.
Government. The Diversity Czar who was appointed, not vetted
and confirmed by the U.S. Senate, wanted Chavez to succeed and
did not want the communist revolution to fail.[22]

The Perfect Station

Our Diversity Czar has a long resume when it comes to
developing policies of fighting conservative talk shows and
private broadcasters. He has written extensively about various
government measures that can drive conservative views off the
air. His proposals include 100% taxes on operating expenses,
increased licensing fees, larger penalties, skewed spectrum sales,
content rationing, regional and local quotas, as well as ownership
requirements. Lloyd openly admits that the Fairness Doctrine is
not good enough for him because it would not suppress the voices
of the opposition as efficiently as his own proposals could.

Mark Lloyd was hand-picked and placed into a perfect position
where he can finally put his anti-free-market, speech-squelching
theories into practice.

1 FCC Press Release, July 29, 2009 -
http://fjallfoss.fcc.gov/edocs_public/attachmatch/DOC-292368A1.txt
2 Fox News, Glen Beck, August 26, 2009.
3 FCC Press Release, July 29, 2009 -
http://fjallfoss.fcc.gov/edocs_public/attachmatch/DOC-292368A1.txt
4 FCC Press Release, July 29, 2009 -
http://fjallfoss.fcc.gov/edocs_public/attachmatch/DOC-292368A1.txt
5 *Townhall*, "The Fairness Doctrine is Dead, But Here Comes the Chief
Diversity Officer" by Jillian Bandes, August 12,2009.
6 FCC Press Release, July 29, 2009 -
http://fjallfoss.fcc.gov/edocs_public/attachmatch/DOC-292368A1.txt
7 LCCR Website - http://www.civilrights.org/about/
8 *Townhall*, "The Fairness Doctrine is Dead, But Here Comes the Chief
Diversity Officer" by Jillian Bandes, August 12,2009.
9 FoxNews.com "FCC's New Hire Targeted Conservative Radio Stations
in Writings", Monday August 10, 2009.
10 The Heritage Foundation, "Why the Fairness Doctrine is Anything But
Fair" by Adam Their, October 29, 1993.
11 FoxNews.com "FCC's New Hire Targeted Conservative Radio Stations
in Writings", Monday August 10, 2009.
12 *CNSNews*, "FCC's Chief Diversity Officer Wants Private Broadcasters
to Pay a Sum Equal to Their Operating Costs to Fund Public
Broadcasting" by Matt Cover, August 13, 2009.
13 Prologue to a Farce: Communications and Democracy in America by
Mark Lloyd, University of Illinois Press; 1 edition, December 29, 2006, P.
279-279.
14 Center for American Progress, "The Structural Imbalance of Political
Talk Radio" by John Halprin, James Heidbreder, Mark Lloyd..., June 20,
2007.
15 Center for American Progress, "The Structural Imbalance of Political
Talk Radio" by John Halprin, James Heidbreder, Mark Lloyd..., June 20,
2007.
16 Center for American Progress, "The Structural Imbalance of Political
Talk Radio" by John Halprin, James Heidbreder, Mark Lloyd..., June 20,
2007.
17 FoxNews.com "FCC's New Hire Targeted Conservative Radio Stations
in Writings", Monday August 10, 2009.
18
19 *CNSNews*," FCC Diversity Chief Asked Liberals to Copy FDR, Take on
Limbaugh, Murdoch, Supreme Court" by Matt Cover, August 27, 2009.

---

[20] Center for American Progress, "Forget The Fairness Doctrine" by Mark Lloyd, July 24, 2007.
[21] Fox News, Glen Beck, August 26, 2009.
[22] Fox News, Glen Beck, August 26, 2009.

Drug Czar — Gil Kerlikowske

Official title:	Director of the Office of National Drug Control Policy
Official responsibilities:	Establish policies, objectives, and priorities for the National Drug Control program
Reports to:	President
Senate confirmation:	Yes
Salary:	$
Ideology / political affiliation:	Politics of surrender; focus primarily on medical treatment rather than supply curtailment

Leave It to Obama — Appoint the Father of a Drug Dealer to Be Drug Czar

President Obama has outdone himself in appointing Gil Kerlikowske as his czar in charge of drug control policy — not an inconsiderable feat given the inappropriateness of many of his czar choices thus far. Kerlikowske has a long history of surrendering in the face of difficulty in fighting the availability, distribution, and use of illicit drugs on America's streets. While serving as chief of police in Seattle, Kerlikowske refocused police drug policy more on treatment and intervention than on drug arrests, which of course declined after he took that office in 2000. Repeatedly lamenting that stopping trafficking in illegal drugs was too difficult to accomplish, he threw up his hands and decided that maybe it would be better to put users into rehab programs rather than jail.

Jeffrey Kerlikowske, the son of Obama's new drug czar, was arrested recently for violating probation from a July 2007 felony battery charge and the two drug-related charges on his record. Among the charges from Florida agencies were marijuana possession and distribution, aggravated assault with a deadly weapon, theft, cruelty to animals, and larceny, according to police officials and public records.[1] Jeffrey Kerlikowske was arrested February 27 for a violation on a warrant related to an original conviction of felony battery in Broward County, Fla., said a spokeswoman for the Martin County, Fla., sheriff's office. In June

2007, after pleading no contest to battery, he was sentenced to one year and one day in state prison, to be followed by two years of drug-offender probation and an additional year of regular probation.

Our new drug czar stated, "Our nation's drug problem is one of human suffering," according to his prepared remarks. "As a police officer, but also in my own family, I have experienced first-hand the devastating effects that drugs can have on our youth, our families, and our communities." Unfortunately, his difficult family experiences appear to have left their emotional scars on this once fine police officer. Obama has now enabled Kerlikowske to bring his message of resignation to the national stage, unilaterally announcing that he will no longer wage a war on drugs.

What Is a Drug Czar?

The position of director of the Office of National Drug Control Policy and the office were created by the Anti-Drug Abuse Act of 1988. The position, first filled in 1989, was given cabinet-level status from 1993 to 2009. The principal responsibilities of the director of ONDCP, commonly known as the "drug czar," include:

- establishing policies, objectives, and priorities for the National Drug Control program;
- annually promulgating the National Drug Control strategy and coordinating and overseeing the strategy's implementation by the respective drug control agencies of the federal government;
- making recommendations to the president regarding changes in the organization, management, budgets, and allocation of federal personnel engaged in drug enforcement;
- consulting with and assisting state and local governments with respect to their relations with federal drug enforcement agencies;
- appearing before committees and subcommittees of

Congress to represent the drug policies of the executive branch; and

- notifying any federal drug control agency if its policies are not in compliance with the strategy and transmitting a copy of the notification to the president.[2]

The "czar" title was first used to refer to an appointed government official in a *Time Magazine* article in December 1973, referring to William E. Simon's appointment as the head of the Federal Energy Administration. The "drug czar" title was first published in a 1982 news story quoting Joe Biden by United Press International, which reported that "Senators ... voted 62-34 to establish a 'drug czar' who would have overall responsibility for U.S. drug policy."[2] Since then, several ad hoc executive positions in both the United States and the United Kingdom have been established that have been subsequently referred to in this manner.[3]

History of Drug Control Czars

Name	Term of Office	President(s) Served Under
William Bennett	1989 – 1991	George H. W. Bush
Bob Martinez	1991 – 1993	
Lee P. Brown	1993 – Dec. 12, 1995	Bill Clinton
Barry McCaffrey	Feb. 29, 1996 – Jan. 4, 2001	
John P. Walters	Dec. 7, 2001 – Jan. 19, 2009	George W. Bush
Gil Kerlikowske	May 7, 2009 – present	Barack Hussein Obama

Gil Kerlikowske: A Sad, Misguided Case

The position of drug czar is perhaps the most frustrating post among the pantheon of czars and czarinas in the Obama administration. The latest occupant of this post, former Seattle Chief of Police Gil Kerlikowske, appears to have a fine record of service as a policeman and police administrator, but in all likelihood his tenure will be doomed to the ignominy facing any human being occupying that post. That is in the best of circumstances. However, Kerlikowske has staked out a new ideological approach to the drug problem by unilaterally announcing that he is ending the war on drugs and will focus on drug treatment rather than using incarceration and military action to curtail supply.[4]

The war on drugs refers to the prohibition campaign undertaken by the United States government, with the assistance of participating countries, intended to reduce the illegal drug trade. This initiative includes a set of laws and policies that are intended to discourage the production, distribution, and consumption of targeted substances. The term was first used by President Richard Nixon in 1969, and its use of war as metaphor is similar to the war on poverty announced by President Lyndon B. Johnson in 1964.[5]

Ending the 'War on Drugs' — What Is Wrong With These People?

This policy, which on the surface sounds a bit new, is little more than the politics of surrender and conflict avoidance that is fast becoming the hallmark of the Obama administration. The same mentality is characteristic of Obama's Middle East policy and his approach to Iran, North Korea, Libya, and China. In fact, the language uttered by Kerlikowske appears to have been taken directly from Script Central in the Obama Propaganda Ministry. "Regardless of how you try to explain to people it's a 'war on drugs' or a 'war on a product,' people see a war as a war on them," he said. "We're not at war with people in this country."[6] If you switch out a couple of nouns, you have verbatim quotes of Obama's statements regarding his approaches to terrorism and Islamic extremism.

At the same time, it represents a bizarre form of social engineering that fits in well with the darkest features of his Obamacare healthcare initiative. In addition, by stating that the current approach to fighting drugs unfairly persecutes the black population in America, he, once again, wheeled out the race card and the politics of division. Obama has called for an end to the disparity in how crimes involving crack cocaine and powder cocaine are dealt with, saying African-American communities, where crack is more prevalent, are unfairly targeted. Fine: Throw them all in the same jail cell, but don't free them from the responsibility of their actions.

Consider Where He Comes From

Seattle is a city known for experimenting with drug programs. In 2003, voters there passed an initiative making the enforcement of simple marijuana violations a low priority. The city has long had a needle-exchange program and hosts Hempfest, which draws tens of thousands of hemp and marijuana advocates. Seattle is considering setting up a project that would divert drug defendants to treatment programs.[7]

James Pasco, executive director of the Fraternal Order of Police, the nation's largest law-enforcement labor organization, said that he holds Kerlikowske in high regard but that police officers are wary. "While I don't necessarily disagree with Gil's focus on treatment and demand reduction, I don't want to see it at the expense of law enforcement. People need to understand that when they violate the law there are consequences."[8]

Kabuki and the Useful Idiots

It is a shame that a police officer as distinguished as Kerlikowske, whose own son faces drug charges, has allowed himself to be the frontman for the ongoing Obama campaign to demean America by deepening dependency relationships, declaring drug possession and/or addiction to be a noncriminal disease or societal failure, and absolving criminal behavior[9] through the creation of an anything-goes, no-one-is-to-blame, we-are-all-victims-of-circumstance society that has no rules, only publicly financed consequence management. The decriminalization of dangerous illicit activities that hold nothing but negative consequences for humanity is a certain step forward in the managed disintegration of civil society in America.

It is interesting to note that Obama has not given the drug czar position the rank of cabinet member as it was in some prior administrations. Perhaps this signals Obama's disingenuous approach to the drug problem, or it may be a means of shielding the position from serious congressional oversight — who knows?

— *Lucy Leitner*

---

[1] http://www.washingtontimes.com/news/2009/mar/12/drug-czar-picks-stepson-charged-with-marijuana/

[2] Congressional Research Service. *War on Drugs: Reauthorization of the Office of National Drug Control Policy.*
http://www.fas.org/sgp/crs/misc/RL32352.pdf

[3] http://en.wikipedia.org/wiki/Drug_czar

[4] Gary Fields. *The Wall Street Journal,* "White House Czar Calls for End to 'War on Drugs'
Kerlikowske Says Analogy Is Counterproductive; Shift Aligns With Administration Preference for Treatment Over Incarceration" (May 14, 2009), A3.

[5] http://en.wikipedia.org/wiki/War_on_drugs

[6] Ibid.

[7] Fields, op. cit.

[8] Ibid.

[9] *National Journal,* " 'I've Ended the War on Drugs': Q&A: Gil Kerlikowske," (May 28, 2009)
http://www.nationaljournal.com/njonline/ii_20090526_6945.php

Economic Czar — Paul Volcker

Official title:	Chair of the President's Economic Recovery Advisory Board
Official responsibilities:	To advise the president on how to stop the recession
Reports to:	President
Senate confirmation:	None
Salary:	Unpaid
Ideology / political affiliation:	Has given money to Republicans and Democrats alike, essentially a universally respected economic mind

While the current economic crisis is going to be difficult for anyone to handle, it would be very hard to come up with a more qualified guiding hand than Paul Volcker. He has come closer than almost anyone else to dealing with this type of situation before. Volcker was named chairman of the Federal Reserve in 1979 and immediately had to deal with the repercussions of what was and still is the largest government intervention in the private economy since World War II, Nixon's wage and price controls of 1971. The controls were removed in 1974,[1] and what followed was the worst inflationary crisis America had seen in decades. Volcker showed foresight by dramatically raising interest rates, which caused the worst economic downturn since the Great Depression, brought the unemployment rate into double digits, and ultimately ended the crisis. Though controversial at the time, this tactic is now considered a necessary step when combating inflation. This helped Volcker gain a reputation for being strong, fair, and capable of making the tough decisions that are called for in times of crisis.[2]

Looking to Volcker for Legitimacy

Obama, with his limited economic credentials, is leaning heavily on the 81-year-old Volcker to both design his policy and establish his credibility. But it is difficult to divine either how strongly or how permanently Volcker is tied to the administration. He was discussed as a potential secretary of the treasury, but he ended up not taking a full-time job. Still, those close to Obama say that the president listens to Volcker's opinion above all others on economic issues.[3]

Volcker seems quite concerned about the way the bailout has gone thus far. He was skeptical of the Federal Reserve's decision to risk $29 billion on the sale of Bear Stearns. He stated that the actions of the Federal Reserve "extend to the very edge of its lawful and implied powers, transcending in the process certain long-embedded central banking principles and practices."[4] All around, he seems concerned by how much power central banks, treasuries, and regulatory agencies have gained in order to attempt to stop the economic meltdown. "It is evident," he said, "in the United States, and not just in the United States, the central bank is taking on a role that is way beyond what a central bank should be taking."[5] Yet the appointment of a czar like Volcker may be an attempt by Obama to seem more centrist than he actually is, as Volcker's task is not ideologically important to Obama. It is simply something that has to be done, and Volcker is one of the most capable people to help do it. Yet, he could be unfairly held up as an example of centrist politics, when he is actually involved in something rather apolitical.[6]

Heavy Tax Increases on the Way

Volcker is also heading Obama's six-member tax commission. The commission essentially has to raise taxes in one way or another to cover Obama's proposed budget, and this will most likely mean heavy tax increases on the rich and corporations. Putting the pragmatic Volcker in this spot means that, regardless of his own views, he will be forced to find solutions within a situation that requires him to go along with Obama's wishes.[7]

— *Rick Rush*

[1] Robert Samuelson, "Rescue Risk: Panic Now or a Mess Later," 23 September 2008, Investor's Business Daily, <http://www.ibdeditorials.com/IBDArticles.aspx?id=307056049536197&kw=paul%20volcker>

[2] "Paul Volcker," Who Runs GOV, <http://www.whorunsgov.com/Profiles/Paul_Volcker>

[3] Ibid.

[4] Ibid.

[5] Eileen AJ Connelly, "Paul Volcker: Economic Crisis May Be Worse Than Great Depression," 20 February 2009, The Huffington Post, <http://www.huffingtonpost.com/2009/02/20/paul-volcker-financial-cr_n_168772.html>

[6] Charles Krauthammer, "Obama's 'Shift' to the Center Masks Agenda," 11 December 2008, Investor's Business Daily, <http://www.ibdeditorials.com/IBDArticles.aspx?id=313890516143932&kw=paul%20volcker>

[7] "Trojan (Tax) Horse," 25 March 2009, Investor's Business Daily, <http://www.ibdeditorials.com/IBDArticles.aspx?id=322873875315887&kw=paul%20volcker>

Education Czar — Arne Duncan

Official title:	Secretary of Education
Salary / Direct cost to taxpayers:	Unavailable
Responsibilities:	Head of the Department of Education; primary administrator of federal education policy
Reports to:	President
Senate confirmation:	Yes: Jan. 20, 2009
Relation to Obama:	Met Obama in early 1990s in Chicago through Michelle Obama's brother. Obama and Duncan often played basketball together. When Duncan was chief executive of Chicago Public Schools and Obama was a senator in Illinois, Duncan helped shape Obama's education policy.
Ideology / political affiliation:	Indoctrinate them while they are young

Who Is the Education Czar?

Conservatives have many concerns about Education Secretary Arne Duncan, a longtime Chicago crony of President Obama, which include promoting the creation of a high school for homosexuals in Chicago, a controversial sex education curriculum passed under Duncan's leadership, and Duncan's connection with Weather Underground terrorist Bill Ayers. Conservatives have also noted that progress made in the Chicago Public Schools during his tenure as chief executive stands in absolute contrast to claims by Obama upon Duncan's nomination. And despite the fact that Duncan is not technically qualified to teach even at the first-grade level in many states, Obama moved quickly to add him to his cabinet.

Not Qualified to Be a Public School Teacher

Though Duncan has seven years' experience as chief executive of the Chicago Public Schools, he has very little background even for that position, let alone enough to be named secretary of education.

He has an undergraduate degree in sociology from Harvard. Virtually all the administrators and many of the teachers he oversees hold higher degrees (master's and doctorates) and, of course, in the field of education. Duncan could hold a license as a substitute teacher, but he would need more education to work as a classroom teacher. Therein lies the question: If he is not qualified because of his lack of education, does he at least possess expertise in management? According to an article in the *New York Times*[1], "Duncan … has little of the national political experience that education secretaries often need in representing the White House's educational agenda before Congress and negotiating with the leaders of the 50 state school systems and the myriad interest groups that make up the educational establishment …." The *Kansas City Star*[2] reported that although he helped manage a "small, non-profit education program" for a few years and worked for three years "under predecessor Paul Vallas, [Duncan] never had a high enough post to merit his own secretary."

Purely an Ideological Creature of Chicago Politics

Promoting his sociological liberal agenda, as chief executive of Chicago's schools, Duncan spearheaded a plan to open the Social Justice Solidarity High School–Pride Campus, a homosexual-friendly high school. According to *Investor's Business Daily*[3], Duncan was quoted in October as saying, "If you look at national studies, you see gay and lesbian students with high dropout rates … Studies show they are disproportionately homeless … I think there is a niche there we need to fill." The Family Research Council[4] says that the school "would have been committed to affirming homosexuality in adolescents, have been publicly subsidized and included homosexuality-affirming curricula." The school, however, has not come to fruition. According to Ken Shepherd, the managing editor of *NewsBusters*[5], the proponents of the school "withdrew their proposal at the last minute, pledging to return with another version of the plan in time for an opening in the fall of 2010."

Social Engineering Point Man

Again pushing his liberal agenda in the Chicago school system, Duncan supported the adoption of the Family Life and Comprehensive Sexual Health Education Policy in 2006. The policy was created in coordination with the Illinois Caucus for Adolescent Health, a group that promotes sex education curricula that according to the Family Research Council[6] "among other things, teach students subversive views of sexual conduct, abortion, and homosexuality."

On June 20, 2006, the website of Concerned Women for America reported that the controversial Illinois Caucus for Adolescent Health organization held its spring 2006 fundraiser at the Playboy headquarters in Chicago.

Affiliated With William Ayers

In addition to his lack of experience and radical views on sex education, Duncan keeps some questionable company. Duncan served at the Chicago Annenberg Challenge organization founded by terrorist William Ayers — the same organization that tried to cover up the tie between Obama and Ayers during the presidential campaign. According to *Investor's Business Daily*[7], Ken Rollins, executive director of the Chicago Annenberg Challenge, stated that Duncan relied on the Annenberg Challenge to assist him in programming the Chicago Public Schools agenda: The CAC was "founded and financed through the efforts of … William Ayers. Ayers saw the CAC as a chance to radicalize Chicago public school teachers and students." Also, the Family Research Council[8] writes that "Duncan worked in promoting the Annenberg Challenge, a radical education group formerly run by Barack Obama and Bill Ayers. The CAC's agenda flowed from Mr. Ayers's educational philosophy, which called for infusing students and their parents with radical political commitment, and which downplayed achievement tests in favor of activism." In 2002, Ayers endorsed Duncan with language that seemed to suggest that Duncan was a fellow traveler on the road to revolution: "Arne Duncan is the brightest and most dedicated school leader Chicago has had in memory, and he comes to this post from a long and deep experience in neighborhood community development and education."[9]

Overstated Achievements

It appears now that Duncan's successes at the helm of Chicago's schools, as touted by Obama when announcing Duncan's nomination to be secretary of education, were somewhat embellished. A June 30, 2009, *USA Today* article[10] by Greg Toppo details some of these embellishments, beginning even with the article's title: "Chicago Schools Report Contradicts Obama and Duncan." Toppo writes that the Civic Committee of the Commercial Club of Chicago "puts a new spin on the academic gains made during the seven years that Arne Duncan led the Chicago schools before he was named U.S. Education Secretary." Though the group supported Duncan and Mayor Richard M. Daley's quest for more control of city schools, *USA Today*'s report says that "the schools have made little progress since 2003." Regarding Obama's inflated endorsement, Obama said that during Duncan's seven-year tenure he boosted elementary school test scores 29 percent, "from 38 percent of students meeting standards to 67 percent." The civic group's study shows that the students' pass rates rose only approximately 8 percent. *USA Today*[11] quotes Scholastic website writer Alexander Russo, who covers Chicago schools, as saying that the study's findings show the Chicago school system "isn't nearly as improved as many have been led to believe .... What I find particularly appalling is that Duncan and Obama—supposed champions of transparency and using research rather than ideology—have cited Chicago's inflated tests scores, even though they knew the increases were exaggerated."

Obama and Duncan have also forced their Democratic "more spending and less accountability" approach on the Head Start program, according to a May 11 article in *Investor's Business Daily*[12]. Duncan has pledged $10 billion a year to the Head Start program, which provides preschool for poor children, even though numerous studies have shown that the program doesn't work. *IBD* reports that children enrolled in the program "at an average cost of $7,700 were able to name only about two more letters than disadvantaged kids who were not in Head Start, according to the Hoover Institution's 'Education Next' reform project. They also didn't show any significant gains in early math, pre-reading, pre-writing, vocabulary or oral comprehension." *IBD* says that Obama has said he will do whatever works and is "backed up by evidence and facts and proof that [it] can work." Education Secretary Duncan also states that "we must stop doing what doesn't work." In true liberal-ideological form, they "preach accountability and pragmatism, but their proposals don't match their rhetoric," notes the *IBD* report.

Hypocrisy and School Choice

Another area of hypocrisy from Duncan and the Obama administration is that of school choice. The *Wall Street Journal*'s John Fund writes, "Mr. Obama's Education Secretary, Arne Duncan, professes to support the D.C. choice program, but his actions speak louder than words. He has taken back 200 scholarship offers that had already been made to local parents for the next school year." Fund adds, "Mr. Duncan himself knows the value of choice. He told *Science* magazine that he thought carefully where to send his daughter to school in the D.C. area when he moved from Chicago to join the Obama cabinet. He explained his decision to live in Virginia thusly: 'My family has given up so much so that I could have the opportunity to serve; I didn't want to try to save the country's children and our educational system and jeopardize my own children's education.' Would that the parents of the Washington, D.C., children who will be thrown out of their current schools had that same option of relocating in upper-income Arlington and enjoying its relatively good public schools." It is also significant to note that while living in Chicago, the Obamas elected not to send their daughters to the Chicago Public Schools under the supervision of Duncan but instead sent them to the University of Chicago Laboratory Schools, ironically the private school that Duncan himself attended[13].

Duncan has placed $4.3 billion toward a program called "Race to the Top," which will link teachers' pay to student standardized test scores. It almost has the ring of a conservative education proposal. However, *Investor's Business Daily*[14] sees the potential for something much more sinister. "Plainly speaking, this is a kind of soft nationalization. It comes at the expense of locally elected school boards that, historically, have served as laboratories of experimentation and innovation. From now on, the feds know best. And since money's involved, you'd better listen. Of course, preconditions may be good for many schools. But they open the door to federal micromanagement. Let's see: How long will it take before political indoctrination of students becomes a precondition for receiving government funds? Maybe not as long as you think. Perhaps not coincidentally, Venezuela is gripped by riots over a takeover of that country's schools .... Will riots in Caracas turn into riots in Cleveland? This could get out of hand very fast."

It is without question that Duncan will be increasing government control as quickly and aggressively as he can. The day following the passage of the $787 billion stimulus package, Duncan was interviewed by *Chicago Magazine*[15]. The interview, published in April 2009, notes that the stimulus package includes "$100 billion in new federal money for education ... nearly double what the department spent in 2008." Asked if he had read Geoffrey Canada's book *Whatever It Takes,* about the Harlem Children's Zone, Duncan replied, "Geoff Canada's a good, good friend of mine. I'm actually meeting with him Monday. ... I'm going to create 20 Harlem Children's Zones around the country. I am." The interviewer asked, "Really? Do you think you'll face opposition to the federal role expanding in that way?" Duncan arrogantly replied, "I don't care. I'm going to fund it."

— *Angie Wheeler*

1. *New York Times,* "Arne Duncan," 2009.
2. *Kansas City Star, Prime Buzz,* "Obama Names Education Czar" by Bill Dalton, Dec. 16, 2008.
3. *Investor's Business Daily,* "Choice, Not Echo," Dec. 17, 2009.
4. Family Research Council, "Change Watch Backgrounder: Arne Duncan" by David Nammo, Jan. 8, 2009.
5. *NewsBusters,* "WaPo Ignores Obama EdSec's Controversial Push to Open Gay High School in Chicago" by Ken Shepherd, Dec. 17, 2008.
6. Family Research Council, "Change Watch Backgrounder: Arne Duncan" by David Nammo, Jan. 8, 2009.
7. *Investor's Business Daily,* "Choice, Not Echo," Wednesday, Dec. 17, 2008.
8. Family Research Council, "Change Watch Backgrounder: Arne Duncan" by David Nammo, Jan. 8, 2009.
9. Phi Delta Kappan, "Private Management of Chicago Schools Is a Long Way From Mecca" by William Ayers and Michael Klonsky, February 2006.
10. *USA Today,* "Chicago Schools Report Contradicts Obama and Duncan" by Greg Toppo, July 12, 2009.
11. Ibid.
12. *Investor's Business Daily,* "More Head Start? Not Smart," May 11, 2009.
13. *Kansas City Star, Prime Buzz,* "Obama Names Education Czar" by Bill Dalton, Dec. 16, 2008.
14. *Investor's Business Daily,* "Is Education Next?" Aug. 17, 2009.
15. *Chicago Magazine,* "What Arne Learned," by Jennifer Tanaka, April 2009.

Energy Czar — Carol Browner

Official title:	Assistant to the President for Energy and Climate Change - a newly created position
Official responsibilities:	Coordinating energy and climate policy while emphasizing regulation and conservation
Reports to:	President Obama
Senate confirmation:	None
Relation to Obama:	Financial supporter, giving $4,600 to Obama's election campaign in the 2008 election cycle[1]
Direct cost to taxpayers:	$172,200 annually[2]
Ideology / political affiliation:	Socialist / Democrat

On the surface, this Clinton administration veteran has an impressive environmental policy resume. Carol Browner worked for former Senators Lawton Chiles (D-FL) from 1986 to 1988 and Al Gore (D-TN) from 1988 to 1991. She headed up Florida's Department of Environmental Regulation and was tapped to run the Environmental Protection Agency (EPA) by President Bill Clinton from 1993 to 2001. According to the EPA's website, she was the longest-serving administrator in the history of the Agency.[3]

But the unsightly reality behind the respectable veneer reveals a single-minded fringe radical who considers global warming "the greatest challenge ever faced,"[4] campaigned to ban offshore drilling, pushed to give the EPA the authority to regulate carbon emissions to the detriment of the American manufacturers, and most recently championed the failed Cap and Trade legislation that could potentially cripple U.S. economy.

Her radical environmental agenda and socialist policies, as well as her membership in a socialist organization[5] might explain why President Obama chose to create a new office for Browner, rather than to nominate her to an existing position that would have been subject to the typical Senate confirmation process. As a result, an unelected radical socialist was given control over the Secretary of Energy, Secretary of Interior and the Administrator of the Environmental Protection Agency[6] - positions confirmed by the

U.S. Senate, while her own position does not require any confirmation. She showed her appreciation, and lack of scruples, by doing a complete 180 on nuclear power. Before taking her czar position, Browner was a member of Al Gore's Alliance for Climate Protection, an organization which staunchly opposes opening nuclear power plants. Once a member of the administration, she supported Obama's plan to do exactly that.[7]

Socialist Ties

As recently as December 2008, Carol Browner was listed as a commissioner in Socialist International, the worldwide organization of social democratic, socialist, and labor parties[8] that is harshly critical of U.S. policies. She was one of fourteen official leaders of this umbrella socialist organization's so-called "Commission for a Sustainable World Society" - a nice-sounding name for a sinister goal of establishing a shadow world government with an agenda of controlling the world's wealthiest economies under the pseudo-scientific pretext of global warming. That would be the only real-life outcome of the Commission's euphemistic calls for "global governance" and its assertions that global warming can be stopped if only wealthy developed countries shrink their economies, decrease consumption, and commit to binding and punitive limits on greenhouse gas emissions[9].

In early January of 2009, as Carol Browner's appointment began to stir controversy, the Socialist International expediently scrubbed Browner's name, position, and biography from its website[10]. However, she still appears on the site as an "individual" participant at the June 30 - July 2, 2008 conference titled "XXIII Congress of the Socialist International, Athens Global Solidarity: The Courage to make a difference"[11].

But the one thing that Socialist International cannot scrub from history is its organizing document, which blasts capitalism as the root of mass unemployment, social insecurity, imperialist expansion, and colonial exploitation. This collection of historically inaccurate and discredited notions is crowned by an insane assertion that capitalism helped "the barbarism of the past raise its head again in the form of fascism and Nazism."[12] While a serious look at the historical origins of fascism and Nazism would, in fact, reveal them as clearly socialist ideologies, such a discussion is beyond the scope of this book. A question relevant to the issue at hand is, do we really want a national Energy Czar who has been a member of and worked with a group that blames capitalism for the likes of Adolph Hitler?

The "Aims and Tasks of Democratic Socialism" adopted at the First Congress of Socialist International held in 1951 in Frankfurt, Germany, includes the following declarations:[13]

- From the nineteenth century onwards, capitalism has developed immense productive forces. It has done so at the cost of excluding the great majority of citizens from influence over production. It put the rights of ownership before the rights of man. It created a new class of wage-earners without property or social rights. It sharpened the struggle between the classes.

  Although the world contains resources, which could be made to provide a decent life for everyone, capitalism has been incapable of satisfying the elementary needs of the world's population. It proved unable to function without devastating crises and mass unemployment. It produced social insecurity and glaring contrasts between rich and poor. It resorted to imperialist expansion and colonial exploitation, thus making conflicts between nations and races more bitter. In some countries powerful capitalist groups helped the barbarism of the past to raise its head again in the form of Fascism and Nazism.

- Socialism was born in Europe as a movement of protest against the diseases inherent in capitalist society. Because the wage-earners suffered most from capitalism, Socialism first developed as a movement of the wage-earners.

- Socialism aims to liberate the peoples from dependence on a minority which owns or controls the means of production. It aims to put economic power in the hands of the people as a whole, and to create a community in which free men work together as equals.

- Socialists oppose capitalism not only because it is economically wasteful and because it keeps the masses from their material rights, but above all because it revolts their sense of justice.

- Socialism stands not only for basic political rights but also for economic and social rights. Among these rights are:
  - *the right to work;*
  - *the right to medical and maternity benefits;*
  - *the right to leisure;*
  - *the right to economic security for citizens unable to work because of old age, incapacity or unemployment;*
  - *the right of children to welfare and of the youth to education in accordance with their abilities;*
  - *the right to adequate housing.*

As if this was not utopian enough, In 1987 Socialist International also adopted a list of misguided principles that favor the nationalization and internationalization of industry, outline deep skepticism in economic growth, and call for the establishment of a more "equitable international order,"[14] which in plain language means placing the control over world's capitalist economies into the hands of a global socialist government.

These economically illiterate principles, which Browner worked to apply as a member and as a commissioner, include:

- #78. In order to generate employment and prosperity all across the world, there is a need for ecologically balanced development. Growth which is not designed to meet ecological and social imperatives runs counter to progress, since it will cause environmental damage and destroy jobs. The market system alone can never ensure the attainment of the social goals of economic growth. It is the legitimate function of democratic economic policy to promote development, which opens up future opportunities while improving the quality of life.

- #79. To achieve these objectives on a global basis, it is imperative to establish a genuinely new international economic order. This must reconcile the interests of both industrialized and developing countries. A fundamental reform of financial relations must create the conditions for international economic cooperation. A more equitable international economic order is necessary not only for reasons of solidarity, but also in order to create a more efficient, productive and balanced world economy.

Why should this worry American citizens concerned with the preservation of liberty? The Obama Administration has already displayed its adherence to socialist principles by taking over the auto industry and large chunks of the financial sector, and is currently attempting to take over the nation's health care industry. If one wanted to continue this trend and nationalize the entire energy sector, a socialist environmentalist like Carol Browner would be a perfect choice for Energy Czar.

Pushing for Radical Reform

As the Czarina of Energy, Carol Browner has played a major role in pushing one of the Obama Administration's top priorities, Cap and Trade legislation, which is designed to place all private energy and manufacturing companies under a total control of the manipulative government bureaucracy, putting an end to the concept of free enterprise as we know it.

Forced through the U.S. House of Representatives earlier this spring, this economically disastrous plan would give the Obama Administration the power to set a cap on the total amount of CO2 that can be emitted nationally, with the presumption that over time it would be lowered even further. Such a measure would require companies to buy or sell permits to emit CO2,[15] which among other things would raise production costs, stifle growth, disadvantage small businesses and startups, and cause American companies to outsourse the remaining manufacturing jobs overseas.

The Cap and Trade scheme has been criticized as one of the largest tax increases in the history of the world and one of the largest transfers of wealth from consumers to special interests in American history.[16] No wonder one of the bill's proponents, Senator Ben Cardin (D-MD) has called Cap and Trade "the most significant revenue-generating proposal of our time".[17] But for whom will it generate revenue? Not for the American businesses, their employees, and the consumers whose budgets will be badly hurt by the resulting price increases.

Ben Lieberman, Senior Policy Analyst at the Heritage Foundation, testified at a Senate Republican Conference, "If you look at the total cost of Waxman-Markey [Cap and Trade Legislation], it works out to an average of $2,979 annually from 2012-2035 for a household of four. By 2035 alone, the total cost is over $4,600.... We estimate job losses averaging 1,145,000 at any given time from 2012-2035."[18]

Despite the enormity and importance of the Cap and Trade bill - it totaled more than 1,000 pages and covered a very complicated array of issues - Democrat leadership pushed it through committee and to the floor without giving members time to read and understand the legislation.

Congressman Joe Barton (R-TX), the Energy and Commerce Committee's ranking member, accused the Democrat leadership of ramming through legislation that neither Members of Congress nor their constituents fully understood in an effort to avoid a real debate on the proposal. He famously quipped, "The majority's motto: Pass it now! Explain it later." [19]

Congressman Barton was not kidding about the speed and lack of time to read the full bill. On June 29, 2009, a week after the House passed the legislation, Carol Browner, our Energy Czar, appeared on Fox News Channel's *Fox and Friends* morning show to discuss the legislation, and was stumped when co-host Steve Doocey asked her if she had read what's in it.[20]

The Energy Czar's lack of familiarity with details of the bill she helped to push through Congress would suggest that she deemed the social engineering goals contained therein important enough on their own merits to warrant passage - the economy be damned along with the lives of the common American citizens who will suffer from it.

Lack of Transparency Could be Illegal

On May 19, 2009, President Obama announced new federal Corporate Average Fuel Economy (CAFE) Standards. The new regulations would require automakers to manufacture vehicles with a standard of 39 miles per gallon for cars and 30 miles per gallon for trucks by 2016.[21]

Carol Browner was given the authority to coordinate the development of the new CAFE policy with officials at the Environmental Protection Agency, Council on Environmental Quality and the Department of Transportation and Energy.[22] Apparently there was little to no transparency to the meetings Browner coordinated or hosted while preparing the new standards. In fact, U.S. Congressmen Darrel Issa (R-CA) and James Sensenbrenner, Jr. (R-IL) have questioned the legality of the secrecy employed by Browner.[23]

Sensenbrenner and Issa wrote a letter to the Chairman of the Oversight and Government Reform Committee and the Select Committee on Energy Independence and Global Warming, demanding a joint investigation into the process in which the standards were developed. Their letter stated:

> We are writing out of grave concern over the lack of transparency and accountability that the Administration has exhibited in the development of regulations of carbon dioxide (CO, and other greenhouse gasses (GHGs) under the Clean Air Act (CAA). Regulations that give the Environmental Protection Agency (EPA) unprecedented power and authority to intervene in the U.S. economy in the name of reducing carbon emissions

have been crafted behind a deliberate veil of secrecy and under a vow of silence. This is deeply troubling and demands Congressional attention....

Mary Nichols, the head of the California Air Resources Board (CARB), revealed to the *New York Times* that the White House held a series of secret meetings with select special interests as they were crafting the new CAFE standards. Nichols was a key player in these negotiations because of California's determined efforts to regulate fuel economy standards at the state level. Nichols admitted there was a deliberate "vow of silence" surrounding the negotiations between the White House and California on vehicle fuel economy [standards]. According to Nichols' interview, "[Carol] Browner [Assistant to the President for Energy and Climate Change] quietly orchestrated private discussions from the White House with auto industry officials." Great care was taken to "put nothing in writing, ever." This coordinated effort, led by Carol Browner, to leave no paper trail of the deliberations within the White House appears to be a deliberate and willful violation of the Presidential Records Act. This Act requires the President to take, "all such steps as may be necessary to assure that the activities, deliberations, decisions, and policies that reflect the performance of his constitutional, statutory, or other official or ceremonial duties are adequately documented and that such records are maintained as Presidential records." Clearly, Browner's actions were intended to leave little to no documentation of the deliberations that lead to the development of stringent new CAFE standards. [24]

On January 20, 2009, following up on a campaign trail promise, the Obama Administration posted a message on the White House website stating "President Obama has committed to making his Administration the most open and transparent in history..."[25] Either the Energy Czar didn't get the memo, or President Obama himself didn't read the full text of his promise to the American people. In any event, the Obama Administration appears to be in violation of the law.

On December 28, 2009, the public interest group Judicial Watch filed a Freedom of Information Act lawsuit against the

Environmental Protection Agency and the Department of Energy seeking all records of communications they have had with Browner. Judicial Watch alleges that during Browner's secret negotiations she instructed participants to "put nothing in writing, ever."[26]

Tremendous Power without Checks

Not only has President Obama appointed an avowed socialist as his Energy Czar, he has also created a new, exceedingly powerful government position that allows Carol Browner to oversee entire departments, such as Energy, Interior, and Transportation, as well as agencies, such as the EPA and the Council on Environmental Quality. Remember that the head of each of those Departments and Agencies was required by law to be fully vetted and approved by the U.S. Senate. But Mrs. Browner answers only to the President.

---

[1] The Kudlow Report, The Czar Money Trail, www.cnbc.com/id/31315388

[2] The Glenn Beck Program, List of Obama's Czars, August 17, 2009

[3] www.epa.gov/history/admin/agency/browner.htm

[4] *New York Times*, "Title, but Unclear Power, for a New Climate Czar" by John M Broder, December 11, 2008.

[5] *Newsbusters*, "Obama's proposed Energy Czar Scrubbed from Socialists Website" by Noel Sheppard, January 8, 2009.

[6] *Time*, "Energy Czar: Carol Browner" by Frances Romero, December 15, 2008.

[7] Aaron Klein, "Climate chief reverses view of nuclear plants," Feb. 18, 2010, WorldNetDaily, <http://www.wnd.com/index.php/index.php/index.php?pageId=125444>

[8] *Newsbusters*, "Obama's proposed Energy Czar Scrubbed from Socialists Website" by Noel Sheppard, January 8, 2009.

[9] *The Washington Times*, "Obama Climate Czar Has Socialist Ties" by Stephen Dinan, January 12, 2009.

[10] *Newsbusters*, "Obama's proposed Energy Czar Scrubbed from Socialists Website" by Noel Sheppard, January 8, 2009.

[11] http://www.socialistinternational.org/viewArticle.cfm?ArticlePageID =1269

[12] Fox News, Browner: Redder than Obama Knows by Steven Milroy, January 15, 2009.
[13] Aims And Tasks Of Democratic Socialism, *Declaration Of The Socialist International -*
http://www.socialistinternational.org/viewArticle.cfm?ArticleID=39
Adopted At Its First Congress Held In Frankfort-On-Main On 30 June-3 July 1951 -
http://www.socialistinternational.org/viewArticle.cfm?ArticleID=39
[14] Fox News, "Browner: Redder than Obama Knows" by Steven Milroy, January 15, 2009.
[15] *Wall Street Journal*, "The Cap and Tax Fiction", June 26, 2009. P. A 12
[16] *Human Events*, "Congress Must Defeat Clean Energy and Security Act", May 5, 2009.
[17] Climate Depot, "Updated: Climate Depot Editorial: Climate bill offers (costly) non-solutions to problems that don't even exist" by Marc Morano, June 26, 2009.
[18] Testimony before the Senate Republican Conference, The Economic Impact of the Waxman-Markey Cap-and-Trade Bill by Ben Lieberman, Senior Policy Analyst for Energy and Environment in the Thomas A. Roe Institute for Economic Policy Studies at The Heritage Foundation, June 22, 2009.
[19] CNSNews, "Democrats Are Fast-Tracking Nearly 1,000-Page 'Cap-and-Trade' Bill That Would Increase Electricity Bills" by Matt Cover, May 19, 2009
[20] http://newsbusters.org/blogs/nb-staff/2009/06/29/fncs-steve-doocy-presses-carol-browner-cap-trade-bill
[21] *Politico* "Obama Announces New Fuel Standards" by Mike Allen and Eamon Javers, May 19, 2009.
[22] *The New York Times*, "Vow of Silence Key to White House-Calif. Fuel Economy Talks" by Colin Sullivan, May 20, 2009.
[23] *The Washington Examiner*, "Put Nothing in Writing" by Marc Tapscott, June 8, 2009.
[24] Text of the entire letter can be found at
http://republicans.oversight.house.gov/media/letters/20090609EPAVowofsilence.pdf
[25]http://www.whitehouse.gov/blog/change_has_come_to_whitehouse-gov/
[26] "Judicial Watch Sues for Records on "Climate Czar" Carol Browner's Role in Crafting Policy," Feb. 23, 2010. Marketwire,

---

<http://www.marketwire.com/press-release/Judicial-Watch-Sues-Records-on-Climate-Czar-Carol-Browners-Role-Crafting-Policy-1120549.htm>

Export Czar and Czarina -
W. James McNerney Jr.
and Ursula Burns

Official title:	Chair and Vice Chair of the Presidential Export Council
Salary / Direct cost to taxpayers:	Unknown
Responsibilities:	Advising Obama on Exports
Reports to:	President Obama[1]
Senate confirmation:	None
Relation to Obama:	Already appointed to lead the federal STEM program
Ideology / political affiliation:	Anti-free market, believes in a "level playing field for American companies and workers."[2]

President Obama has vowed to create 2 billion jobs while both doubling U.S. exports and saving the planet. Though his utopian rhetoric and appeals to the optimistic may have some believing that it is all possible, many also remember that old adage that if something sounds too good to be true, it probably is. And most likely, it will create another spacious wing in the colossal mansion that the federal government has become.

By reactivating the Presidential Export Council, Obama has once again used his power to further expand the already massive wingspan of the government. Once again merging business with the White House, he has appointed Xerox CEO Ursula Burns as the vice chair to serve alongside chairman and Boeing CEO W. James McNerney Jr. as part of the National Export Initiative. As American accountant Irwin Stelzer writes for the U.K.'s *Times Online*, "This approach is consistent with the administration's philosophy that the best way to solve a problem is to erect yet another government apparatus."[3]

With the National Export Initiative, Obama says he aims to create 2 million jobs by doubling exports in the next five years and help farmers and small businesses sell their goods overseas. Unfortunately, many pundits believe that it will accomplish no such goal. "There's just one problem: Growing exports is almost entirely out of the president's -- and even business's – hands," writes Jia Lynn Yang on *CNN.com*, "The United States' chief exports -- sophisticated manufacturing items like planes and semiconductors -- benefited from the countries' need to rebuild (or, in many cases, to just build) nationwide infrastructures. But a nation can only stock up on so many Caterpillar tractors at a time. Then the demand inevitably slowed. To get back to the mid 2000s-kind of growth, the U.S. would have to bank on other countries' stimulus plans working flawlessly."[4]

Who is McNerney?

Providence, Rhode Island native W. James (Jim) McNerney, Jr., was named chairman of the board, president and CEO of Boeing in 2005. He had already been with the company as a board member starting in 2001, while he was the CEO of 3M. Before that, he worked at General Electric for 19 years. McNerney is a Yale graduate, with an MBA from Harvard. Boeing is the largest manufacturer of commercial jets and military aircraft. They produce helicopters, electronic and defense systems, missiles, satellites and advanced information and communications systems.[5] Unfortunately Boeing has historically been involved the most egregious violations of U.S. Export Control Laws. In fact, Boeing's corporate acquisitions of Hughes and McDonnell Douglas make them into a Rogues Gallery of criminal assistance to the military capabilities of the Peoples Republic of China. The CEO of Boeing is going to lead the reform of the U.S. Export Control regulations? The greatest beneficiary is likely to be Communist China.

So President Obama has appointed the new CEO of the struggling Xerox to advise him on exports. Ursula Burns, a mechanical engineer by trade with a Masters from Columbia University. She joined the company as a summer intern 30 years ago and was soon after offered a full-time position, working in product development and planning. She was on the company's radar for a potential promotion to CEO since the 1990s and led several business teams within Xerox. In 1990, she was appointed special assistant to the president of marketing and customer operations and worked her way up general manager in 1997. Two years later she was named vice-president for worldwide manufacturing and began to work closely with Anne Mulcahy who became CEO in 2001. During this time, Xerox was struggling as customers started to gravitate towards cheaper office supplies and means of copying. Burns was responsible for cutting 40 percent of the staff and outsourcing production to other companies to streamline costs. She was named president of the company in 2007 and in May 2009 became the first black female CEO of a Fortune 500 company.[6] In November of that year, Obama appointed her to lead the federal STEM (science, technology, engineering and math) Education Coalition to support these subjects in schools. Educated, experienced and seemingly quite capable, Burns appears a great fit for Xerox, but her position in the government is questionable and appears to mark the federal addition of color copiers to its collection of minivans.

Xerox Fits Right into the Obama, George Mitchell Israel Hater Club

It is impossible to overlook that Obama's choice of Xerox as one of his favored Corporations may be based upon the fact that Xerox has also been found guilty of criminal violations of U.S. Export Control and foreign policy regulations to include illegally supporting the Arab Blacklist of Israel – which seems to fit right into the administration's anti-Israel theme that is becoming more visceral and apparent every day. Burns should get along well with McNerney if for no other reason than their shared corporate history in violating the very regulations Obama has appointed them to change. While Rank Xerox, their U.K. subsidiary has previously run afoul of both U.S. and U.K. export control laws Burns will be playing catch-up to equal Boeing's horrific record of export violations.[7]

But how does Burns' knowledge of mechanical engineering and decades of business experience translate into an export expertise? And why does Xerox — a company that got busted for failing to correctly report earnings in 2002 — have representation in the White House? Ursula Burns is part of Obama's Business Roundtable, a premier group of CEOs of corporations that boast almost $6 trillion in annual revenues and the Xerox executive has been known to back many of Obama's initiatives.[8]

The President's National Export Initiative has been met with criticism for the disparity between its goals and the means by which it will achieve them. Since the recession grew to a worldwide scale, exporting more goods will be far more difficult than Obama naively suggests. Other nations are also attempting to recover, and they will be looking to export, too. Critics have pointed out that domestic sales are for important to revive a lagging economy.

And so much of it is riddled in contradiction. Obama has chastised CEOs, Wall Street and business for just about everything they do and now two powerful executives are White House appointees. Something is amiss.

Boeing's Sordid History

Of all Obama's canoodling with business leaders, his decision to allow Boeing into the White House may be the most inexplicable. Boeing has a long and sordid history of violations regarding the overseas sale of military technologies. In 2006 Boeing paid a $15 million fine for violating Arms Export Control Act regarding the unlicensed sale of commercial airplanes carrying the QRS-11 gyrochip, particularly 19 planes to China. The QRS-11 is listed among defense items specifically not to be sold to China. Before this settlement, Boeing senior vice president and general counsel Douglas Bain declared export control to be the "biggest issue we face" at Boeing. So, naturally, Boeing's CEO has been appointed to a position overseeing this "issue." And it certainly has been an issue for Boeing in the past.[9]

The QRS-11 issue is far from their first brush with arms-export-control overseers. In 1998, Boeing illegally shared technologies with Russian, Ukrainian, Norwegian and German partners as part of the Sea Launch space rocket project, resulting in a $10 million fine. In 2001, Boeing was hit with a $4.3 million dollar fine for technology transfer without an export license to Australia, Malaysia, Turkey and Singapore. In 2003 Boeing subsidiary Hughes Space and Communication and Loral were fined $32 million for illegally exporting satellite technology to China. The violations occurred before Boeing acquired Loral and Hughes, but still show Boeing's willingness to associate with fellow violators.[10] The State Department Directorate of Defense Trade Controls (DDTC) stated that Boeing has a "serious, systemic, and longstanding" problem with export violations. Clearly, there is plenty to back that up. And while the government has taken action by fining the company repeatedly, the fines are simply not enough of a deterrent to force Boeing into compliance.[11]

Even from a financial perspective, McNerney has been largely unsuccessful as CEO. Boeing has repeatedly been delaying the release of its new airplanes. The company has been reporting increasing losses, which seem to get worse each month. McNerney fired his head of commercial aircraft, which seems to isolate the blame for the delays on McNerney himself. In 2009, Boeing shares had dropped 43% from two years prior, and people were calling for McNerney's registration.[12]

In a *Washington Examiner* article about the annual Export-Import Bank's conference in mid-March, columnist Timothy P. Carney details the comments made by Obama introducer GE CEO Jeff Immelt, in which he praises the near merger between government and business in countries such as Germany and China. "It's not hard to translate Immelt, who is much blunter than the president. The economics Immelt derides -- "let whatever happens happen" -- is also known as the free enterprise system. The economics Immelt advocates -- "government and business working as a pack" -- is also known as corporate socialism, or corporatism. President Obama is too savvy, and much too scripted, to use the same words as Immelt. But he has the same vision," he writes. Carney also criticizes the Obama's double-talk as the President states that he is aiming his plan to aid small businesses while the actual systems have always favored the big, established businesses.[13] One being General Electric who critics argue is acting as its own arm of the Obama administration, from starting its own PAC that gave more money to Obama than any other politician to hiring former senators — such as Trent Lott and John Breaux — as lobbyists.[14]

Others have pointed out how difficult it would be for businesses with small staffs and modest means to operate outside of the United States.

Obama has also emphasized going green to create jobs however, as multiple pundits have pointed out, the wind machines he prefers are manufactured in China. John Dimsdale reported for *American Public Media*, "To sell American products overseas, the president is backing financing for the Export-Import Bank, which lends money to potential exporters. But last year the Ex-Im Bank backed the exports of oil, gas, and mining technology and power plants. That represents a tripling of the pollution from the previous year's underwriting."[15]

As posted on *American Elephants*, "That's just the ticket. To create jobs, always erect another government bureaucracy. If you don't create any jobs in the private sector, at least you're creating a whole bunch in government. Unfortunately the only way you can pay all the new bureaucrats is by taking more out of the wallets of all those people looking for jobs."[16]

Many pundits have also noted that the true way to revive the economy is to produce more goods in America that are consumed domestically. "Mr. Obama can only realize his export and economic recovery ambitions if he addresses the nation's still-excessive imports — and recognizes that, because America's dismal economic and financial realities have been ignored for so long, greater short-term pain has become inevitable. If the president's trade and related policies don't quickly start making these hard choices, then his talk of doubling exports will be unmasked as double-talk," Alan Tonelson wrote in *The Washington Times*, where he also pointed out several flaws in the export program.[17] He notes in an online addendum to his column that the plan to increase exports is immaterial if the United States does not start replacing imported goods with domestically produced ones.

Another issue resides in the restrictions that are still in place that have discouraged other nations from importing U.S. goods. In 2009 Obama signed a law that ended Mexican trucks' access into the United States, causing our neighbors to the south to place tariffs on a variety of American goods that resulted in the loss of 25,000 jobs and $2.6 billion in trade revenue.[18] As Tonelson writes, "Obama's export-doubling rhetoric ignores the biggest realities about our global economy – not only since the economic and financial crisis broke out, but in recent decades. Principally, America's trade competitors were loath to import from the United States robustly – especially on a net basis – even when times were good around the world. Now, with "uncertain" being the kindest way to describe the world's prospects, these countries are going to become more enthusiastic about U.S. products?"

The initiative has also been criticism for being superfluous, just another bunch of appointees who will be too bogged down in bureaucracy to accomplish anything. Obama's unwillingness to get tough with China has also come under fire. As written in a *Christian Science Monitor* editorial, "Another step is tougher enforcement of current trade rules to prevent foreign bias against US goods and services. So far, however, Obama has been reluctant to force China - the country with the largest trade deficit with the US - to end manipulation of its currency rate that favors Chinese exports and discourages imports. China also ranks high as a thief of US intellectual goods, such as software." He has also been slow to approve pending free-trade agreements with Columbia, Panama and South Korea and challenge members of Congress opposed to the ideas.[19]

So, under the guise of helping small businesses and creating jobs, the President has appointed big business CEOs to advise him on doubling exports. As Ursula Burns is already aiding the White House in the science education programs, shouldn't she and Xerox expect something in return? And if Jim McNerney's company sees export control as an "issue" to fight against, why would he ever be expected to influence policy without putting Boeing's interests first and continuing to jeopardize national security?

---

[1] "President's Export Council History." International Trade Administration, Department of Commerce. Mar. 10, 2003. Apr. 8, 2010 < http://www.ita.doc.gov/TD/PEC/history.html>.

[2] Hill, Bob. "How 10 of the Most Well-Known CEOs in America Rate Obama's Policies." PBP Media. Aug. 10, 2009. Apr. 13, 2010 <http://www.businessbrief.com/how-10-of-the-most-well-known-ceos-in-america-rate-obamas-policies/>.

[3] Stelzer, Irwin. "Trade rows sap Obama's plan to create 2m jobs." *Times Online* March 14, 2010. March 22, 2010 < http://business.timesonline.co.uk/tol/business/columnists/article7061010.ece>.

[4] Yang, Jia Lynn. "Why Obama's export push won't save jobs." *CNN.com* Jan. 29, 2010. March 24, 2010 < http://money.cnn.com/2010/01/29/news/state_of_the_union_obama.fortune/index.htm>.

[5] "Executive Biographies: W. James McNerney, Jr.," Boeing.com, Jan. 2010 <http://www.boeing.com/companyoffices/aboutus/execprofiles/mcnerney.html>

[6] Byrnes, Nanette and Roger O. Crockett. "Ursula Burns: An Historic Succession at Xerox." *Business Week.com* May, 28 2009. March 25, 2009 < http://www.businessweek.com/magazine/content/09_23/b4134018712853.htm>.

[7] http://news.google.com/newspapers?nid=1755&dat=19830917&id=PjAcAAAAIBAJ&sjid=hmgEAAAAIBAJ&pg=3852,5378798

[88] King, Neil Jr. "CEOs' Club Issues Non-Statement on Obama's Health Care Overhaul." *WSJ.com*. The Wall Street Journal March 23, 2010. March 24, 2010 < http://blogs.wsj.com/washwire/2010/03/23/ceos-club-issues-non-statement-on-obamas-health-care-overhaul/>.

[9] Dominic Gates, "Boeing Pays $15 Million Fine," *The Seattle Times*, 2006, <http://gflorencescott.wordpress.com/2009/05/22/ boeing-arms-export-control-violations-and-continuing-problems-at-boeing/>

[10] Ibid.

[11] "Boeing's Arms Export Control Violations and Continuing Problems at Boeing," May 20, 2009, <http://www.pmddtc.state.gov/compliance/ ... mpany.html>

[12] Douglas A. McIntyre, "Boeing (BA) Earnings: Time for CEO Jim McNerney to Leave," Oct. 21, 2009. <http://247wallst.com/2009/10/21/boeing-ba-earnings-time-for-ceo-jim-mcnerney-to-leave/>

[13] Carney, Timothy P. "Obama's export plan imports Europe's corporatism." *The Washington Examiner.com* March 12, 2010. March 23, 2010 < http://www.washingtonexaminer.com/opinion/columns/Oba ma_s-export-plan-imports-Europe_s-corporatism-87389757.html>.

[14] Dougherty, Michael Brendan. "Big Government, Big Business, Big Rip-Off." *The American Conservative.com* Feb. 1, 2010. March 23, 2010 < http://www.amconmag.com/article/2010/feb/01/00047/>.

[15] "A Conflict with Obama's Trade Pledge." *American Public Media*. March 11, 2010. March 23, 2010 < http://marketplace.publicradio.org/display/web/2010/03/11/ pm-exports/>

[16] "Is this Any Way to Create Export Jobs?" [Weblog entry.] American Elephants. March 15, 2010. March 24, 2010 < http://americanelephant.wordpress.com/2010/03/15/is-this-any-way-to-create-export-jobs/>.

[17] Tonelson, Alan. "Doubling Exports or Double-Talk?" *The Washington Times*. Feb. 2, 2010: A9.

[18] Stelzer, Irwin. "Trade rows sap Obama's plan to create 2m jobs." *Times Online* March 14, 2010. March 22, 2010 <

http://business.timesonline.co.uk/tol/business/columnists/art icle7061010.ece>.

[19] Jobs, Jobs, Jobs: For Obama, They Lie in More Exports." *The Christian Science Monitor*. March 11, 2010.

Faith-Based Czar : Joshua DuBois

Official title:	Director of the White House Office of Faith-
icial title:	ector of the White House Office of Faith- .ed and Neighborhood Partnerships
icial responsibilities:	.rks with secular and religious groups to .ist them with social issues; also assists ups apply for federal grants
)orts to:	sident Obama
.ate confirmation:	ne
ary:	,000
ology / political liation:	eral Pro-abortion Democrat

Who Is the Faith-Based Czar?

Joshua DuBois was named the Director of the White House
Office of Faith-Based and Neighborhood Partnerships on
February 5, 2009. A faithful follower of Obama, DuBois was
seen as the obvious choice for this position by those close to the
administration. At the youthful age of 26, the question has been
raised as to whether DuBois possesses the maturity and
temperament required to manage a position for which he has no
real experience. With no experience working with charities, one
would logically ask why DuBois was awarded this position.
What is already known of him seems to suggest his role will be
that of a front man for Obama's leftist agenda to be dressed up
as religion, something liberals claim to hate when they accuse
conservatives of it.

Inexperienced Obama Crony

Even more than the concern of his youth and inexperience is his
liberal ideology and his loyal following to President Obama's
radical agenda. DuBois became a Senate Aide for Obama in 2005
after persistently pursuing the position, having been turned
down three times. His allegiance to the Senator was eventually
recognized and his abilities to use religion to aid Obama in his

political gain were soon being exploited. DuBois was tapped by Obama as the director of religious affairs for the Obama campaign in 2008 because of his ability to reach out to religious leaders and present Obama as "a man motivated by his faith" (*New York Times*)[1]. Paradoxical to the way the *New York Times* usually mocks religious people, in Obama's case the *Times* saw it very positive to present Obama as a man of faith.

DuBois tells the *Boston Globe* that he "[grew] up in the church", as he was raised by a stepfather that was a minister in the African Methodist Episcopal Church[2]. In college at Boston University, DuBois attended the United Pentecostal Council of the Assemblies of God, "a small predominantly African-American denomination"[3]. At the age of 18, DuBois would occasionally preach when the pastor was away. To add to his experience and credibility, many pro-Obama news organizations have described DuBois as being a pastor or associate pastor for the church he attended in Boston, but the *Washington Times* reported on January 31, 2009 that "a spokeswoman for the denomination said he does not have pastoral credentials with them."[4]

Democrat Hypocrisy Run Amok

One can find no criticism of DuBois in the mainstream pro-Obama media, and in fact, they have taken the opposite approach than they did when they harshly criticized the position in the Bush administration. MSNBC's Mark Murray not only didn't criticize, but with staggering duplicity, actually praised the position, "Rather than cut the Bush-created office, Obama is expanding it. Including neighborhood and community groups may be an Obama administration nod to secular non-profit organizations who felt excluded by the Bush Administration's office."[5]

There is also a duplicitous view from the media regarding DuBois' religious affiliation with the United Pentecostal Council of the Assemblies of God. The liberal-dominated media portrayed Sarah Palin a religious extremist because of her religious views and her upbringing in the similar-in-doctrine Assemblies of God church. Ken Shepherd of *NewsBusters* made the point during the 2008 presidential campaign: "In a *Newsweek* Web exclusive, Lisa Miller and Amanda Coyne set out to find something juicy about Alaska Governor Sarah Palin's house of worship, Wasilla Bible Church. But finding a 'staid' worship environment that 'steer[s] clear of politics' and whose main attraction is Biblical preaching, they opted to focus on where the governor used to worship regularly years ago, an Assemblies of God church: [The *Newsweek* article says]

'Pentecostalism is one of the fastest growing branches of Christianity in the world, and the Assemblies of God is one of the largest Pentecostal denominations in the country, claiming 1.6 million members. Pentecostals are generally characterized by a strict adherence to moral codes--no tobacco, no alcohol, no social dancing, no sex outside of marriage--and by their belief that the Holy Spirit bestows upon some the gift of 'speaking in tongues,' a reference to Acts 2: 'And they were all filled with the Holy Ghost and began to speak with other tongues.' A spokeswoman for the McCain-Palin campaign has said that Palin attends many churches and does not consider herself to be Pentecostal. […] When Palin worships in Juneau, she attends an Assembly of God church there. Sarah Palin may not call herself a Pentecostal, but she has deep and long experience in Pentecostal churches. And as the race wears on, this biographical fact will likely become another religious Rorschach test--pleasing to some, discomfiting to others." Compare that to Joshua DuBois, who the media not only has no problem associating with the Pentecostal sect, but actually claims that it gives him credibility because he has worked as "an associate pastor."[6] Will this become, as *Newsweek*'s Miller and Coyne pointed out regarding Palin "another religious Rorschach test?" It is evident that this is not a test of religion; it's a test of politics. DuBois is being used as a political evangelist for the administration – faith in Obama is the gospel.

DuBois stated that in college he was "struggling whether [to] go into ministry or politics."[7] While garnering experience in politics, before working as an aide for then-Senator Obama, DuBois worked as an aide to Representative Rush Holt (D-NJ) and as a fellow for Representative Charles Rangel's (D-NY) office. Though DuBois claims a steadfast faith and belief in Jesus Christ, all of the political offices for whom he has worked were politically positioned far left and strongly pro-abortion. Indeed Mr. DuBois' first display of social activism was not that to defend the life of the unborn, but that of an unarmed immigrant mistakenly killed by four New York police officers. When DuBois was a freshman at Boston University, he became outraged because the police officers that killed the Guinean immigrant, Amadou Diallo, were acquitted. Although a tragedy, the jury recognized the innocence of the officers, as they shot Diallo when he reached into his pocket to get his wallet, and they all believed him to be reaching for a gun. DuBois, however, felt the officers were guilty and so this led to his first social-activism protest. In an interview with the *Boston Globe*, DuBois "wrote 'NO MORE' on a placard, planted himself on the expanse of pavement along Commonwealth Avenue, in front of a memorial to Martin Luther King Jr., and stood there – 41 hours for 41 shots."[7] In this situation, DuBois was moved by the killing of a seemingly innocent man. The question could be asked if DuBois has ever stood for hours to defend the millions of innocent lives killed through abortion. Though DuBois had "struggled" to decide between politics and faith, because of his association with all liberal, pro-choice politicians, and though he works under the guise of religion, he has undeniably chosen politics.

He has tried to coerce Catholic voters into becoming Obama supporters by comparing the value of human life to healthcare and having food. The *Wall Street Journal* reported, "At a recent house party in Cincinnati, 15 Catholic voters packed into a small living room. They snacked on cookies and punch as Mr. DuBois played a DVD of Sen. Obama sitting in front of a fireplace talking about the role of faith in politics. When the short video ended, Mr. DuBois led a discussion about how religious voters can come to terms with voting for a pro-choice Democrat. 'Abortion is certainly a deeply moral issue, but so is struggling to afford decent health care for your family, or straining to put food on your table,' he recalls telling the group."8 It is interesting to note here that the Obama campaign and the religious Left use scripture and religion as a battering ram to advance their political agenda – the very thing the Left accuses conservatives of doing. In many ways DuBois has learned the fine art of using his Christian faith when it is convenient for him and the Obama administration.

In true political fashion he told *Christianity Today*, "Our democracy demands that when people are religiously motivated, you have to translate your [policy] concerns into universal rather than religion-specific values. We're no longer just a Christian nation; we're also a Jewish nation, a Hindu nation, a Muslim nation, and a nation that does not adhere to a particular religion."9

Forcing Churches to Hire Non-believers?

According to the *New York Times*, the most controversial issue DuBois will face is "whether Mr. Obama should rescind a Bush administration legal memorandum that allows religious groups that receive government money to hire only those who share their faith. Mr. Obama said in a campaign speech last June, 'If you get a federal grant, you can't use that grant money to proselytize to the people you help and you can't discriminate against them – or against the people you hire – on the basis of their religion."10 In a *Washington Times* article, Bill Donohue of the Catholic League commented regarding Obama's campaign promise, "If a Catholic agency cannot work according to its religious precepts, then it's no longer Catholic. For the state to impose a secular vision on religious agencies is to neuter them."11 Echoing that sentiment, Tom McClusky, vice president of governmental affairs for Family Research Council, stating the same concerns as Donohue, said "Most churches have concerns they'd be forced to hire people who do not believe or follow their church's core mission," he said. "Traditionally, not a lot of conservative groups have worked with the faith-based office because of those kind of regulations.

President Bush went a long way towards lowering those barriers. It'd be a shame to turn the clock back."12 But now that the Obama administration is in full-swing and those campaign promises are being neglected, forgotten, altered – whatever the case may be – it now appears Obama has decided that instead of changing the policy as to whether "faith-based groups accepting federal money can hire and fire according to their religious beliefs", DuBois has said such decisions will be made on a "case by case" basis.13 Along with the banking industry, the car industry, healthcare, etceteras, Obama's quest for total control is again implied in the area of religion. By making these decisions on a "case by case basis", which is not what he promised in his campaign, Obama now can grant these privileges to only the federal-money recipients that he wants to, and deny those he does not want to have the privileges, thus creating a well-funded religious militia of the Left.
— *Angie Wheeler*

1 *New York Times*, "Leaders Say Obama Has Tapped Pastor for Outreach Office" by Laurie Goodstein, January 2, 2009 - http://www.nytimes.com/2009/01/29/us/politics/29faith.html?_r=3&ref=politics
2 *Boston Globe*, "Obama's Man of Faith" by Michael Paulson, July 10, 2008, http://www.boston.com/news/nation/articles/2008/07/10/obamas_man_of_faith/?page=1
3 *Boston Globe*, "Obama's Man of Faith" by Michael Paulson, July 10, 2008, http://www.boston.com/news/nation/articles/2008/07/10/obamas_man_of_faith/?page=1
4 *Washington Times*, "Faith Panel Chief Seen as Inexperienced" by Julia Duin, January 31, 2009 -

http://washingtontimes.com/news/2009/jan/31/faith-panel-pickseen-lacking-experience/

5 MSNBC, "Obama's Faith-based Rollout, February 4, 2009 - http://firstread.msnbc.msn.com/archive/2009/02/04/1780367.aspx

6 *NewsBusters*, "Newsweek Takes on Sarah Palin's Religion" by Ken Shepherd, September 2, 2008 - http://newsbusters.org/blogs/kenshepherd/2008/09/02/newsweek-takes-sarah-palins-religion

7 *Boston Globe*, "Obama's Man of Faith" by Michael Paulson, July 10, 2008, http://www.boston.com/news/nation/articles/2008/07/10/obamas_man_of_faith/?page=1

8 *Wall Street Journal*, "Young Clergyman Leads Obama's Drive to Attract 'Faith Voters'" by Amy Chozick, August 16, 2008 - http://online.wsj.com/article/SB121883753433545501.html?mod=googlenews_wsj

9*Christianity Today*, "Conservatives Talk Abortion Reduction with White House" by Adelle M. Banks, Religion News Service, March 25, 2009 - http://blog.christianitytoday.com/ctpolitics/joshua_dubois/

10 *New York Times*, "Leaders Say Obama Has Tapped Pastor for Outreach Office" by Laurie Goodstein, January 28, 2009 - http://www.nytimes.com/2009/01/29/us/politics/29faith.html?_r=3&ref=politics

11 *Washington Times*, "Faith Panel Chief Seen as Inexperienced" by Julia Duin, January 31, 2009 - http://washingtontimes.com/news/2009/jan/31/faith-panel-pickseen-lacking-experience/

12 *Washington Times*, "Faith Panel Chief Seen as Inexperienced" by Julia Duin, January 31, 2009 http://washingtontimes.com/news/2009/jan/31/faith-panel-pickseen-lacking-experience/

13 *World Magazine*, "Stay Tuned" by Edward Lee Pitts, June 12, 2009 - http://www.worldmag.com/webextra/15523

Government Performance Czar — Jeffrey Zients

Official title:	Chief Performance Officer, OMB's Deputy Director of Management
Official responsibilities:	Improving relationships with DHS partners at home and abroad, leading efforts to reduce violence along the Southwest border
Reports to:	Office of Management and Budget Director
Senate confirmation:	Yes
Salary:	Information unavailable
Ideology / political affiliation:	This is his first government job, but he has made many campaign donations, almost exclusively to Democrats

Jeffrey Zients has never worked for the government before, but Obama is counting on his ability to make himself very rich to translate into an ability to make the government more efficient. A very shrewd businessman, Zients joined the Washington D.C. consulting and research company The Advisory Board in 1992, was the chief operating officer by 1996 and the chief executive officer by 1998. In 1999, he took the Corporate Executive Board branch of the company public, making $155 million. The company made $90 million more in 2001 when the rest of The Advisory Board went public. In 2002, these moves proved successful enough to land Zients on Fortune's list of the richest Americans under 40.[1]

A lifelong baseball fan, Zients played a key role in bringing Major League Baseball back to the nation's capital, as he helped orchestrate the transformation of the Montreal Expos into the Washington Nationals. He had a group of investors ready to purchase the team and a management group that included former Secretary of State Colin Powell, but ultimately lost out on his bid to buy the franchise.[2]

He will essentially be functioning as an efficiency expert in his new job, and will have to find ways to cut out as much fat as possible from the federal budget so Obama can continue with his many spending projects with as small a deficit as is possible considering what he wants to implement. From his post in the Office of Management and Budget, the avid Democratic political donor[3] "will work to streamline processes, cut costs, and find best practices throughout our government," says Obama.[4] As the first Chief Performance Officer, Zients will have to come up with a system to evaluate program performance, revamp the government's hiring practices, lead an expanded e-government initiative, and work on contract reform. He will be involved with stimulus plans as well, helping out other agencies and studying the effects of the stimulus.[5]

[1] "Jeffrey D. Zients," Who Runs GOV,
<http://www.whorunsgov.com/Profiles/Jeffrey_D._Zients>
[2] "Jeffrey D. Zients," Who Runs GOV,
<http://www.whorunsgov.com/Profiles/Jeffrey_D._Zients>
[3] "Jeffrey Zients Contribution List in 2004," CampaignMoney.com,
<http://www.campaignmoney.com/political/contributions/jeffreyzients.asp?cycle=04>
[4] "Getting your 'money's worth?'" 18 April 2009, Political Ticker,
<http://politicalticker.blogs.cnn.com/2009/04/18/obama-namesperformance-and-technology-czars/>
[5] Robert Brodsky, "Zients confirmed as OMB's director of management," 22 June 2009, Govexec.com,
<http://www.govexec.com/story_page_pf.cfm?articleid=43003&printerfriendlyvers=1>

Great Lakes Czar — Cameron Davis

Official title:	Special advisor to the U.S. EPA, Great Lakes Restoration Plan Oversight
Salary / Direct cost to taxpayers:	Unknown
Responsibilities:	Will coordinate federal programs on the Great Lakes (Huron, Ontario, Michigan, Erie and Superior)
Reports to:	Environmental Protection Agency Administrator Lisa Jackson
Senate confirmation:	No
Relation to Obama:	Met in 1998 on a volunteer beach cleanup in Obama's district when Obama was a state senator.[1] Davis became a political supporter of Obama, blogging for his group Organizing For America during the 2008 presidential campaign.[2]
Ideology / political affiliation:	Gullible environmental activist, wide-eyed Obama supporter

No one can deny the importance of preserving the environment, including that of the Great Lakes. But like many other feel-good issues, environmental protection has long ago been hijacked by the Left as a backdoor way to increase the government's control over the industries and individual lives.

A wide-ranging strategy for protecting and restoring the lakes had already been developed in 2005 by the Bush administration. As usual, environmental activists complained about the lack of federal dollars - and Barack Obama answered their plea during his campaign, promising to spend over $5 billion of taxpayers' dollars over a ten-year period for the Great Lakes' project.

In June 2009, President Obama appointed Cameron Davis to a newly-created czar position to oversee the project. No congressional confirmation was required - despite the fact that Davis will be managing a $475 million budget that Obama has proposed just for 2010 alone, while the entire restoration program is expected to cost more than $20 billion.

Who is Cameron Davis?

Like many environmental enthusiasts, Cameron Davis is not a scientist. In fact, he is a lawyer with a history of participating in environmental advocacy organizations that are driven by ideological considerations rather than science.

Upon graduating from Boston University in 1986, Davis joined the Alliance for the Great Lakes, an environmental advocacy organization of which he is now President and CEO. While working as a litigating attorney and serving as an adjunct clinical assistant professor of law at the University of Michigan Law School, he continued to advocate for environmental issues regardless of their credibility or scientific value. This led him to join the United Nations Environment Program in Nairobi, Kenya, working on the Montreal Protocol project designed to protect the Earth's ozone layer.

The great Ozone Scare of the 80s and 90s, which consumed billions of dollars and increased government control over the industries worldwide, culminated into nothing. When "man-made ozone holes" were proven to be a scientific hoax, the anti-capitalist ideologues dropped the issue of saving the ozone layer and shamelessly recycled the same scare tactics and strategies to achieve their perpetual goal by accusing industrialized nations of "man-made global warming." Some of them went back to the more familiar activism. Cameron Davis returned to his Alliance for the Great Lakes.

For Davis, who boasted of having worked with and supporting Barack Obama for an entire decade, environmental activism is inseparable from proselytizing. An official blogger for the pro-Obama group Organizing For America during the 2008 presidential campaign (my.barackobama.com), Davis wrote that one of the important lessons we could all learn from Obama is that "If you want to save the environment, don't hug a tree. Get a college student or 20-something involved."[3]

Activism Over Economic Reality

"One challenge Davis will face is making sure the federal money is used effectively -- particularly when the government already has about 140 programs dealing with the Great Lakes environment," reported AP writer John Flesher.[4] Conserving the Great Lakes, the world's largest freshwater resource, is certainly a noble endeavor, but with 140 programs already in place was it necessary to create another salary positon -- not to mention the added billions of federal dollars that will be going toward the program? It was reported that Davis, when president of the Alliance for the Great Lakes, pushed for the Great Lakes restoration program which is expected to cost more than $20 billion.[5]

Flesher's AP report stated that George Kuper, president of the Council of Great Lakes Industries said that despite his background as an environmental activist, Davis has been willing to consider the region's business interests: "I hope he'll reach out and get guidance on that," Kuper said. "We've worked quite closely on legislation and other things in the basin. He understands the value of multi-stakeholder participation."[6]

In an interview with Czar Davis, *Chicago Life Magazine*'s Jane Ammeson asked Davis if there is really a way to balance business and environmental concerns. Davis replied, "This assumes that business and environmental concerns sit on either end of the seesaw — or teeter-totter if you grew up here in the Midwest. They don't. I think of things not so much in terms of businesses versus other entities, but more in terms of whether we're going to be shortsighted or take the long view. We need to provide for the Great Lakes of today so that the Great Lakes can provide jobs, recreation and renewal for the next generation."[7]

Though George Kuper believes that Davis "understands the value of multi-stakeholder participation", Davis' comments to *Chicago Life Magazine* indicate that his enviromental activism will always come first.

On the Wrong Side of Issues

On his blog at my.barackobama.com Davis praised Obama for challenging Detroit auto makers to fight global warming.[8] Having now become the White House official policy, the tendency to put questionable theories and ideological slogans above jobs and well-being of American economy have proven disastrous. Both Cameron Davis and Barack Obama are on the wrong side of the issue of advancing American economy, without which there can be no funding for any of the environmental projects, no matter how urgent or realistic they are.

— *Angie Wheeler*

---

[1] *Evanston Review*, "Obama Picks Evanston Man for Post of Great Lakes 'Czar'" by Bob Seidenberg, June 22, 2009 -- http://www.pioneerlocal.com/evanston/news/1634292,evanston-obama-appoints-resident-062209-s1.article

[2] Conservative Thoughts, "Obama's Czars September Update", August 23, 2009 -- http://conservativethoughts.us/2009/08/23/obamas-czars/

[3] Cameron Davis's Blog, Organizing For America, http://my.barackobama.com/page/community/blog/cameron_davis

[4] Associated Press, "EPA Head Names Cameron Davis to Oversee Federal Initiative to Restore Great Lakes Environment" by John Flesher, June 4, 2009.

[5] Associated Press, "EPA Head Names Cameron Davis to Oversee Federal Initiative to Restore Great Lakes Environment" by John Flesher, June 4, 2009.

[6] Associated Press, "EPA Head Names Cameron Davis to Oversee Federal Initiative to Restore Great Lakes Environment" by John Flesher, June 4, 2009.

[7] *Chicago Life Magazine*, "Great Lakes Czar" by Jane Ammeson, August 9, 2009 -- http://www.chicagolife.net/content/environment/Great_Lakes_Czar

[8] Cameron Davis's Blog, Organizing For America, http://my.barackobama.com/page/community/blog/cameron_davis

Green Jobs Czar — Van Jones

Official title:	Special Advisor for Green Jobs, Enterprise and Innovation at the White House Council on Environmental Quality[1]
Responsibilities:	Promote environmentally friendly employment and generate support for the idea nationwide (control the green-jobs related cash in the stimulus bill)
Appointed:	March 9, 2009
Senate confirmation:	None
Salary:	Information unavailable
Reports to:	Head of the Council on Environmental Quality (Nancy Sutley)[2]
Ideology / political affiliation:	A self-avowed communist, critic of capitalism and environmental activist

While in theory the mission of the Green Jobs Czar is "to help create and promote environmental friendly jobs across the country," in practice it seems to be a nice-sounding excuse to advance Obama's agenda of putting large sectors of U.S. economy under government control and make an "inspiring" show designed to get more Americans to think favorably of central economic planning.

Four months into his role as the Green Jobs Czar, Van Jones admitted that he still could not explain exactly what a "green job" was. In a July 2009 interview with Newsweek magazine, the former community organizer from Oakland stated: "Well, we still don't have a unified definition, and that's not unusual in a democracy. It takes a while for all the states and the federal government to come to some agreement. But the Department of Labor is working on it very diligently. Fundamentally, it's getting there, but we haven't crossed the finish line yet."[3]

The real reason for such confusion might just be that in a free market economy this job would have been completely unnecessary: the same goals and much more could have been accomplished with the right tax incentives and technological innovation. But the free market is being disposed of, and Obama couldn't have chosen a more dedicated accomplice in dismantling the capitalist system than Van Jones, a self-avowed Marxist-Leninist-Maoist.

Who is Van Jones?

A 41-year-old Yale Law School graduate, Van Jones began his career of a radical activist in the Oakland, CA, grassroots organizing scene - first as a prison-reform advocate, and then moving on to becoming a leading member of Standing Together to Organize a Revolutionary Movement (STORM), a Bay Area Marxist-Maoist group. A "multi-racial activist collective with Marxist influences," STORM became the guiding force behind several notable front groups, one of which was an anti-police unit called Bay Area Police Watch, which viewed police officers as the arch-enemies of black people. Another STORM front was the School of Unity and Liberation (SOUL), which was a Marxist training organization; yet another was People Organized to Win Employment Rights (POWER), which agitated on behalf of the jobless.

In 1993 Jones was arrested during the Rodney King riots and again in 1999 during the Seattle protest against the World Trade Organization.[4] Having been converted by radical prison inmates from a self-described "rowdy black nationalist" to a full-blown communist, by the late 1990s Jones was already a committed Marxist-Leninist-Maoist who loathed capitalism for allegedly exploiting nonwhite minorities worldwide. In 1996 he founded the Ella Baker Center for Human Rights, which seeks to promote alternatives to incarceration, claiming that the American criminal-justice system is infested with racism. He also co-founded Color of Change, a racial grievance group that later spearheaded an advertising boycott of the Glenn Beck show on Fox News when the popular host questioned President Obama's judgment in nominating Van Jones for a government position.[5]

Having realized that his Marxist agenda could be more effectively achieved under the fashionable guise of the more respectable "green" movement, Jones applied his community organizing skills to creating and promoting radical groups with correspondingly benign names and noble-sounding goals. Soon after attending the Clinton Global Initiative in September 2007, Jones launched Green For All, a non-governmental organization "dedicated to building an inclusive green economy strong enough to lift people out of poverty ... advocating for local, state and federal commitment to job creation, job training, and entrepreneurial opportunities in the emerging green economy - especially for people from disadvantaged communities."

In October 2008 Jones published his first book, *The Green Collar Economy: How One Solution Can Fix Our Two Biggest Problems*, in which he promoted his crypto-Marxist approach on environmental and economic issues. The book received favorable reviews from such notables as Al Gore, Nancy Pelosi, Laurie David, Winona LaDuke, environmentalist Paul Hawken, and NAACP President/CEO Ben Jealous.

In 2008, Time magazine named Jones one of its "Environmental Heroes."[6] In this new capacity Jones has served as a board member of numerous environmental and nonprofit organizations, including the Rainforest Action Network; Free Press; Bioneers, the National Apollo Alliance, the Social Venture Network, Julia Butterfly Hill's "Circle of Life" environmental foundation, and was a Fellow at the Institute of Noetic Sciences.

Most recently he worked for John Podesta's Center for American Progress - a George Soros-funded far-left think tank that became a reliable source of ideologically committed cadres for the Obama Administration. Jones served as a Senior Fellow at the Center working on green issues and writing the book *Green Collar Economy.*[7]

Luckily for Van Jones and many other Obama's Czars with unsavory credentials and disturbing backgrounds, his new job was not dependent upon the vetting and confirmation process in the U.S. Senate.

Blaming America for 9-11

One day after the 9/11 attacks, Van Jones led a cynical anti-American vigil[8] at Snow Park in Oakland, CA., that blamed America for this tragedy. Organized by Jones' radical Marxist groups STORM and Elle Baker Center for Human Rights, the vigil immediately politicized the human suffering and mourned, not as much the people who died at the Twin Towers, the Pentagon, and the passengers of the hijacked planes, but rather the alleged victims of "U.S. imperialism" around the world, as well as "Arab and Muslim Americans" who Jones expected to become the "new victims."[9]

Already on 9-11, STORM and Elle Baker Center issued a joint press release titled *People Of Color Groups Gather to Stand In Solidarity With Arab Americans and to Mourn the East Coast Dead.*[10] Written in the ridiculously archaic and stilted style of Leninist Pravda editorials, the document stated:

> "Anti-Arab hostility is already reaching a fever pitch as pundits and common people alike rush to judgment that an Arab group is responsible for this tragedy," said Van Jones, national executive director of the Ella Baker Center for Human Rights. "We fear that an atmosphere is being created that will result in official and street violence against Arab men, women and children."

And so that you would have no doubts that the real criminal here was the United States, Van Jones and his unwavering commissars declared the following:

> The system, in the United States and worldwide, has continually denied peaceful, "legitimate" attempts by those seeking justice and freedom. Through its own reckless, violent and oppressive actions against poor people and people of color, the United States government has fueled frustration, grief and outrage here and around the world... Neither police repression at home nor U.S. bombs abroad will ease this

fundamental despair; instead, they will only continue
this vicious cycle of frustration and violence.[11]

STORM's official manifesto "Reclaiming Revolution" also blamed
the U.S. for 9-11. According to the leftist victimology template
based on the "divide and conquer" strategy, Jones and his
Politburo disdainfully separated the deaths of "innocent working
class people" from the deaths of presumably not-so-innocent
American citizens who did not belong to the working class or
minorities and, therefore, could be classified as legitimate targets.

> That night, STORM and the other movement leaders
> expressed sadness and anger at the deaths of innocent
> working class people. We were angry, first and
> foremost, with the U.S. government, whose worldwide
> aggression had engendered such hate across the globe
> that working class people were not safe at home. We
> honored those who had lost their lives in the attack --
> and those who would surely lose their lives in
> subsequent U.S. attacks overseas.[12]

The same cynical strategy to "divide and conquer" under the guise
of unity penetrated the 9-11 press release that announced the vigil.
Using a formula that implied the presumed culpability of those
excluded from it, the press release repeatedly stated:

> All people and especially African-Americans, Asian-
> Americans, Latinas/os and Native Americans must
> stand in solidarity with our Arab and Muslim sisters and
> brothers.[13]

Consistent with the leftist tactics of using any excuse, no matter
how tragic, to undermine American economy, security, and image
in the world, the press release called to disarm the nation in the
face of the foreign and domestic threat:

> We oppose any and all efforts to increase the funding and authority
> of U.S. police and intelligence agencies as a "solution" to this crisis.
> ... We must now be extraordinarily vigilant against threats directed

against the people - not from underground cells, but from the highest levels of government. [14]

It is dismally ironic that Van Jones, who has never distanced himself from his past statements and subversive communist activities, is now part of the Obama administration's push to turn September 11 into a National Day of Service focused on the promotion of the radical environmentalist agenda.

Radical Ties to Marxist Revolutionary Radicals

Following 9-11, Jones and STORM were active in the anti-Iraq War demonstrations organized by International ANSWER, a front group for the Marxist-Leninist Workers World Party. Prior to that Jones had also collaborated on numerous STORM projects, including antiwar protests, with local activist Elizabeth "Betita" Martinez, who served as a "mentor" for members of the Ella Baker Center.

According to David Horowitz's DiscoverTheNetworks.org website, "Martinez was a longtime Maoist who went on to join the Committees of Correspondence for Democracy and Socialism (CCDS), a Communist Party USA splinter group, in the early 1990s. To this day, Martinez continues to sit on the CCDS advisory board alongside such luminaries as Angela Davis, Timuel Black (who served on Barack Obama's 2004 Senate campaign committee), and musician Pete Seeger. Martinez is also a board member of the Movement for a Democratic Society, the parent organization of Progressives for Obama. Martinez and Van Jones together attended a 'Challenging White Supremacy' workshop which advanced the theme that 'all too often, the unconscious racism of white activists stands in the way of any effective, worthwhile collaboration' with blacks.

"STORM also had ties to the South African Communist Party and it revered Amilcar Cabral, the late Marxist revolutionary leader (of Guinea-Bissau and the Cape Verde Islands) who lauded Lenin as 'the greatest champion of the national liberation of the peoples.'

In 2006 Van Jones would name his own newborn son "Cabral" -- in Amilcar Cabral's honor." [15]

In 2005, Van Jones gave an in-depth interview to the *East Bay Express,* in which he described his radicalization.

> Jones had planned to move to Washington, DC, and had already landed a job and an apartment there. But in jail, he said, "**I met all these young radical people of color -- I mean really radical, communists and anarchists. And it was, like, 'This is what I need to be a part of.'**"

> Although he already had a plane ticket, he decided to stay in San Francisco. "**I spent the next ten years of my life working with a lot of those people I met in jail, trying to be a revolutionary.**"

> In the months that followed, he let go of any lingering thoughts that he might fit in with the status quo. "**I was a rowdy nationalist on April 28th, and then the verdicts** [Rodney King police trial] **came down on April 29th,**" he said. "**By August, I was a communist.**"

> In 1994, the young activist formed a socialist collective, Standing Together to Organize a Revolutionary Movement, or STORM, which held study groups on the theories of Marx and Lenin and dreamed of a multiracial socialist utopia.[16]

One of the most influential and active radical groups in the San Francisco Bay area, STORM was involved in organizing blacks to protest the first Gulf War.[17] The group has worked with known communist leaders and "led the charge in black protests against various issues," including the unsuccessful attempt to defeat Proposition 21, a ballot initiative that sought to increase the penalties for violent crimes and require more juvenile offenders to be tried as adults.

Together with James Rucker, a former Moveon.org organizer, Jones co-founded Color of Change, the extremist racial grievance group that views the United States as a profoundly racist country. The group has removed references to Jones off its site but the nonprofit's tax forms list Jones as the Director as recently as 2007.[18]

In 2005, Color of Change launched a petition to spare the life of convicted multiple murderer and co-founder of the notorious Crips street gang, Stanley Tookie Williams.[19]

Jones was a founding member and served on the board of the Apollo Alliance, a radical environmentalist group that describes itself as a "coalition of labor, business, environmental, and community leaders working to catalyze a clean energy revolution."[20] The outfit is generously supported by MoveOn.org and the Tides Foundation, two organizations heavily funded by liberal activist George Soros, as well as Ted Turner's United Nations Better World Fund.[21] Connected with ACORN, The Sierra Club, and the Service Employees International Union,[22] the Apollo Alliance had a significant role in drafting the stimulus package signed into law, and was even thanked by Senate Majority Leader Harry Reid.

Phil Kerpen, National Policy Director of *Americans for Prosperity*, described the group's aspirations as a "centrally-planned, organized massive mobilization to reorder society and take control of energy and their various other objectives."

According to DiscoverTheNetworks.org, at some point in his activist career, Jones "toned down the overt hostility and defiant rage that he previously had worn as badges of honor. 'Before, we would fight anybody, any time,' he said in 2005. 'No concession was good enough; we never said Thank you. Now, I put the issues and constituencies first. I'll work with anybody, I'll fight anybody if it will push our issues forward.... I'm willing to forgo the cheap satisfaction of the radical pose for the deep satisfaction of radical ends.'"[23]

> Jones' new approach was modeled on the tactics outlined by the famed radical organizer Saul Alinsky, who stressed the need for revolutionaries to mask the extremism of their objectives and to present themselves as moderates until they could gain some control over the machinery of political power. In a 2005 interview, Jones stated that he still

considered himself a revolutionary, but a more effective one thanks to his revised tactics.[24]

Where are the Green Jobs?

Van Jones has been in his Green Jobs Czar role since March. In late January, the Congress passed, and President Obama signed, a massive $787 Billion stimulus package designed to create jobs[25]. President Obama specifically set aside nearly $60 Billion of the stimulus package for building a new green economy.[26] One would assume with nearly half a year and billions of dollars to work with that the Green Jobs Czar could claim some sort of success. However, a *Newsweek* article in late July stated that not one green job has been created.[27]

Jones responded to *Newsweek* claiming, "Well, we still don't have a unified definition, and that's not unusual in a democracy," suggesting that it was the reason for not having any countable green jobs.

Speaking with the *Los Angeles Times* regarding the creation of green jobs, Jones stated, "You can employ a lot of people very quickly with off-the-shelf technology like caulk guns... This isn't George Jetson stuff."[28] Indeed, it might not be "George Jetson stuff" but it is highly dubious that caulking is going to revitalize our economy or create a so-called green economy.

The Apollo Alliance, which Jones helped to launch, released a green jobs study in the fall of 2008, which concluded that five million green jobs could be created with a $500 billion investment. When asked about the numbers by the *Wall Street Journal*, Kate Gordon, co-director of the Alliance, said the numbers were not as critical as the message. "Honestly," she says, "it's just to inspire people."[29]

Conn Carol editor of the Heritage Foundation's *Foundry* writes:

The lie at the core of the green-collar myth is that new jobs are being created. There is no new employment, just a transfer of employment from the "non-green" sector to the "green sector" - and often at a net loss of jobs. If regulations force power companies to forgo natural gas for solar power, then sure, the people who manufacture and install the solar panels will have "new" jobs, but those who mined and distributed the natural gas will be out of jobs. And then there are the higher energy costs. Carbon taxes and renewable energy mandates do not create new energy: they simply drive up the price of existing supplies. And higher energy prices mean less jobs for everyone.[30]

Van Jones' vision of his own role in the Obama Administration can best be summed up in his own words:

This movement is deeper than a solar panel! Deeper than a solar panel! Don't stop there! Don't stop there! We're gonna change the whole system! We're gonna change the whole thing. We're not gonna put a new battery in a broken system. We want a new system. We want a new system![31]

The Green Job Czar

In the aftermath of 9-11, Jones' STORM outfit declared, "We express our disgust at the present attempts by the U.S. security and surveillance establishment to turn this tragedy into a cash-cow bonanza - or to use it to mask a cynical power grab."[32] And yet this is exactly what Van Jones is doing today. Enabled by the Obama Administration's exploitation of the economic downturn, Jones has become a willing accessory in transforming the self-perpetuating crisis into "a cash-cow bonanza" and using it "to mask a cynical power grab."

But even to those who still feel "inspired" by Obama's promises and believe that the Green Jobs Czar's mission is a noble and worthy cause, it should be clear now that the numbers haven't demonstrated any benefit to the economy. Van Jones is an unlikely champion of jobs as he has spent a great deal of time and effort promoting communist and other radical far-left ideas that have never been the hallmark of job creation or a healthy economy.

Resignation

In the end, all of these issues just needed a little publicity. On September 5, 2009, Jones resigned from his post amid the firestorm that was generated when details of his past began to reach the public. Despite his czar status, a White House official claimed that Jones was not vetted as stringently as most advisors because his rank was so low. He suggested that the White House was unaware of Jones' past, and the controversy caught the administration off guard.[33] This directly contradicts statements from one of Obama's Senior Advisors Valerie Jarrett. Jarrett said that they had been following Van Jones his entire career, and praised his "creative ideas."[34] White House spokesman Robert Gibbs stated that Obama does not support what Jones has done in the past, but thanked Jones for serving the administration.

Glenn Beck has been given much of the credit for forcing Jones out, as he railed about Jones' past publicly, which inspired Republican congressmen to question Jones' suitability for his position.[35] Jones has not been replaced.

---

[1] http://www.whitehouse.gov/blog/09/03/10/Van-Jones-to-CEQ/.

[2] The Glenn Beck Program, "List of Obama's Czars", August 17, 2009.

[3] *Newsweek*, "What Green Jobs" by Daniel Stone, July 28, 2009.

[4] The Glenn Beck Program, "List of Obama's Czars", August 17, 2009.

[5] *The Huffington Post*, "GEICO Pulls Its Ads from Glenn Beck Show" by James Rucker, August 13, 2009.

[6] *Van Jones: Heroes of the Environment 2008* by Elliot, Michael, Time Magazine
http://www.time.com/time/specials/packages/article/0,28804,1841778_1841781_1841811,00.html

[7] Center for American Progress Website -
http://www.americanprogress.org/issues/2008/10/green_collar_economy.html.

[8] *Obama 'czar' on 9/11: Blame 'U.S. imperialism'!* By Aaron Klein, August 28, 2009, WorldNetDaily,
http://www.wnd.com/index.php?fa=PAGE.view&pageId=108180
[9] *Van Jones and His STORMtroopers Denounced America the Night After 9/11* by Matthew Vadum, August 28, 2009, The American Spectator
http://spectator.org/blog/2009/08/29/van-jones-and-his-stormtrooper
[10] People Of Color Groups Gather to Stand In Solidarity With Arab Americans and to Mourn the East Coast Dead, Press Release by Ella Baker Center for Human Rights
http://base21.jinbo.net/new/show/show.php?p_cd=0&p_dv=0&p_doc nbr=17775
[11] People Of Color Groups Gather to Stand In Solidarity With Arab Americans and to Mourn the East Coast Dead, Press Release by Ella Baker Center for Human Rights
http://base21.jinbo.net/new/show/show.php?p_cd=0&p_dv=0&p_doc nbr=17775
[12] *Reclaiming Revolution* by STORM, Spring 2004,
http://www.leftspot.com/blog/files/docs/STORMSummation.pdf
[13] People Of Color Groups Gather to Stand In Solidarity With Arab Americans and to Mourn the East Coast Dead, Press Release by Ella Baker Center for Human Rights
http://base21.jinbo.net/new/show/show.php?p_cd=0&p_dv=0&p_doc nbr=17775
[14] People Of Color Groups Gather to Stand In Solidarity With Arab Americans and to Mourn the East Coast Dead, Press Release by Ella Baker Center for Human Rights
http://base21.jinbo.net/new/show/show.php?p_cd=0&p_dv=0&p_doc nbr=17775
[15] Van Jones, an article on David Horowitz's DiscoverTheNetworks.org website
http://www.discoverthenetworks.org/individualProfile.asp?indid=240 6
[16] *East Bay Express*, "The New Face of Environmentalism" by Eliza Strickland, November 2, 2005.
[17] *World Net Daily*, "Will a 'Red' Help Blacks Go Green" by Aaron Klein, April 12, 2009.
[18] *American Spectator*: AmSpecBlog: Communist Green Jobs Czar's Group Takes Aim at TV's Glenn Beck.
[19] *American Spectator: AmSpecBlog*, "Communist Green Jobs Czar's Group Takes Aim at TV's Glenn Beck".

[20] *American Spectator*: AmSpecBlog: Communist Green Jobs Czar's Group Takes Aim at TV's Glenn Beck.

[21] Cato Institute, "Blowing Smoke on Gas Savings" by Alan Reynolds, April 3, 2005.

[22] Foxnews.com, Glen Beck, "Linking Social Justice to Green Jobs", July 29, 2009 - http://www.foxnews.com/story/0,2933,535284,00.html.

[23] Van Jones, an article on David Horowitz's DiscoverTheNetworks.org website

http://www.discoverthenetworks.org/individualProfile.asp?indid=240 6

[24] Van Jones, an article on David Horowitz's DiscoverTheNetworks.org website

http://www.discoverthenetworks.org/individualProfile.asp?indid=240 6

[25] *Washington Post*, "Congress Passes Stimulus Package" by Shailagh Murray and Paul Kane, February 14, 2009.

[26] *Newsweek*, "What Green Jobs" by Daniel Stone, July 28, 2009.

[27] *Newsweek*, "What Green Jobs" by Daniel Stone, July 28, 2009.

[28] *Los Angeles Times*, "Why Obama's Grenn Jobs Might Work" by Marla Dickerson, January 4, 2009.

[29] *Wall Street Journal*, "Does Green Energy Add 5 Million Jobs? Potent Pitch, but Numbers Are Squishy," by Jeffery Ball, November 7, 2008.

[30] The Heritage Foundation, *The Foundry*, "The New Marshall Green Apollo Deal Plan" by Conn Carol, August 26, 2008.

[31] *Van Jones, in His Own Words* by Glenn Beck, September 2, 2009 http://www.glennbeck.com/content/articles/article/198/29999/

[32] People Of Color Groups Gather to Stand In Solidarity With Arab Americans and to Mourn the East Coast Dead, Press Release by Ella Baker Center for Human Rights

http://base21.jinbo.net/new/show/show.php?p_cd=0&p_dv=0&p_doc nbr=17775

[33] Scott Wilson and Garance Franke-Ruta, "White House Adviser Van Jones Resigns Amid Controversy Over Past Activism," Sep, 6, 2009. The Washington Post.
<http://voices.washingtonpost.com/44/2009/09/06/van_jones_resigns.html>
[34] "Van Jones was Vetted by Obama, Valerie Garrett says so..."
<http://www.youtube.com/watch?v=gDoYoCBusZ4&feature=related>
[35] Scott Wilson and Garance Franke-Ruta, "White House Adviser Van Jones Resigns Amid Controversy Over Past Activism," Sep, 6, 2009. The Washington Post.
<http://voices.washingtonpost.com/44/2009/09/06/van_jones_resigns.html>

Guantánamo Closure Czar—Daniel Fried

Official title:	Special Envoy to Guantánamo Bay
Official responsibilities:	To carry out President Obama's commitment to close the detention facility at Guantánamo Bay by January 2010
Reports to:	Secretary of State Hillary Clinton
Senate confirmation:	None
Salary:	Information unavailable
Ideology / political affiliation:	Career Foreign Service officer, focus on Eastern Europe

On Jan. 22, 2009, President Obama signed the first executive order of his new administration, to close the detention facility in Guantánamo Bay within one year.[1] Daniel Fried, world citizen, will be brokering the deals as the Obama administration attempts to exchange monetary aid and favors for a desperately needed public relations victory.

Framing the order as a return to the "moral high ground" in the war on terrorism, the president himself has avoided the real question of what to do with the detainees when Gitmo closes.[2] After failing to make the case for the American people to play host to the detainees, how will the Obama administration persuade foreign leaders to accept them? The answer: send Daniel Fried, with powers of persuasion augmented by money your children will be paying off for years.

Who Is the Guantánamo Closure Czar?

Daniel Fried is a career Foreign Service officer who has specialized in the former Soviet bloc countries and has held several interesting positions. An assistant secretary of state in the Bureau of European and Eurasian Affairs in 2005, he also served as special assistant to the president and senior director for European and Eurasian affairs at the National Security Council and was ambassador to Poland in the late 1990s.

Whom Is He Freeing?

Seventeen of the 241 terrorist detainees currently being held at Guantánamo Bay are Chinese Muslims known as Uighurs. These Uighurs have been allied with and trained by al Qaeda-affiliated terrorist groups. The goal of the Uighurs is to establish a separate *sharia* state. At Guantánamo Bay, the Uighurs are known for picking up television sets on which women with bare arms appear and hurling them across the room. By their own admission, Uighurs being held at Guantánamo Bay are members of or associated with the Eastern Turkistan Islamic Movement, an al Qaeda-affiliated group designated as a terrorist organization under U.S law. The goal of the ETIM is to establish a radical Islamist state in Asia. Last year, during the Beijing Olympics, the ETIM released a video in which an ETIM member stood in front of an al Qaeda flag and threatened anyone who attended the games.[3]

Prior to 9/11, the Uighurs received jihadist training in Tora Bora, Afghanistan, a known al Qaeda and Taliban training ground. What's more, they were trained, most likely in the weapons, explosives, and ideology of mass killing, by Abdul Haq, a member of al Qaeda's *shura,* or top advisory council. President Obama's own interagency review board found that at least some of the Uighurs are dangerous.[4]

How Much Are We Paying for Countries to Take Them?

The question of what we are giving Bermuda, Palau, Spain, Lithuania, or any other location to take the Gitmo detainees is a very real concern. President George H. W. Bush provided huge economic concessions to many Latin American states to bribe them into joining the coalition of nations in the first Gulf War. Remember the Latin American debt crisis that threatened the collapse of the international banking system in the late 1980s? It disappeared almost overnight — in the early 1990s — when President Bush provided massive debt forgiveness to those countries that agreed to join his crusade to oust Saddam Hussein from Kuwait. The military value of those nations in that conflict was nil, but they were of inestimable propaganda value for the internationalization of an overwhelmingly U.S. military action.

Immediately after World War II, Gen. George Marshall carried an enormous bag of U.S. dollars to entice European nations to stay out of the Warsaw Pact and remain loyal to the anti-communist West. Daniel Fried is no George Marshall, so how much is in the bag he is carrying, and who is getting our money?

Take a Uighur, Please: $10,000 for Each Resident of Palau

The Republic of Palau is a nation composed of eight principal islands in the Pacific.[5] With 20,000 citizens and a per capita income of $8,412, Palau is among the wealthier Pacific Island states, according to the State Department, with tourism (much of it Japanese sex tours) the largest industry.[6] What does it cost to relocate 13 allegedly risk-free Guantánamo inmates to this island paradise? As far as we know, a commitment of $200 million in aid.[7] That's $10,000 for each resident of Palau. The pledge is $30 million more than Palau's annual GDP. Imagine what it will cost to relocate the "dangerous" detainees.

Bermuda will also receive unspecified "routine reimbursements" for the four detainees that it has agreed to take.[8] For an administration that once touted the merits of transparency, the negotiation was apparently concluded in secret, behind the backs of our British allies. As The Independent reported on June 13, "An official in Washington said: 'We did talk to them before the Uighurs got on the plane.' This, however, was flatly denied by the governor, Sir Richard Gozney, who maintained yesterday: 'We were only told this morning.' The secret deal allows the Uighurs – detained in Afghanistan and Pakistan in 2001 but who have since been deemed not to be enemy combatants – to settle in Bermuda. This raises the prospect of them getting British citizenship and the right to travel (and technically settle) in the U.K."[9]

A Whitehall official responded to the affront, "The Americans were fully aware of the foreign-policy understanding we have with Bermuda, and they deliberately chose to ignore it. This is not the kind of behavior one expects from an ally."[10]

With over 200 more detainees to relocate from the Guantánamo Bay facility, one can only imagine how many more bridges (and how much more money) will be burned in the process.

---

[1] CNN Politics, "Obama Signs Order to Close Guantánamo Bay Facility" by Ed Henry, Barbara Star, and Deirdre Walsh, Jan. 22, 2009.

[2] Ibid.

[3] Newt Gingrich, "Let's NOT Meet the Uighurs," *Washington Examiner*, May 15, 2009.
http://www.washingtonexaminer.com/opinion/columns/Newt-Gingrich/Lets-NOT-meet-the-Uighurs-45080387.html

[4] Ibid.

[5] Department of State website

[6] Ibid.

[7] Associated Press, "Pacific State Palau to Take Uighur Detainees" by Ray Lilley, June 10, 2009.

[8] *New York Post*, "Prisoner Paradise — Bermuda Takes in 4 Ex-Gitmo Detainees" by Geoff Earle, June 12, 2009.

[9] *The Independent*, "America's 'Bermuda Solution' Angers Britain; Decision to Send Guantánamo Inmates to British Colony Sours 'Special Relationship' " by Kim Sengupta, June 13, 2009.

[10] Ibid.

Healthcare Czar — Nancy-Ann DeParle

Official title:	Counselor to the President and Director of the White House Office of Health Reform
Official responsibilities:	Coordinates the development of the administration's healthcare policy agenda
Reports to:	President
Senate confirmation:	Yes
Salary:	$158,500
Ideology / political affiliation:	Crony capitalism, self-aggrandizement, financial reward, public service as the means toward personal ends

In Nancy-Ann DeParle we appear to have been saddled with the Obama administration's conflict of interest queen, who is masquerading as a healthcare reformer. The extent of her ties to a variety of healthcare-related corporations is very deep, and her history has been to parlay government appointments into lucrative lobbying and influence-peddling activities. So far, DeParle is the poster child of the Obama administration for hypocrisy, self-promotion, and personal gain.

As a fair example of Obama administration transparency and openness in government, her White House biography mentions that she had served on corporate boards but doesn't name any of them. Though it dwells on her government career, it states that she "also brings a unique industry perspective from her work in the private sector."[1]

A Pig at the Trough

DeParle has made a nice little career out of spinning the government's "revolving door" with periodic forays into the government sector where she builds up her Rolodex of contacts and then leaves to peddle her list to the highest bidders in the private sector. Her pattern is particularly insidious as she floats conscience-free between the regulatory agencies she worked for and the corporations subject to those very same regulations. She does more pirouettes than a prima ballerina. After leaving government, DeParle accepted director positions at half a dozen companies suspected of violating the very laws and regulations she had enforced for Medicare. Those companies got into further trouble on her watch as a director. Now she's back in government as a leading voice in deciding the shape of healthcare reform.[2]

In touting DeParle's accomplishments when appointing her in March, Obama didn't mention the lucrative private-sector career she built after September 2000, when she left her government job running Medicare for the Clinton administration. Records show she has earned more than $6.6 million since early 2001, according to a tally by the Investigative Reporting Workshop. No wonder the White House kept DeParle's background under wraps; after all, her ties and past compensation within the medical industry expose deep conflicts of interest for the woman who will have direct control over which companies benefit and which suffer under Obamacare.[3]

As director of the White House Office of Health Reform, DeParle is the point person in pushing for the administration's plans for changing healthcare and the ways Americans pay for it—changes in which her former companies have a great deal at stake.[4]

Lipstick Cannot Disguise This One

According to MSNBC and the Investigative Reporting Workshop at American University, DeParle made more than $6.1 million over the past nine years serving on the boards of directors of many companies that she may soon have federal control over.[5]

From 2002 to 2005, DeParle served on the board of Accredo Health, which would later be bought out by Medco. At the time of the buyout, DeParle exercised more than 72,000 stock options netting over $3.5 million. In October of 2008, DeParle rejoined the board of directors at Medco. DeParle was also a member of the boards of Guidant and Boston Scientific (Boston Scientific purchased Guidant but appointed DeParle to the board) up until her White House appointment. She also served as a director of Specialty Laboratories, CareMore Health Plan, and Triad Hospitals.[6]

Among her other earnings achievements over the past eight years:

> More than $2 million in compensation from DaVita Inc.
> More than $680,000 in compensation from Cerner
> More than $1.2 million in compensation from Triad
> Hospital Systems
> More than $66,000 from Specialty Laboratories Inc.

DeParle also served as a senior adviser to JP Morgan Partners LLC (compensation undisclosed) and earned more than $1 million as a member of the board of CCMP Capital Partners (yes, that is a private equity fund).[7]

Her financial relationship with Cerner is particularly problematic as the Obamacare initiative demands the automation of all healthcare records. Cerner, one of the world leaders in electronic medical records software, stands to gain enormously if such an intrusive, privacy-destroying, national requirement is implemented. Also troubling is her record at DaVita. In recent years, the *Fortune* 500 company — one of the country's largest dialysis providers — has filed at least six suits in five states against physicians and competing dialysis centers that pose a threat to its profits, according to court documents examined by the *Colorado Springs Gazette*. In those suits, the publicly traded company or its subsidiaries have alleged a list of wrongdoings, from breaching contracts and ignoring noncompete arrangements to slander.[8]

In each one, the company contends physicians and its competitors have secretly conspired to harm its business. The doctors say DaVita is waging a legal war to crush its competition.

Recently, a citizen watchdog group filed suit to force the White House to disclose which healthcare lobbyists and executives it had met with this year to discuss insurance takeover legislation. White House counsel Greg Craig refused to disclose which administration officials attended the meetings. But at least two of the industry visitors have ties to DeParle. William C. Weldon is chairman of Johnson & Johnson, which paid DeParle $7,500 for a recent speech. Wayne Smith is chief executive of Community Health Systems, which merged with Triad Hospitals — where DeParle served on the board of directors. DeParle's options were converted to cash payments worth $1.05 million.[9]

Over the past 10 years, DeParle has used her political influence to earn millions. Because of limited disclosure and no scrutiny in her White House position, it is unknown how many shares or stock options she still holds in these companies, which stand to either benefit or suffer under her oversight. There is a reason that the White House has kept DeParle in the background of the healthcare debate, and it is the same reason that her official White House website biography doesn't mention her private-sector roles. The administration doesn't want the American people to know of DeParle's corporate connections, especially considering its demonization of past White Houses that appointed lobbyists (although it has also done that).[10]

The Worst Government Has to Offer

The level of cronyism within this administration is unbelievable considering the open and transparent White House that the people were promised. A majority of Americans oppose Obama's transformational healthcare legislation, and perhaps now they have one more reason to maintain that opposition. The idea that the White House would give control of this area to an individual who has such extensive ties to major healthcare players is an exercise in hypocrisy.[11]

By the way, don't expect the mainstream media to cover DeParle any time soon. After all, she is married to an editor at the *New York Times*.[12][13]

[1] http://investigativereportingworkshop.org/investigations/deparle-portfolio/
[2] Larry Anderson, "Oh, to Be an Obama Czar!" *American Thinker* (July 3, 2009)
http://www.americanthinker.com/blog/2009/07/oh_to_be_an_obama_czar.html
[3] http://politicallydrunk.blogspot.com/2009/08/revolving-door-conflict-of-interest.html

[4] http://investigativereportingworkshop.org/investigations/deparle-portfolio/
[5] Ibid.

[6] Kenneth P. Vogel, "Health Firms Paid Nancy-Ann DeParle $5.8 Million," *Politico* (June 12, 2009)
http://www.politico.com/news/stories/0609/23688.html

[7] http://politicallydrunk.blogspot.com/2009/08/revolving-door-conflict-of-interest.html

[8] http://djsilverfish.wordpress.com/2009/07/06/nancy-ann-deparle-obama-the-industrys-health-care-czar/

[9] http://noisyroom.net/blog/2009/08/11/health-czar-nancy-ann-deparle/

[10] http://politicallydrunk.blogspot.com/2009/08/revolving-door-conflict-of-interest.html

[11] Ibid.

[12] Ibid.

Information Czar—Vivek Kundra

Official title:	Federal Chief Information Officer
Salary / Direct cost to taxpayers:	Unknown
Responsibilities:	Overseeing and streamlining $71 billion technology budget
Reports to:	Director of the Office of Management and Budget Peter Orszag
Senate confirmation:	None[1]
Relation to Obama:	Donated $3,300 to Obama's presidential campaign
Ideology / political affiliation:	Has donated $4,760 to political causes since 2002, including the Virginia Democratic Party

Information Czar in Charge of $71 Billion Tech Budget Has History of Stealing

In 1997, Vivek Kundra pleaded guilty to shoplifting $134 in shirts from JC Penney. Now, as Obama's chief technology officer, Kundra, the convicted thief, is responsible for a $71 billion budget. What, was Winona Ryder unavailable? The White House calls his arrest a "youthful indiscretion."

Kundra is another in a seemingly endless list of Obama czars whose appointments are tainted with bizarre irony. Is there really no one more qualified to streamline and oversee the massive budget than someone who is a known thief? Or was it the $3,300 that Kundra donated to Obama's campaign that put him first in line for the information czar position? [2]

Of course, just days after his appointment to the position of federal CIO, Kundra was placed on administrative leave after his former office was raided by the FBI.

Advocate of Cloud Computing

Kundra is a major proponent of "cloud computing,"[3] the practice of companies—and in this case, government agencies—purging themselves of their own databases to host their documents and information on a remote server. The practice outsources information to a third party whose sole job is to host the data and cut costs of maintaining individual corporate servers. Cloud computing has been relatively controversial, with supporters praising its cost-effectiveness and the ability to access files from anywhere, as opposed to saving them all on a single desktop computer. Opponents say that it is a dangerous system that will trap subscribers into a long-term contract with companies like Google that sponsor this technique and will cost more over time. "One reason you should not use Web applications to do your computing is that you lose control," Richard Stallman, founder of the Free Software Foundation, said. "It's just as bad as using a proprietary program. Do your own computing on your own computer with your copy of a freedom-respecting program. If you use a proprietary program or somebody else's Web server, you're defenseless. You're putty in the hands of whoever developed that software."[4]

The Kind of Advice You Would Expect From a Shoplifter

Attempting to steer the government in the direction of placing its data in the hands of private entities gives substance to the concern of many that the Obama administration is dedicated to gathering information on individual Americans and using it for political purposes. This cloud-computing nonsense will provide the mechanism whereby politically selected "contractors" may be authorized access to these off-site databases, and one can readily imagine the intrusive, privacy-violating uses they can find for such a resource. Kundra's arguments are couched in false cost-savings mumbo jumbo similar to what was very likely going through his head when he decided to save his own money by shoplifting his shirts from a department store.

"The idea is that those 'others' can do those things a lot better than you can, because it's their business to deal with it," blogged tech business lawyer David Canton. "On the other hand, we lose control over all that. That means we are dependent on others to ensure our data is secure, private, confidential, backed up, and available. The consequences of losing all of one's data because of some vendor issue can be massive."[5]

Kundra embarked on his cloud-computing transformation while CIO of Washington, D.C., the position he occupied before Obama appointed him to the same position on a national level. His current job is to oversee the technology budget, streamline costs, and decide where the annual $71 billion will be spent. While serving the District of Columbia, he cut costs by switching the government's e-mail, documents, and spreadsheets to the Google platform, thus removing the burden of hosting duties from the offices themselves. Eliminating responsibilities from city employees led to trouble for Kundra earlier this year.

FBI Raids Kundra's Former Office

In March, right after Kundra's presidential appointment, the FBI raided his former office. In order to trim expenses, the then city CIO paid an outside company to hire subcontractors for government technology projects. The FBI arrested Yusuf Acar, the chief security specialist who was also responsible for hiring contractors for the city, and Sushil Bansal, the CEO of one of the subcontracting companies. The FBI alleges that the two men operated as a team, along with help from at least one other office employee, to defraud the city of $500,000 by creating "ghost employees" who did not actually exist but were on the city's payroll. Another scheme involved placing orders at a discount from Bansal's company but billing the city for the full amount.[6] Kundra was not arrested, and authorities state that he is not involved, but he was placed on administrative leave for a few weeks immediately after the papers broke the scandal.

"Consultants who work with the technology office said yesterday that the bribery allegations emphasize their long-standing complaints that the agency lacks sufficient oversight to ensure that contracts are awarded fairly," wrote David Nakamara in his coverage of the scandal for *The Washington Post.* "They described a system in which project managers have virtually unabridged authority to issue 'purchase orders' for consultants and then decide which ones receive the contracts."[7]

Gee, Why Wouldn't We Want to Follow Kundra's Advice?

Though Kundra was not arrested in the scandal, the bribery scheme that occurred in a system that he created clearly makes his judgment appear questionable. Silicon Valley has also expressed disappointment in Kundra's appointment:

> It's taken a while, but President Obama has his technology team in place. What's most striking to us in California is how few of them have any association with the foremost regional generator of tech innovation (which would, ahem, be us). Take Vivek Kundra, the new chief information officer. He was previously in charge of technology for the District of Columbia. While he certainly has tech management bona fides, they are all from companies in the D.C. area.[8]

The unnamed writers continue to call Kundra's job, along with that of chief technology officer Aneesh Chopra, "thankless" and "bureaucracy-fighting."

Thieves Invading Your Privacy

Kundra, along with Michael Fitzpatrick, associate administrator of the Office of Management and Budget's office of information and regulatory affairs, posted a blog that detailed the federal government's proposed use of cookies to track the use of government websites. The program seeks to end the ban—in place since 2000—on use of this technology to invade citizens' privacy[9]. Currently, the ban can be bypassed only if an agency has a "compelling need" to collect this information. OMB officials have stated that the ban is in place for government sites only, not private companies. A source at YouTube told *The Washington Post* that although the government cannot access personal information through the action of a viewer's accessing the White House website itself, the Obama administration can circumvent the prohibition by posting videos on the site embedded with cookies that would track a viewer's personal information. "[The move would] allow the mass collection of personal information of every user of a federal government website," said American Civil Liberties Union spokesman Michael Macleod-Ball.

Others have voiced concern about companies such as Google being tied so closely to the White House that these private enterprises have started to influence the government. Google, a Kundra favorite since he converted all the District of Columbia government's files to the company's free applications, signed a deal with an unnamed government agency in February that allows use of the YouTube player so that the agency can violate the ban. Marc Rotenberg, executive director of the Electronic Privacy Information Center, has objected to this contract, stating that the General Services Administration has "failed to protect the privacy rights of U.S. citizens." He adds, "The expectation is they should be complying with the government regulations, not that the government should change its regulations to accommodate these companies."[10]

Foxes Guarding the Henhouse

The use of tracking cookies is just one of the many campaigns the government has launched that would result in the invasion of privacy for millions of U.S. citizens. The appointment of so many tech-savvy czars like Vivek Kundra is merely a means to compartmentalize each fiercely invasive agenda, creating separate arguments from a variety of departments, so that they will not be recognized as a massive affront to American liberty.

— *Lucy Leitner*

[1] "CEA Applauds New CIO, Trade Rep." Dealerscope. Mar. 10, 2009. Apr. 8, 2010 <http://www.dealerscope.com/article/the-consumer-electronics-association-has-praised-president-obama-appointing-vivek-kundra-ron-kirk-positions-federal-chief-information-officer-us-trade-representative-404218/1>.

[2] "Vivek Kundra." Who Runs Gov? 2009. *The Washington Post.* Sept. 5, 2009 < http://www.whorunsgov.com/Profiles/Vivek_Kundra>.

[3] Weier, Mary Hayes. "Federal CIO Vivek Kundra Sees Potential of Cloud Computing." *Information Week.* April 24, 2009. Sept. 4, 2009 <http://www.informationweek.com/cloud-computing/blog/archives/2009/04/federal_cio_viv_1.html>.

[4] Johnson, Bobbie. "Cloud Computing Is a Trap, Warns GNU Founder Richard Stallman." *The Guardian* Sept. 29, 2008. Sept. 5, 2009 <http://www.guardian.co.uk/technology/2008/sep/29/cloud.computing.richard.stallman>.

[5] Canton, David. "Cloud Computing Controversy." [Weblog entry]. *E-Legal.* Meritas. Oct. 1, 2008 < http://canton.elegal.ca/2008/10/01/cloud-computing-controversy/>. Sept. 4, 2009.

[6] Cox, John. "FBI Probe of Kundra's Former D.C. Technology Office May Widen." *Network World* March 13, 2009. Sept. 4, 2009 <http://www.networkworld.com/news/2009/031309-kundra-probe-widens.html>.

[7] Nakamara, David. "D.C. Technology Office Scandal Revives Questions of Cronyism." *The Washington Post* March 14, 2009. Suburban Edition: p. B1.

[8] "Shunned by Obama, but It's Probably for the Best." *The Evening Standard* July 17, 2009.

[9] "Feds Seek Input on Web Site Cookie Policy." *Techweb.* July 27, 2009.

[10] Hsu, Spencer S. and Cecilia King. "U.S. Web-Tracking Plan Stirs Privacy Fears." *The Washington Post* Aug. 11, 2009, Suburban Edition: p. A2.

Intelligence Czar–Dennis Blair

Official title:	Director of National Intelligence
Salary / Direct cost to taxpayers:	$197,700
Responsibilities:	Coordination of intelligence from all agencies
Reports to:	President Obama
Senate confirmation:	Yes, January 28, 2009
Relation to Obama:	Occasional advisor
Ideology / political affiliation:	unknown

Who Is The Intelligence Czar?

A graduate of the Naval Academy and a Rhodes Scholar (spending time at Oxford with Bill Clinton) as well as a former White House fellow. He served as the Central Intelligence Agency's first associate director of military support, and also worked on the National Security Council.

Glaring Errors of Judgment

Defense Secretary Donald Rumsfeld, chary of Blair's independence and labeling him as one of the "Clinton Generals" that he sought to purge, passed him over as a possible chairman of the Joint Chiefs. After retiring from the Navy in 2002, he served as head of the Institute for Defense Analyses (IDA), a Pentagon-funded think-tank. He was forced to give up his IDA post after the Pentagon inspector general reported he had violated conflict-of-interest rules when the think tank assessed the wisdom of a multiyear contract for F-22 fighter jets while Blair was serving on the board of one of the F-22 project's subcontractors.[1]

Sometimes it is impossible to not question which side these guys are on. Obama's Intelligence Czar, Dennis Blair raises that sort of question. In February, Blair tapped the extremely controversial Charles "Chas" Freeman to chair the National Intelligence

Council. Frank Gaffney, former Reagan National Security advisor issued this stinging rebuke of Freeman, "that the Obama administration would turn over the job of preparing National Intelligence Estimates to a man whom Saudi Arabia, China, Iran and Hamas surely consider an agent of influence calls to mind an old axiom about Charles 'Chas' Freeman's new line of work — 'Garbage in, garbage out.'"[2]

Another Obama Arabist in Disguise?

Freeman was forced to withdraw his name for the post, but the fact that he was selected to begin with raises significant concerns about Blair's judgment and points directly to where the Obama administration is taking the national security of the US. It is precisely what many Obama critics predicted since before the election.

"Mr. Freeman has viewed the Middle East through the prism of one of Foggy Bottom's most successful Arabists. He justifies Arab enmity towards us on the grounds that we are associated with Israel. He decries the liberation of Iraq for having 'catalyzed anarchy, sectarian violence, terrorism, and civil war in that country.' He makes excuses for 'democratically elected' Hamas and urges its embrace by the United States," says Gaffney.[3]

Newsweek Magazine was also critical of Blair's judgment in his defense of Freeman against evidence of an overwhelming conflict of interest. "As he vigorously defended Freeman, Blair also underplayed evidence of substantial financial ties between the Middle East Policy Council, a think tank Freeman used to run, and Saudi interests. Blair had told Congress that 'no more than one 12th' of the council's $600,000 budget came from the Saudi government. But Freeman told NEWSWEEK that the council had also received a $1 million endowment from Saudi King Abdullah in 2005, plus another $1 million pledge for operating support from Saudi Prince Alwaleed" reported Newsweek[4], which is viewed by many to be a very sympathetic publication to the Obama administration.

A Really Bad Judge of Character

But Blair's lack of judgment doesn't end with Freedman's failed appointment according to Newsweek, "Now both Republican and Democratic intel experts are raising questions about another Blair pick: John Deutch, a former CIA director once accused of major security lapses, who's been appointed to a temporary panel reviewing troubled, top-secret spy-satellite programs."[5]

Again, the irony of paradoxes never ends with this administration. Of all the qualified trained and cleared candidates for the "top-secret spy-satellite programs", Blair picks a man who was stripped of his top-secret security clearance for downloading classified material onto his unclassified computer when he was Director of Central Intelligence. A criminal investigation led to Deutch pleading guilty to mishandling of classified material. President Clinton ultimately pardoned Deutch on his last day in office.

Who Would Even Think of Bringing Deutch Back?

"Given Deutch's history, congressional officials want to know why Blair placed him on a panel so sensitive that its work should require an ultra-top-secret security clearance known as SI/TK (Special Intelligence/Talent-Keyhole). 'The decision to grant [Deutch] a security clearance again is an affront,' GOP Sen. Kit Bond, the vice chair of the Senate Intelligence Committee, told NEWSWEEK, adding that it 'should be reversed immediately'."[6]

In addition to the questions of judgment about his staff selections, the *Wall Street Journal* pointed out that there is evidence of personal baggage as well. "When Mr. Blair was president of the Institute for Defense Analyses, a nonprofit corporation that administers federal research programs, he didn't recuse himself from involvement in a study of a contract for the F-22 fighter jet. At the time, he was sitting on the board of a subcontractor on that program, EDO Corp. The inspector general found in a 2006 report that Mr. Blair violated the institute's conflict-of-interest standards but didn't influence the outcome for the study. Mr. Blair resigned from IDA over the matter, and he also stepped down from the EDO board."[76]

Despite all of this, by comparison to the other czars, Admiral Blair appears to be one of Obama's least controversial appointments.

— *Angie Wheeler*

---

[1] Mark Thompson, "Dennis Blair: 2 Minute Bio," *Time Magazine* (Monday, Jan. 12, 2000).
http://www.time.com/time/politics/article/0,8599,1870985,00.html
[2] *Washington Times*, "Garbage In, Garbage Out" by Frank Gaffney, March 3, 2009 --http://washingtontimes.com/news/2009/mar/03/garbage-in-garbage-out/
[3] Ibid
[4] *Newsweek Magazine*, "The Intel Czar's Picks: Not Too Intelligent?" by Mark Hosenball and Michael Isikoff, March 14, 2009 --
http://www.newsweek.com/id/189282
[5] Ibid
[6] Ibid
[7] *Wall Street Journal*, "Obama Picks Military Man, Blair, as Top Spymaster?" by Siobhan Gorman, December 19, 2008 --
http://online.wsj.com/article/SB122970963384222109.html

Labor Czar–Andy Stern

Official title:	Member, National Commission on Fiscal Responsibility and Reform
Official responsibilities:	To make recommendations to reign in national debt
Reports to:	Commission leaders Alan Simpson and Erskine Bowles
Senate confirmation:	None
Salary:	Information unavailable
Ideology / political affiliation:	Borderline communist

Who Is the Labor Czar?

Born in West Orange, New Jersey and educated at the University of Pennsylvania, labor czar Andy Stern made a power grab in 1996 and has been president of the Service Employees International Union (SEIU) ever since. In this capacity, Stern controls over two million service workers such as nurses, bus drivers and janitors.[1] He is notorious for his brutish business tactics and his union's widespread corruption. So naturally Obama is turning to him for advice on fiscal responsibility.

Strange favoritism

Obama and Stern have an unusual relationship to say the least. Dating back to SEIU endorsing Obama's 2004 senate campaign in Illinois, the two have spent an inordinate amount of time together. On Inauguration Day Stern was with Obama and his family on the reviewing stand watching the parade. Since then, Stern estimates that he visits the White House once a week. SEIU shelled out $60 million campaigning for Obama, and provided 100,00 volunteers toward the cause, 3,000 of whom worked full-time on the election.[2]

In turn, Obama has taken union officials into his administration. Staffers such as White House political Director Patrick Gaspard, economic recovery board member Anna Burger and Federal Election Commission member John Sullivan all hold or have held high-ranking positions at SEIU. Rival union boss John Wilhelm of Unite Here believes Stern receives preferential treatment to other union executives in terms of White House invitations.[3]

The relationship between Stern and Obama is so close that Americans for Tax Reform and the affiliated Alliance for Worker Freedom sent letters requesting a probe into Stern's possible violation of the Lobbying Disclosure Act. Despite Stern's near-constant presence in the White House, he is not registered as a lobbyist, which may constitute a violation of the law regarding disclosure and reporting of lobbying activity. A similar request was made regarding Burger. Federal prosecutors are in the process of reviewing the request.[4]

Corruption

It is strange that Obama chooses to associate with Stern at all, considering the rampant corruption he has presided over at SEIU. One of his appointees, Tyrone Freeman, the president of SEIU's Local 6434, the Los Angeles union and the largest local branch in California representing low-wage caregivers, was exposed for overseeing the payout of hundreds of thousands of dollars to firms owned by his wife and mother-in-law. Almost $300,000 was additionally spent on a Four Seasons Resorts golf tournament, a Beverly Hills cigar club and similar indulgences.[5]

The only reason there was so much money to misuse is Stern's own consolidation campaign, which caused enormous growth the local union. So Stern, who has denounced excessive pay and perks for officials, decided it was important to consolidate things under his chosen leader, Freeman who was being paid $213,000 in salary in addition to other compensation in 2007 while clearly creating even more perks for himself.[6]

Rickman Jackson, another of Stern's protégés, and Tyrone Freeman's former chief of staff was also implicated while he was in charge of Michigan's largest SEIU chapter. In addition to his six-figure salary in Michigan, he was collecting a salary in California and $33,500 in housing payments on a residence that Freeman was listing as the business address of the false non-profit corporation he was funneling money through.[7]

Annelle Grajeda was another of Stern's leaders, who arranged an eight-month leave of absence for her ex-boyfriend Alejandro Stephens, who was collecting myriad salaries from the company before eventually being fired for refusing to return to work. Grajeda ended up quitting her SEIU job in California after this information became public, and managed to find a new job as Anna Burger's special assistant in Washington, where she will help strengthen SEIU's bond with the Obama administration.[8] These are the people that Stern surrounds himself with, and promotes instead of punishing.

Questionable business tactics

Even without the corrupt culture of SEIU, there are plenty of problems with Stern's business practices. Wilhelm of Unite Here has publicly chastised Stern for SEIU's attempt to absorb about a third of Unite Here's membership. Wilhelm stated that SEIU has failed to grow within its core jurisdictions and as a result is attempting to poach members from other unions. In Wilhelm's words:

> Yet today, in spite of, or perhaps because of, his lackluster performance in SEIU's own traditional industries, Stern is planning to raid our union jurisdiction. Faced with his inability to organize inside SEIU's traditional industries, Stern's messianic mindset has led him to seek membership growth by conquest.
>
> His undemocratic practices threaten the entire labor movement's agenda. While criticizing employers for their undemocratic intimidation of workers, he has carried out numerous intimidation campaigns against other unions - all in support of his growth-by-conquest scheme.[9]

In San Francisco, Stern's own members are turning on him. SEIU Local 1021 voted to oust Stern's leadership team, and have published a letter signed by many top political officials condemning SEIU's hostile takeover of the National Union of Healthcare Workers. NUHW criticized Stern for his autocratic leadership style and undemocratic methods. [10]

An excerpt from the letter:

> These allegations, made in sworn testimony before the California Public Employment Relations Board, include that SEIU officials directed staff to open, mark, and alter workers' ballots; threaten the deportation of immigrants; and tell workers they would suffer the loss of wages, benefits and hours to scare them into voting for SEIU. The complaint alleges further that SEIU organizers physically removed ballots from workers' mailboxes and homes.
>
> Caregivers in San Francisco have complained of similar intimidation and harassment at the hands of SEIU officials trying to block union representation elections requested by them and tens of thousands of other California healthcare workers who have petitioned to join NUHW.[11]

Stern seems to have SEIU employing the same election procedure as a third world fledgling democracy in San Francisco. He has taken is bullying style into his government work, as his SEIU members intimidated and at times assaulted opponents of the Obama's health care plan in town hall meetings. Yet when he ranted about the Senate's failure to pass the health care legislation while the Democrats held the filibuster-proof supermajority, he declared "There are a lot of terrorists in the Senate who think we're supposed to negotiate with them when they have their particular needs that they want met," said Stern.[12] Republicans are terrorists, and it is acceptable to attempt to coerce them into supporting your ideas with force and intimidation. Ladies and gentlemen, your Labor Czar, Andy Stern.

— *Rick Rush*

---

[1] "Andy Stern," Who Runs Gov,
<http://www.whorunsgov.com/Profiles/Andy_Stern>
[2] Peter Nicholas, "Obama's Curiously Close Friendship," Jun. 28, 2009. Los Angeles Times,

<http://articles.latimes.com/2009/jun/28/nation/na-stern28>
[3] Ibid.
[4] Fred Lucas. "U.S. Attorney Reviews Call for Probe of SEIU Activities with White House, Congress," Feb. 1, 2010, CNS News. <http://www.cnsnews.com/news/article/60735>
[5] Paul Pringle, "Union charity paid thousands to firms owned by official's relatives," Aug. 9, 2008. Los Angeles Times, <http://www.latimes.com/news/local/la-me-union9-2008aug09,0,7839120,full.story>
[6] Ibid.

[7] Michelle Malkin, "Inside SEIU president Andy Stern's culture of corruption," Sep. 21, 2009. Michelle Malkin.com <http://michellemalkin.com/2009/09/21/inside-seiu-president-andy-sterns-culture-of-corruption/>
[8] Ibid.
[9] Ben Smith, "Wilhelm blasts SEIU Czar Stern," Mar. 23, 2009, Politico <http://www.politico.com/blogs/bensmith/0309/Wilhelm_blasts_SEIU_Czar_Stern.html>
[10] Stephen T. Jones "SF leaders condemn SEIU tactics" Mar. 2, 2010, SFBG Politics Blog <http://www.sfbg.com/politics/2010/03/02/sf-leaders-condemn-seiu-tactics>
[11] Ibid.
[12] Matthew Vadum, "Stern Talk," Jan. 27, 2010, American Spectator <http://spectator.org/archives/2010/01/27/stern-talk>

Middle East Peace Czar–George Mitchell

Official title:	Special Envoy to the Middle East
Official responsibilities:	To negotiate a lasting peace in the Middle East
Reports to:	Secretary of State Hillary Clinton
Senate confirmation:	None
Salary:	Information unavailable
Ideology / political affiliation:	Career Democrat, generally focused on fairness over political machinations

Who Is the Middle East Peace Czar?

A Waterville, Maine, native, George Mitchell entered the Senate as an appointee to fill the seat left open when Edward Muskie was named secretary of state in 1980, and he was elected to a full term in 1982.[1] He quickly became very popular and was voted "the most respected member of the Senate" six years in a row by a bipartisan group of congressional aides. Mitchell was elected Senate majority leader in 1989 and remained in that capacity until 2005.[2] Always known for his fairness, Mitchell was offered an appointment to the U.S. Supreme Court by Bill Clinton. Mitchell declined the offer to continue to focus on healthcare issues. He decided to leave the Senate in 1995, at which time he took on his first envoy position and chaired peace negotiations to stop violence in Northern Ireland. After nearly two years, he managed to arrange the historic Good Friday agreement. In 1999, he received the Presidential Medal of Freedom for his role in the peace process.[3]

In 2000, he was made chairman of a presidential committee overseeing a one-year study of the causes of violence in Israel.[4] His team produced a report in 2001 that called for Israelis to dismantle existing settlements and urged Palestinians to crack down on militant activity. Outside of his government work, Mitchell has served on the boards of Disney, Xerox, and the Boston Red Sox. In 2006, Mitchell led an investigation into the use of steroids in Major League Baseball.[5] Mitchell and his successor as Senate majority leader, Bob Dole, worked together at lobbying firm Verner, Liipfert, Bernhard, McPherson & Hand, studying the independent counsel statute for the American Enterprise Institute and the Brookings Institution.[6] Dole has a great deal of respect for Mitchell, saying, "He's just very smart, very quick, very patient. He's never stopped — he's still one of the most important figures in America, but many people may never know it. He's not looking for visibility." Dole went as far as to say, "If I ever get in trouble, I'm going to call George Mitchell."[7]

A Palestinian State

Mitchell does support the creation of a Palestinian state, which he feels is necessary to create a safe Israel. Because of this, some Jewish leaders are not happy with his appointment. The national director of the Anti-Defamation League said that while Mitchell is "fair and decent," this may not be the time to be completely fair, as Israel deserves some privileges as an American ally.[8] Some Israeli officials seem to feel the same way. They have described Mitchell as "too balanced" and said that his zero-tolerance policy on freezing new settlements "would likely put Israel and the new administration on a collision course." Mitchell has said, "Israel has a state, but its people live in unbearable anxiety, so security for the people is an overriding objective. The Palestinians don't have a state, and they want one, an independent, economically viable, and geographically integral state; that is their overriding objective. I believe that neither can attain its objective by denying to the other side its objectives."[9] The worries seem to be based not on concerns about Mitchell as a person, but rather on the fact that Obama may be taking a decidedly more anti-Israeli position than previous American presidents and that Mitchell will simply attempt to implement that policy as even-handedly as possible.

Steroids

Mitchell has taken some flak for his investigation into the use of steroids in Major League Baseball. The integrity of the inquiry has been challenged via allegations of bias toward the Boston Red Sox, a team for which Mitchell was serving as a director when he was given the assignment. Jack Cust, a designated hitter on the Oakland Athletics who was named in the Mitchell Report as a steroid user, still denies ever having used performance-enhancing drugs. Cust told the Associated Press, "To me, it's kind of funny they spent all that money on the Mitchell Report and a bunch of hearsay, and the guy who made all the money off it happened to work for the Red Sox.... Were there any Red Sox on the report? To me, that's kind of a joke. How does that happen? It's coming out now with guys on that team. The guy worked for the Red Sox — they spent all kinds of millions of dollars — and then no one there had their name brought up."[10] Cust was referring to the fact that according to the *New York Times,* former Boston teammates Manny Ramirez and David Ortiz were among 104 players who allegedly tested positive for performance-enhancing drugs in 2003, according to a list compiled by the federal government, yet they were not named in the Mitchell Report.[11]

Failing and Quitting

By late February 2010, Mitchell had already decided to give up on his mission for peace in the Middle East. He has taken issue with the State Department for not being pro-Palestinian enough for his tastes. He seems to think certain people in the state department have are favoring Israel too much, which flies in the face of the history of Department history, and the fact that the Obama administration in general has been pushing for restrictions on Israeli construction that the Palestinians never even asked for. But Mitchell most likely wants out simply because he is failing. He has been unable to set up any peace negotiations, and cannot even establish America as the intermediary it has so often been in Arab-Israeli dealings. The man even failed in his attempt to quit, as Obama rejected his resignation.[12]

— *Rick Rush*

---

[1] Alex Altman, "Middle East Envoy George Mitchell," Jan. 22, 2009, Time.com,

<http://www.time.com/time/world/article/0,8599,1873532,00.html>
[2] "George Mitchell," Who Runs GOV,
<http://www.whorunsgov.com/Profiles/George_Mitchell>
[3] Alex Altman, "Middle East Envoy George Mitchell," Jan. 22, 2009,
Time.com,
<http://www.time.com/time/world/article/0,8599,1873532,00.html>
[4] "George Mitchell," Who Runs GOV,
<http://www.whorunsgov.com/Profiles/George_Mitchell>
[5] Alex Altman, "Middle East Envoy George Mitchell," Jan. 22, 2009,
Time.com,
<http://www.time.com/time/world/article/0,8599,1873532,00.html>
[6] "George Mitchell," Who Runs GOV,
<http://www.whorunsgov.com/Profiles/George_Mitchell>
[7] Matt Whickenheiser, "Mitchell Again Finds Himself Peace Broker
Amid a Sea of Hostility," Aug. 9, 2009, Portland Press Herald.com,
<http://pressherald.mainetoday.com/story.php?id=275822&ac>
[8] "George Mitchell," Who Runs GOV,
<http://www.whorunsgov.com/Profiles/George_Mitchell>
[9] Ibid.
[10] Janie McCauley, "Cust Calls Mitchell Report a 'Joke,' " Aug. 18, 2009,
Associated Press,
<http://www.google.com/hostednews/ap/article/ALeqM5j_CPkgZu
WHcBDR2Vb5d_FSCkSBkAD9A5HMHG2>
[11] Janie McCauley, "Cust Calls Mitchell Report a 'Joke,' " Aug. 18, 2009,
Associated Press,
<http://www.google.com/hostednews/ap/article/ALeqM5j_CPkgZu
WHcBDR2Vb5d_FSCkSBkAD9A5HMHG2>
[12] Marty Perez, "George Mitchell Wants To Quit. Yipee!" Feb. 26,
2010. The New Republic.
<http://www.tnr.com/blog/the-spine/george-mitchell-wants-quit-
yipee>

Pay Czar — Kenneth Feinberg

Official title:	Special Master for Compensation
Official responsibilities:	Vetting compensation for executives of large corporations that have received federal bailout funds
Reports to:	Secretary of Treasury Timothy Geitner
Senate confirmation:	None
Salary:	None
Ideology / political affiliation:	Longtime Donor to Democrats and Obama, Arbiter

Do you make too much money? In the Obama administration, that question is answered by long-time democratic donor Kenneth Feinberg. As "special master for compensation," Feinberg has been tasked with keeping executive compensation packages for companies receiving federal bailout dollars small enough that they won't embarrass the administration.

The Washington lawyer served as the Special Master of the Federal September 11th Victim Compensation Fund, which distributed nearly $7 billion to more than 5,000 families and victims of 9/11. And if that wasn't enough, three years later he agreed to administrate the Hokie Spirit Memorial Fund, set up for the benefit of victims' families in the wake of the 2007 Virginia Tech mass shooting.[1] He has donated over $120,000 to democratic candidates and causes, including $6,900 to Barack Obama in 2007.

An attorney, Feinberg has come under criticism for his lack of experience in the business world. "Nothing in his background seems to make him qualified to determine how much firms should compensate executives," read an October, 2009 editorial in *The Washington Times*. Also included in the story is Feinberg's strange decision to pay government-controlled financial corporation executives negative salaries, such as Bank of America president Kenneth Lewis who expectedly left the company when being billed for the right to work. Supporters of this plan claim that this will inspire the execs to work their ways back up to higher salaries, but opponents believe that they will merely leave for companies that are not subject to government regulation.[2]

Since assuming his post, Feinberg has been bombarded with criticism from both Democrats and Republicans in Congress, both for being too strict and not strict enough. He has been tough on the seven companies that received "exceptional" government assistance while allowing corporate bonuses and large salaries at the 200 others that have received taxpayer money. *The Los Angeles Times* quoted Rep. Jim Jordan (R-Ohio) summing up Feinberg's autonomous power, "We're the largest economy in the world. And now one person, one single person, is deciding what people make," said Rep. Jim Jordan (R-Ohio). "That's a dangerous, dangerous place we're going."[3] Luckily, Feinberg has expressed reluctance in handling any of the corporations aside from the "exceptional" seven.

In informal, private conversations, Feinberg conferred with Goldman Sachs CEO Lloyd Blankfein on rather or not the executive should take his $9-million year-end bonus. Feinberg claims that he thought the bonus was "too high," but Blankfein took it anyway, leaving pundits and bloggers to wonder what exactly Feinberg does control?[4] In early February, the bailed out AIG (one of the "exceptional" seven that Feinberg claims he does oversee) granted employees $100-million in bonuses, causing outrage amongst taxpayers. Feinberg insisted that these payments were, though lavish, legal as they were mandated as part of legally binding contracts.[5] Feinberg's efforts at controlling the outrageous abuses of bailout money are inconsistent to say the least and one wonders what taxpayer dollars are paying him to do.

Flexible Moral Compass

Feinberg began his career in politics in 1975, serving as junior counsel and later as chief of staff to Edward Kennedy.[6]

In 1981, Feinberg took one of his first high-profile cases in defending corrupt Democratic New Jersey Senator Harrison Williams, who stepped down to avoid the dubious honor of being the first Senate expulsion since the Civil War.[7] The bi-partisan ethics panel found Williams' conduct in office to have been "ethically repugnant."[8] The Senator was caught attempting to sell his influence for a stake in a titanium-mining venture and served twenty-one months in prison.[9] Even Bill Clinton denied his request for pardon.[10]

In Feinberg's worldview, such a betrayal of the public trust has no bearing on a person's fitness to hold public office. Feinberg argued that the Senator never *intended* to do anything wrong, dismissing his actions as a simple "error in judgment."[11] He argued that it would be doing a "grave disservice" to the Senator to move for expulsion.[12] This sounds like the type of lesson one would learn working for Ted Kennedy.

Given a Blank Check Over Executive Pay

Kenneth Feinberg, the Obama administration's pay czar, said he has broad and "binding" authority over executive compensation, including the ability to "claw back" money already paid, and he is weighing how and whether to use that power. . . Feinberg said that decisions he makes will be "binding," but the law limits his power over contracts signed before February 11, 2009.

He also said he has the authority to use a "clawback" provision to go after compensation for executives from any company that received money from the U.S. Treasury's Troubled Asset Relief Progr.am (TARP). "I have the discretion, conferred upon by Congress, to attempt to recover compensation that has already been paid to executives not only in these companies, but in any company that received federal assistance," Feinberg said. Asked . . . if he could use that ability to target a firm like Goldman Sachs Group Inc, which paid back $10 billion in bailout money, Feinberg said: "Anything is possible under the law."[13]

This imperious attitude displayed by Feinberg was very much in evidence throughout his tenure setting compensation amounts for 9-11 victims and their families. He was resented by many and despised by others for locking himself away while issuing edicts like the Wizard of Oz behind the curtain. While there is little in the way of a smoking to paint him as unfit for this position there is a deep disquiet present when one realizes just how much this guy enjoys wielding unaccountable power. Accounts from many 9-11 victims and their representatives will attest to their view of the darker side of Feinberg's character.

Arrogance and Power is a Bad Formula

Feinberg said the law requires him to take market forces into account, but also to consider performance and past deals between a company and an employee. "The statute provides these guideposts, but the statute ultimately says I have discretion to decide what it is that these people should make and that my determination will be final," Feinberg said. "The officials can't run to the Secretary of Treasury. The officials can't run to the courthouse or a local court. My decision is final on those individuals," Feinberg added.[14]

Does this sound like a person who will tend to adjudicate matters fairly or one who is salivating over the opportunity to hurt corporate executives and teach them a lesson?

---

[1] Frances Romero, <u>Kenneth Feinberg Compensation Czar</u> *Time*, June 10, 2009
http://www.time.com/time/nation/article/0,8599,1903547,00.html
[2] "Formenting Financial Disasters." *The Washington Times*. 26 Oct. 2009: A20.
[3] Puzzanghera, Jim. "Don't expand my authority, 'pay czar' says; Kenneth Feinberg tells a panel that to have his role go beyond seven

bailed-out firms would be 'a mistake.'" *The Los Angeles Times*. 29 Oct. 2009: B3.

[4] Blodget, Henry. "Pay Czar Kenneth Feinberg: Yes, I am Completely Irrelevant." [Weblog entry.] Business Insider. Business Insider, Inc. 8 Feb. 2010. 4 March 2010. (http://www.businessinsider.com/henry-blodget-pay-czar-kenneth-feinberg-yes-i-am-completely-irrelevant-2010-2).

[5] Kennedy, Helen. "Bailed-out AIG to lavish execs with an 'outrageous' $100M in bonuses: pay czar Kenneth Feinberg." *NY Daily News.com*. 3 Feb. 2010. <http://www.nydailynews.com/money/2010/02/03/2010-02-03_as_aig_preps_to_pay_100m_bonuses_pay_czar_denies_republican_claims_that_aig_outs.html>

[6] The Takeaway, "Ted Kennedy's Former Chief of Staff Remembers" by John Hockenberry, Femi Oke, August 26, 2009.

[7] The Associated Press, "Ethics Panel Meets on Williams' Disciplinary Case" by Skip Wollenberg, August 28, 1981.

[8] The Associated Press, "Ethics Panel Meets on Williams' Disciplinary Case" by Skip Wollenberg, August 28, 1981.

[9] New York Times, "Williams Is Guilty On All Nine Counts in ABSCAM Inquiry" by Joseph P. Freid, May 2, 1981.

[10] Associated Press Online, "Clinton Pardons More than 100," by John Solomon, January 20, 2001

[11] The Associated Press, "Lawyer Says Disservice to Throw Him Out" by Skip Wollenberg, July 28, 1981.

[12] The Associated Press, "Lawyer Says Williams' Mistakes Don't Merit Expulsion" by Skip Wollenberg, July 29, 1981.

[13] Steve Eder, "U.S. pay czar says he can 'claw back' exec compensation" REUTERS, Aug 17, 2009.

http://www.reuters.com/article/newsOne/idUSTRE57G0E820090817

[14] Ibid

Regulatory Czar — Cass Sunstein

Official title:	Administrator of the Office of Information and Regulatory Affairs
Salary:	Information unavailable
Responsibilities:	Oversees government wide standards and regulatory efforts
Reports to:	Peter Orzag, head of the Office of Management and Budget
Senate confirmation:	Pending
Relation to Obama:	Long time friend, political donor and colleague from the University of Chicago
Ideology/ political affiliation:	Democrat / Antigun Animal Rights Activist

All within the state, nothing outside the state, nothing against the state. Attributed to a somewhat different political leader[1], this quote might as well have come from the desk of the "liberal" law professor Cass Sunstein, a fanatical believer in government control of every aspect of human activities - from guns to healthcare to the Internet blogs and free speech in general. A conservative's nightmare, Sunstein's nomination should be closely scrutinized by business owners, gun owners, hunters, Internet users, talk radio hosts and their listeners, and by all proponents of a limited federal government who don't want their individual liberties taken away in the name of Orwellian "security."

An ivory-tower elitist, Cass Sunstein equates humans with animals by advocating the right to bring suit on animals' behalf - hardly a surprising development, given that his snobby attitude towards the American people resembles that of a pet owner towards mindless pets who need to be properly trained, taken care of, and nudged in the right direction. Cass Sunstein openly describes his authoritarian views in a book titled *Nudge: Improving Decisions about Health, Wealth, and Happiness,* which outlines how to use the power of government to "nudge" people into making "better decisions."[2] If confirmed, Sunstein will, in effect, embody such a power, setting the agenda of the regulators who have the ability to do more than just "nudge" Americans to comply with Sunstein's directives. In this capacity Sunstein will be critical to the Obama Administration's plans to impose government control over individual economic, social, and political activities.

Who Is Cass Sunstein?

A Harvard Law School graduate (1978), Cass Sunstein spent several years clerking at the Supreme Court, later moving on to an academic career at the University of Chicago Law School (1981-2008) and Harvard Law School (2008), specializing in constitutional law, administrative law, and regulatory policy. In the academic world of utopian delusions, Sunstein is lauded as "The preeminent legal scholar of our time - the most wide-ranging, the most prolific, the most cited, and the most influential," to quote Harvard Law School Dean Elena Kagan. But in the practical world of stubborn facts and harsh reality, Sunstein's views of society, human nature, and the relationship between the government and the individual are at best controversial, if not outright irrational.

Pet Owners, Hunters, and Farmers, Beware

Senator John Cornyn (R-TX) released a statement calling "numerous aspects of Mr. Sunstein's record troubling, specifically the fact that he wants to establish legal rights for livestock, wildlife and pets which would enable animals to file lawsuits in court."[3] Cornyn is not joking. In the introduction to *Animal Rights: Current Debates and New Directions*, a 2004 book that Sunstein co-edited with then-girlfriend Martha Nussbaum, our potential Regulatory Czar wrote:

> "[A]nimals should be permitted to bring suit, with human beings as their representatives, to prevent violations of current law ... Any animals that are entitled to bring suit would be represented by (human) counsel, who would owe guardian like obligations and make decisions, subject to those obligations, on their clients' behalf."[4]

That's right - if Sunstein has his way, your dog, cat or herd could sue you! Make sure Fido likes his bone!

In a much more sinister development, however, such a legislation would open the floodgates to frivolous lawsuits by environmental and government activists on behalf of wildlife, against any energy or manufacturing company that consumes natural resources and produces waste materials - which pretty much describes all of them. Such a backdoor way to harness intractable businesses is likely to be the real reason why this plan was hatched in the first place.

In addition, Sunstein's view that "we should get rid of the idea that animals are property" is a fair illustration of his far-left position on the issue of property rights in general. Such "animal rights activism" reveals Sunstein as an accomplished master of the Left's clever tactic to use feel-good ideas as a weapon to attack capitalism and undermine the concept of private property.

In a speech at Harvard in 2007, Sunstein called for heavy restrictions on animal testing and asserted that "We ought to ban hunting, if there isn't a purpose other than sport and fun. That should be against the law. It's time now."[5] In addition to hunting Sunstein would like to do away with greyhound racing, cosmetic testing on animals, and meat eating. In Sunstein's brave new world, humans would no longer exterminate rats, but instead, politely purge them from their homes in a way that wouldn't harm the rodents[6] - an idea that could only originate in the mind of an ivory-tower elitist with an utmost disdain for the well-being of ordinary people.

The Right To Bear Arms A Conspiracy By The NRA?

The hunting issue is closely related to the right to bear arms, which in Sunstein's view may not even exist. Under the impression that the federal courts are dominated by conservatives, Sunstein champions liberal judicial activism, believing that the

Constitution is a "living" document whose meanings and mandates change with the passage of time. Arguing against the doctrine of original intent, he contents that Justices should be free to read whatever meanings they wish into the actual words of the founding document. In *Radicals in Robes* he writes,

> [A]lmost all gun control legislation is constitutionally fine. And if the Court is right then fundamentalism does not justify the view that the Second Amendment protects an individual right to bear arms.[7]

In *A Constitutional of Many Minds,* Sunstein opined:

> Consider the view that the Second Amendment confers an individual right to own guns. The view is respectable, but it may be wrong, and prominent specialists reject it on various grounds. As late as 1980, it would have been preposterous to argue that the Second Amendment creates an individual right to own guns, and no federal court invalidated a gun control restriction on Second Amendment grounds until 2007. Yet countless American politicians, in recent years, have acknowledged that they respect the individual right to bear arms, at least in general terms. Their views are a product of the energetic efforts of meaning entrepreneurs – some from the National Rifle Association, who have pressed a particular view of the Second Amendment.[8]

Of course, as the head of OIRA, Sunstein will not be a legislator or a member of the bench. But he will act as the gatekeeper of all regulatory measures and will be able to set the course of all new regulations and future regulatory agendas.

Socialism Through a Second Bill of Rights

Sunstein's book *The Second Bill of Rights: FDR's Unfinished Revolution and Why We Need it More Than Ever* demonstrates his fascination with socialism and desire to increase the size and scope of government. He writes:

> My major aim in this book is to uncover an important
> but neglected part of America's heritage: the idea of a
> second bill of rights. In brief, the second bill attempts to
> protect both opportunity and security, by creating
> rights to employment, adequate food and clothing,
> decent shelter, education, recreation, and medical care.[9]

The fact is, these rights have already been included in the Soviet Constitution and we all know how that ended. If we are to adopt a second bill of rights, why not also add a second "S" into the country's name and make it USSA - the United Socialist States of America?

It is astonishing that such a "preeminent scholar" as Sunstein can lump "opportunity and security" together without realizing that these are two mutually exclusive concepts. In the course of the Soviet experiment, which was conducted over several decades in an array of socialist countries around the globe, the focus on job and income security had completely eliminated any opportunity for individuals to succeed outside of the government apparatus. The inevitable economic, social, and moral decline ended in a catastrophe that eliminated any security whatsoever, all the while creating unlimited opportunities for corruption and organized crime.

The healthcare town halls taking place all across the United States in the summer of 2009 have demonstrated the unwillingness of most Americans to submit to the government-run healthcare system. The resulting debates brought to the forefront the extraordinary expense and inefficiency associated with the government providing services that are normally worked out in a free-market setting. Imagine the expense and inefficiency of a government-controlled totalitarian system proposed in Sunstein's second bill of rights.

Willfully blind to the facts of recent history and economic reality, Sunstein religiously believes that an overreaching centralized government is the answer to all problems, the source of citizens' rights, and the guarantee of their well-being. Apparently, like many of his far-left colleagues, Sunstein is driven by the idea that human progress can only be achieved through socialism, while rationalizing all the previous failures of socialist experiments with assertions that it never, in a hundred years, has been done right. As Obama's Regulatory Czar, he will be in a position to put his "correct" socialist ideas in motion and hope that this time they will succeed.

Hooray for Taxes

Cass Sunstein believes that Americans should "Celebrate Tax Day." Observe the following Orwellian passage in a *Chicago Tribune* editorial written by Sunstein and titled "Why We Should Celebrate Paying Taxes":

> In what sense is the money in our pockets and bank accounts fully 'ours'? Did we earn it by our own autonomous efforts? Could we have inherited it without the assistance of probate courts? Do we save it without the support of bank regulators? Could we spend it if there were no public officials to coordinate the efforts and pool the resources of the community in which we live?... Without taxes there would be no liberty. Without taxes there would be no property. Without taxes, few of us would have any assets worth defending... There is no liberty without dependency. That is why we should celebrate tax day ...[10]

In 2009 we witnessed a great number of spontaneous tea parties taking place all across the nation from small towns to large cities. The hundreds of thousands of Americans participating in them did not gather to celebrate paying taxes.[11] On the contrary, the people were revolting against high taxes and runaway government spending that Sunstein so passionately advocates. Quite tellingly, he credits America's well-being to the government bureaucracy - not to the freedom, opportunity, and entrepreneurial spirit promoted and guaranteed by the U.S. Constitution - and certainly not to capitalism that has brought about America's unprecedented prosperity.

According to Sunstein, "Those of us who have plenty of money and opportunities owe a great deal to an active government that is willing and able to protect what we have."[12] How is this different from a Chicago mobster telling a successful business owner to shell out protection money and be happy that his kneecaps weren't broken? At least Al Capone didn't demand love and adoration from the victims he fleeced.

Attacking Free Speech

Time and again, Sunstein has written about and argued in favor of a reformulation of First Amendment law. In yet another Orwellian twist of logic, he has declared that "the overriding goal of the reformulation is to reinvigorate processes of democratic deliberation, by ensuring greater attention to public issues and greater diversity of views." Claiming that the First Amendment should not stand as an obstacle to "democratic" efforts, he has called for a "New Deal for Speech".[13] According to Sunstein, "A legislative effort to regulate broadcasting in the interest of democratic principles should not be seen as an abridgment of the free speech guarantee."[14]

Unsurprisingly, Sunstein is in favor of bringing back the Fairness Doctrine and regulating talk radio. In his book titled *Republic.com 2.0* he states, "A system of limitless individual choices, with respect to communications, is not necessarily in the interest of citizenship and self-government."[15]

The Fairness Doctrine was a 1949 Federal Communications Commission (FCC) regulation that required broadcasters to present opposing political viewpoints. The regulation was overturned by the FCC in 1987 because it restricted journalistic freedom,[16] specifically with regards to conservative opinions aired on talk radio stations, which was and still remains the main alternative to the left-leaning mainstream media. However, with the election of Barack Obama, the Left has redoubled its efforts to reinstate the Fairness Doctrine as a way to silence the opposition. In the words of U.S. Congressman Mike Pence (R-IN), "bringing back the Fairness Doctrine today would amount to government control over political views expressed on the airwaves."[17]

But controlling radio waves alone is too small a prospect for a wide-ranging totalitarian thinker like Sunstein. In his newest book, *On Rumors: How Falsehoods Spread, Why We Believe Them, What Can Be Done,* Sunstein claims that bloggers have been rampaging out of control and calls for new laws to reign them in. He further supports utilizing the judicial system to impose a "chilling effect" on speech that might offend someone.[18]

Ed Lasky with *the American Thinker* has noted that "Sunstein's book is a blueprint for online censorship as he wants to hold blogs and web hosting services accountable for the remarks of commenters on websites while altering libel laws to make it easier to sue for spreading rumors."[19] While currently bloggers and commenters are immune under *Section 230* of the *Communications Decency Act,* under Sunstein's plan bloggers (of any size or organization) would be forced to remove any comments unless they could be proven.[20]

The expense associated with complying with this type of requirement, as well as the resultant litigation, would be so overwhelming and time consuming that commenters would disappear. Any comment with timely information could easily be forcibly removed and would certainly go stale before any legal proceeding could take place.[21] One can only imagine the full court press and abuse that would be unleashed in an effort to have any critical comment, true or not, removed from blogs prior to any election.

Our Regulatory Czar

While in personal life Cass Sunstein may appear as a soft-spoken, "unusually nice guy," his political attitudes and ideas he has maintained and aggressively promoted throughout his career describe him as a far-left authoritarian elitist with a messianic ambition to establish a total government control over the citizenry "for their own good." Likewise, the title of Administrator for the Office of Information and Regulatory Affairs may sound benign, but this position will provide Sunstein with a perfect platform to effectively "nudge" all of us toward a lifestyle that fits his radical beliefs.

For these very reasons the American Conservative Union, the oldest conservative group in the country, has started a website "stopsunstein.com" in an effort to thwart Sunstein's confirmation. Conservative Senators John Cornyn of Texas and Saxby Chambliss of Georgia placed separate holds on Sunstein's nomination blocking Senate confirmation.[22] According to *Congress Daily*, both Senators have dropped their holds on the nomination but apparently a new anonymous hold has been placed.[23]

---

[1] *Mussolini's Italy: Life Under the Fascist Dictatorship, 1915-1945* by R. J. B. Bosworth (Paperback - Jan 30, 2007)

[2] *Investor Business Daily*, "Behind Agenda Lies Mind-Set That Is Chilling" by Thomas Sowell, August 21 2009.

[3] Foxnews.com, "Obama's Regulatory Czar's Confirmation Held up by Hunting Rights Proponent" by Kelly Beaucar Vlahos, July 22, 2009

[4] *Animal Rights: Current Debates and New Directions* by Cass R. Sunstein and Martha C. Nussbaum, Oxford University Press, USA; (April 1, 2004)

[5] Http://vdeo.google.com/videoplay?docid=2586700127704318361

[6] NRA-ILA, "The World According to Cass: How Obama's New "Regulation Czar" Wants To End Hunting, Allow Animals to File Lawsuits and Strangle Free Speech in the Name of Democracy", March 27, 2009

[7] *Radicals in Robes* by Cass Sunstein, Basic Books, New York, 2005, p.220

[8] *A Constitution of Many Minds* by Cass Sunstein, Princeton University Press, 2009, p. 172-173

[9] *The Second Bill of Rights: FDR's Unfinished Revolution and Why We Need it More Than Ever*, by Cass R. Sunstein, Basic Books, New York, 2004, p. 1

[10] *The Chicago Tribune* "Why We Should Celebrate Paying Taxes," Cass R. Sunstein, April 14, 1999

[11] Cato@Liberty, How Many Attended the Tea Parties by David Boaz, June 18, 2009.

[12] *The Second Bill of Rights: FDR's Unfinished Revolution and Why We Need it More Than Ever*, by Cass R. Sunstein, Basic Books, New York, 2004, p. 4

[13] *Democracy and the Problem of Free Speech* by Cass R. Sunstein, The Free Press,
1995, p. 119

[14] *Democracy and the Problem of Free Speech* by Cass R. Sunstein, The Free Press,
1995, p. 92

[15] *Republic.com 2.0* by Cass Sunstein, Princeton University Press, 2007 p. 137

[16] The Heritage Foundation, "Why the Fairness Doctrine is Anything But Fair" by Adam Their, October 29, 1993.

[17] *Washington Times*, "Republicans seek to bar Fairness Doctrine's return", by Kara Rowland, January 8, 2009.

[18] *New York Post*, "Gag The Internet" by Kyle Smith, July 11, 2009

[19] *American Thinker*, "Cass Sunstein's despicable ideas on regulating the Internet", by Ed Lasky, July 12, 2009

[20] *New York Post*, Gag The Internet, by Kyle Smith, July 11, 2009

[21] *American Thinker*, "Cass Sunstein's despicable ideas on regulating the Internet", by Ed Lasky, July 12, 2009

[22] *The Hill*, "Chambliss Blocks Regulatory Pick Over Animal Lawsuits" by Alexander Bolton, June 28, 2009.

[23] *OMB Watch*, "Sunstein Nomination Will Have to Wait" by Matthew Media, August 6, 2009.

Safe Schools Czar—Kevin Jennings

Official title:	Assistant Deputy Secretary of the Office of Safe and Drug Free Schools within the U.S. Department of Education
Salary:	Information unavailable
Responsibilities:	Promote the health and well being of students, formulate a comprehensive school health education policy and developing policies related to drug and violence prevention.
Reports to:	Secretary of Education and the Deputy Secretary of Policy and Program Administration
Senate confirmation:	None
Relation to Obama:	Financial supporter giving $4,391 during the 2008 election cycle
Ideology / political affiliation:	Democrat / Gay Activist

*** WARNING – This chapter contains graphic language that may be
offensive to some readers***

Kevin Jennings, who was neither vetted nor confirmed by the U.S.
Senate, is an openly gay teacher, writer, and activist with a long
history of promoting homosexuality in schools and distributing
pornographic materials to students. His record shows that as the
Safe Schools Czar, Jennings will readily sacrifice our children's
mental and emotional well-being to the irrational self-indulgence
of his own pro-homosexual agenda.

The appropriateness of this appointment is all the more
questionable considering Jennings' past drug use and terrible
judgment in neglecting to report sexual abuse to the proper
authorities. For all these reasons, the Family Research Council, a
leading Christian group promoting family values, has called upon
Education Secretary Arne Duncan to withdraw Jennings'
appointment. The Council also launched a website
stopjennings.org, which describes Jennings' positions as extreme
and narrow-minded, his rhetoric as harsh and hate-filled, and his
qualifications and ethical standards questionable at best.[1]

Who is Kevin Jennings?

According to Jennings himself, he has had an unhappy, troubled childhood, growing in a family of a Southern Baptist minister, who died when Kevin was very young. Already in high school, resentful Jennings rejected religion and has since been advocating seething hatred and hostile intolerance towards Christianity and its values.[2]

In 1985, Jennings, a Harvard University graduate, helped establish the nation's first Gay-Straight Alliance for students in Concord, Mass., becoming a frequent speaker on Lesbian, Gay, Bi-sexual, and Transgender (LGBT) issues in schools.[3] In 1990, he founded the Gay, Lesbian and Straight Education Network (GLSEN), an organization that uses the guise of "safe schools" to encourage homosexuality in young schoolchildren beginning with kindergarten.

Jennings and GLSEN successfully campaigned to make Massachusetts the first state that officially outlawed discrimination on the basis of sexual orientation against public school students. In 1993 Jennings helped to establish a statewide program called "Safe Schools for Gay and Lesbian Students,"[4] which he used to promote gay sex in public schools and distribute pornographic homosexual instructions to students.[5]

Using "Safety" as a Political Device to Further Homosexual Agenda on Taxpayers' Dime

Concerns for school "safety" alone cannot explain a broad campaign for homosexuality that Jennings and GLSEN conducted among unsuspecting schoolchildren. An article by Tony Perkins in *Human Events* details Jennings' not-so-hidden agenda.

> [In] a 1995 speech, Jennings admitted that the rhetoric about "safety" was a political device, saying that it

"threw our opponents on the defensive, and stole their best line of attack. This framing short-circuited their arguments and left them back-pedaling." In a 1997 speech he embraced the idea of actively "promoting" homosexuality, looking forward to a day when "people, when they would hear that someone was promoting homosexuality, would say, 'Yeah, who cares?'" And an unsigned article on the GLSEN website in 2000 declared, "The pursuit of safety and affirmation are one and the same goal."[6]

Whose safety are Jennings and GLSEN protecting? Shouldn't safety and protection by the law be extended equally to all regardless of their status? Jennings doesn't think so - his concept of "safe schools" extends safety only for designated "victim" groups, especially homosexuals, rather than safety for all.

According to "Model State Anti-Bullying & Anti-Harrasment [sic] Legislation" published by GLSEN, harassment is only qualified as such if the victim has "distinguishing characteristics" such as "race, color, national origin, sex, gender, disability, sexual orientation, gender identity or expression, [and] religion." This seems like an offshoot of the same ideology that spawned the concept of "hate crimes," which would make sense only if mind-reading was a reality. Until then the only feasible and rational way to determine "harassment" and "bullying" is by examining the actual conduct, not the characteristics of the victim.

Pushing Public Schools to Teach Homosexuality to Children

In his book *Always My Child* Jennings calls for a "diversity policy that mandates including LGBT themes in the curriculum." If you think that the author's concept of "diversity" includes straight lifestyle and traditional family values, think again. Jennings wants only one side of this issue to even be aired in schools. While demanding tolerance, he isn't practicing it himself. Seeking to lock sexually confused young people forever into a "gay" identity, Jennings has no tolerance for those who might try to overcome same-sex attractions. "Ex-gay messages have no place in our nation's public schools. A line has been drawn. There is no 'other side' when you're talking about lesbian, gay and bisexual students," Jennings writes.

Apparently to our Safe Schools Czar protecting gay students means, first of all, to shield them from the possibility of switching to the "other side" and having a straight lifestyle with children of their own. If there ever was the straight movement, it may have already lost.[7]

Not limiting himself to teaching homosexuality in high schools and middle schools, Jennings calls for gay and lesbian advocacy at the elementary school level. He wrote the foreword for a book titled *Queering Elementary Education: Advancing the Dialogue about Sexualities and Schooling,* which includes essays by radical gay rights activists who believe adults and children must be taught to "think queerly."[8] In one such essay, written by a lesbian mother, the author boasts of teaching her seven-year-old daughter to masturbate and declares that "'queerly raised' children are agents" using "strategies of adaptation, negotiation, resistance and subversion."

Embracing the book's message, Jennings finds himself in the company of Bill Ayers, the unrepentant domestic terrorist and a co-founder of the Weather Underground, who endorsed the book with a quote prominently featured on the back cover.[9]

Distribution of Pornographic Homosexual Propaganda to Children

On March 25, 2000, GLSEN, where Jennings was the Executive Director, hosted a "Teach Out" for teachers and teenagers at Tufts University. The Traditional Values Coalition has reported that Scott Whiteman, a pro-family activist attended the conference and recorded several of the workshops. One such workshop, titled "What They Didn't Tell You About Queer Sex & Sexuality In Health Class," consisted of two lesbians and a male homosexual who taught children how to "fist" their sex partners.[10] Jennings was a keynote speaker at the conference.[11] Outside the workshops, various pro-homosexual groups set up their tables and distributed materials including condoms and "pocket sex" kits to teens.[12]

A month later, GLSEN held a conference at Brookline High School in Massachusetts for children and teachers to promote homosexuality in elementary schools and high schools[13]. At the event, GLESN distributed the "Little Black Book" to teens. This homosexual propaganda pamphlet was filled with crass instructions and very graphic descriptions and pictures of gay sex acts as well as medical misinformation on the dangers of gay sex.[14]

Then Governor of Massachusetts Mitt Romney strongly objected to these actions by saying:

> Graphic pornographic material on the gay lifestyle has no place in any school. While I agree that medically accurate information is essential in AIDS prevention efforts, this particular publication is grossly inappropriate and should never find its way into the hands of school-aged children.[15]

GLSEN's list of books recommended to school-age children is also quite controversial, with critics calling its contents pornographic. Fox News printed several excerpts on its web site that include accounts of fellatio among first-graders and teenagers engaging in affairs with much older men. Gateway Pundit provides a complete list of GSLEN recommended works that include shockingly explicit content;

> Book after book after book contained stories and anecdotes that weren't merely X-rated and pornographic, but which featured explicit descriptions of sex acts between pre-schoolers; stories that seemed to promote and recommend child-adult sexual

relationships; stories of public masturbation, anal sex in restrooms, affairs between students and teachers, five-year-olds playing sex games, semen flying through the air.[16]

Why not teach the Marquis de Sade alongside Dr. Seuss? There is no reason why high school students shouldn't study a work of literature with homosexual themes if the book has literary value. Poorly written first-person accounts of lewd acts have no place in the classroom. Making schools safe for homosexual youths is about teaching tolerance, not graphic texts. Also, Jennings seems to have forgotten other marginalized groups. Remember Dylan Klebold and Eric Harris? Both were ostracized youths, but neither were gay. And they acted out in a big way. In his overzealous effort to bring homosexuality into the mainstream, has Jennings forgotten about the rest of the youths who the system is supposed to protect?

Choosing NOT to Report the Molestation of a Child

In his book, *One Teacher In 10: Gay and Lesbian Teachers Tell Their Stories,* Jennings acknowledges that he "did not report the sexual victimization of a student to the proper authorities" when he was a school teacher in Concord, Massachusetts.[17]

Under Massachusetts Law one must notify child welfare authorities within 48 hours if a child under 18 suffers from physical, emotional or sexual abuse. State authorities have said that Jennings did not file such a report.[18]

Excerpt from *One Teacher in 10* detailing the incident:

> Toward the end of my first year, during the spring of 1988, Brewster appeared in my office... "Brewster has something he needs to talk with you about," [a student accompanying the boy] intoned ominously... On a hunch, I suddenly asked, "What's his name?" Brewster's eyes widened briefly, and then out spilled a story about his involvement with an older man he had met in

> Boston. I listened, sympathized, offered advice. He left
> my office with a smile on his face.... [19]

Jennings has told several conflicting versions of this story. Drawing facts from other versions, it appears that the boy may have been as young as 15, a sophomore, a substance abuser, very troubled, and finding adult male sexual partners in the bus station restroom in Boston. Jennings did not notify the child welfare authorities, school officials or Brewster's parents. Instead the advice he offered the boy was "I hope you knew to use a condom."[20]

In early October 2010, bloggers unearthed a 1997 speech in which Jennings professed his longtime admiration for the controversial Harry Hay. The deceased gay rights activist was a supporter of NAMBLA (National American Man/Boy Love Association), a controversial organization shunned by mainstream gay rights groups like GLAAD (Gay and Lesbian Alliance Against Defamation). NAMBLA and its supporters advocate "intergenerational relationships" and the abolition of age-of-consent laws that prevent grown men from preying on young boys.[21] Jennings has been associated with militant AIDS awareness group ACT UP that in the late 1980s and early 1990s vandalized churches, homes and businesses.[22]

Protect our Children from the Safe Schools Czar

Kevin Jennings has been described as a "gay militant"[23] who has actively promoted homosexuality to schoolchildren of all ages, as well as on college campuses. If he was able to do this from the small platform of GLSEN, consider how far his efforts could reach with the backing of the federal government. Appointing Kevin Jennings to this office instantly puts our children in a more vulnerable and dangerous situation than they would have been without any Safe School Czar at all.

[1] Family Research Council, *In Focus*, "Talking Points: Why Homosexual Activist Kevin Jennings is Not Fit for the Dept. of Education" by Peter Sprigg, June 2009. http://www.frc.org/infocus/talking-points-homosexual-activist-kevin-jennings-not-fit-for-dept-of-education

[2] Kevin Jennings, speech at Marble Collegiate Church, March 20, 2000; quoted in Peter LaBarbera, "When Silence Would Have Been Golden," Concerned Women for America, April 10, 2002; online at: http://www.cwfa.org/articledisplay.asp?id=2580&department=CFI&categoryid=papers

[3] GLSEN Website - http://www.glsen.org/cgi-bin/iowa/all/library/record/1808.html

[4] GLSEN Website - http://www.glsen.org/cgi-bin/iowa/all/library/record/1808.html

[5] Traditional Values Education & Legal Institute, "Homosexuals Recruit Public School Children" by Rev. Louis P. Sheldon, p.2, Vol.18 No. 11.

[6] Human Events, Kevin Jennings – Unsafe for America's Schools" by Tony Perkins, June 29, 2009.

[7] *Human Events*, "Kevin Jennings – Unsafe for America's Schools" by Tony Perkins, June 29, 2009.

[8] *World Net Daily*, "Bill Ayer's Gay Agenda for Your Kids" by Linda Harvey, October 13 2008.

[9] *World Net Daily*, "Bill Ayer's Gay Agenda for Your Kids" by Linda Harvey, October 13 2008.

[10] Traditional Values Education & Legal Institute, "Homosexuals Recruit Public School Children" by Rev. Louis P. Sheldon, p.2, Vol.18 No. 11.

[11] *The Washington Times*, "NEA Groups Protest Award to Gay Studies Activist" July 2, 2004.

[12] Traditional Values Education & Legal Institute, *Homosexuals Recruit Public School Children* by Rev. Louis P. Sheldon, p.2, Vol.18 No. 11.

[13] MassResistance.org, "The Little Black Book - Queer in the 21st century", contains deadly misinformation on health" by the AIDS Action Committee - http://massresistance.org/docs/issues/black_book/reaction.html

[14] Traditional Values Coalition, "Gay Radical Runs Obama's 'Safe Schools' Program", by Andrea Lafferty, June 4, 2009.

[15] MassResistance.org, "The Little Black Book - Queer in the 21st century", contains deadly misinformation on health" by the AIDS Action Committee - http://massresistance.org/docs/issues/black_book/reaction.html

[16] Hoft, Jim. "Breaking: Obama's "Safe Schools Czar" Is Promoting Child Porn in the Classroom– Kevin Jennings and the GLSEN Reading List." *Gateway Pundit.*

[17] Traditional Values Coalition, "Gay Radical Runs Obama's 'Safe Schools' Program", by Andrea Lafferty, June 4, 2009.

[18] *The Washington Times*, "NEA Groups Protest Award to Gay Studies Activist" July 2, 2004.

[19] Traditional Values Coalition, "Gay Radical Runs Obama's 'Safe Schools' Program", by Andrea Lafferty, June 4, 2009.

[20] *Human Events*, "Kevin Jennings – Unsafe for America's Schools" by Tony Perkins", June 29, 2009.

[21] Gibson, John. "For the Record… Kevin Jennings, Harry Hay and NAMBLA…" FoxNewsRadio.com. 26 Oct. 2009 < http://www.foxnewsradio.com/2009/10/26/for-the-record-kevin-jennings-harry-hay-and-nambla/#axzz0hJkXUAG8>.

[22] "Obama's 'safe schools czar' acts up; Even more troubling news about Kevin Jennings." *The Washington Times*. 22 Oct. 2010: A24.

[23] Traditional Values Coalition, "Gay Radical Runs Obama's 'Safe Schools' Program", by Andrea Lafferty, June 4, 2009.

Science Czar — John Holdren

Official title:	Assistant to the President for Science and Technology, Director of the White House Office of Science and Technology Policy, and Co-Chair of the President's Council of Advisers on Science and Technology
Official responsibilities:	Advise the president on science and technology
Reports to:	President
Senate confirmation:	Yes
Salary:	Information unavailable
Ideology / political affiliation:	Capitalism is an economic system that is inherently harmful to the natural environment.

If you like incompetent science generated by doom-crying ideologues who wield inappropriate analytical tools while advocating drastic changes to our way of life to cure nonexistent problems, you will love John Holdren. Holdren is a long-standing member of an extremist branch of the scientific community that can best be characterized as Malthusians — the ideological offspring of Thomas Robert Malthus (Feb. 13, 1766–Dec. 23, 1834). He was the original British prophet of doom and gloom who predicted that societal improvements such as industrialization, modernization, and increased longevity will lead to uncontrolled population growth, which will spawn famine, disease, and widespread mortality. Malthus and his followers, such as Holdren, do not believe in the inherent goodness of man and the liberty of citizens bound only by the social contract, a form of popular sovereignty that is the underlying principle of American democracy.

Holdren is a globalist who has endorsed "surrender of sovereignty" to "a comprehensive planetary regime" that would control all the world's resources, direct global redistribution of wealth, oversee the "de-development" of the West, control a World Army and taxation regime, and enforce world population limits. He has castigated the United States as "the meanest of wealthy countries," written a justification of compulsory abortion for American women, advocated drastically lowering the U.S.

standard of living, and left the door open to trying global warming "deniers" for crimes against humanity. Such is Barack Obama's idea of a clearheaded adviser on matters of scientific policy.[1]

Holdren and other luminaries from the 1970s radical chic "small is beautiful," "appropriate technology," "the sky is falling, and we will all be resorting to cannibalism by 1995" movement, such as Lester Brown and Paul Ehrlich, have made entire careers out of being completely wrong in their irresponsible misuse of what they try to palm off as science. Planetary starvation, catastrophic resource depletion, the "greenhouse effect" that will cause disastrous global cooling that will threaten mankind's very existence: Remember these issues? This is Holdren's crowd. The group's organizational big brother was the leftist Club of Rome, which promoted one-world government, the United Nations as the only answer, and global redistribution of wealth. The gang's clarion call was a 1972 book entitled *Limits to Growth*, which was published in 30 languages and sold over 30 million copies. According to the book, the depletion of resources would be the ultimate predicament of mankind. In the 1970s, the Club of Rome predicted that the world would run out of oil during the next three to four decades. Wrong again.

So-called scientists who were trying to intrude into the making of public policy gave this rash of doom-crying the patina of analysis and scientific method by misapplying macro-econometric computer models that were designed for the banking industry to issues of population growth, resource depletion, and induced scarcities. They used simplistic assumptions and inappropriate models to forward their ideological agenda, which was related to another popular social change movement rooted in the United Nations in the 1970s: the new international economic order. The NIEO was a joint Third World–Communist bloc effort to weaken the Western industrialized nations by attempting to force the redistribution of wealth and economic power from the developed nations to the so-called underdeveloped nations, all under U.N. auspices.

Unfortunately, Holdren and his cronies have found new chimeras to ride: global warming, redistributive healthcare "reform," and contemporary population and natural resource control measures. It is the same hysterical, nonsensical nonscience Holdren tried to peddle in the past. Of course, like most inveterate true believers in a defective creed, Holdren lashes out, calling climate change skeptics "dangerous" members of a "denier fringe" in a 2008 *New York Times* op-ed.

Who Is Our Science Czar?

Holdren studied aerospace engineering and plasma physics at the Massachusetts Institute of Technology, where he earned his B.S. and M.S., and Stanford University, where he received his doctorate in 1970.

In 1969, Holdren wrote that it was imperative "to convince society and its leaders that there is no alternative but the cessation of our irresponsible, all-demanding, and all-consuming population growth." That same year, he and professor of population studies Paul Ehrlich jointly predicted: "If … population control measures are not initiated immediately and effectively, all the technology man can bring to bear will not fend off the misery to come." In 1971, Holdren and Ehrlich warned that "some form of ecocatastrophe, if not thermonuclear war, seems almost certain to overtake us before the end of the century."

Viewing capitalism as an economic system that is inherently harmful to the natural environment, Holdren and Ehrlich in 1973 called for "a massive campaign … to de-develop the United States" and other Western nations in order to conserve energy and facilitate growth in underdeveloped countries. "De-development," they said, "means bringing our economic system into line with the realities of ecology and the world resource situation." "By de-development," they elaborated, "we mean lower per-capita energy consumption, fewer gadgets, and the abolition of planned obsolescence."

In 1977, Holdren co-authored a book titled *Ecoscience: Population, Resources, and Environment.* The book reportedly includes this statement: "Population-control laws, even including laws requiring compulsory abortion, could be sustained under the existing Constitution." Holdren's office says he "does not now and never has been an advocate of compulsory abortions or other repressive measures to limit fertility."

Also in 1977, Holdren and Ehrlich quantified their anti-capitalist philosophy in a mathematical equation, $I=PAT$, where a negative environmental impact (I) was the product of such undesirable factors as population growth (P), increasing affluence (A), and improving technology (T). In an effort to minimize environmental damage, they prescribed "organized evasive action: population control, limitation of material consumption, redistribution of wealth, transitions to technologies that are environmentally and socially less disruptive than today's, and movement toward some kind of world government."

In 1986, Holdren predicted that "carbon dioxide-induced famines could kill as many as a billion people before the year 2020." In 2006, Holdren suggested that as a result of global warming, sea levels worldwide could rise by 13 feet by the end of the 21st century. A subsequent estimate by the U.N.'s own Intergovernmental Panel on Climate Change placed the figure at 13 inches. In the October 2008 issue of *Scientific American,* Holdren wrote: "The ongoing disruption of the Earth's climate by man-made greenhouse gases is already well beyond dangerous and is careening toward completely unmanageable." "Carbon dioxide (CO2)," he added, "is the most important of civilization's emissions and the most difficult to reduce. About 80 percent comes from burning coal, oil and natural gas; most of the rest comes from deforestation in the tropics."

In 2007, Holdren addressed the American Association for the

Advancement of Science conference, where he served as president; the organization posted his full slide presentation on its website. It revealed his continuing reverence for, and allegiance to, the gurus of population control authoritarianism. He's just gotten smarter about cloaking it behind global warming hysteria. In the opening slide, Holdren admitted that his "preoccupation" with apocalyptic matters such as "the rates at which people breed" was a lifelong obsession spurred by Harrison Brown's work. Holdren heaped praise on Brown's half-century-old book, *The Challenge of Man's Future*, and then proceeded to paint doom-and-gloom scenarios requiring drastic government interventions to control climate change.[2]

Who is Harrison Brown? He was a "distinguished member" of the International Eugenics Society with whom Holdren later worked on a book about — you guessed it — world population and fertility. Brown advocated the same population-control-freak measures Holdren put forth in *Ecoscience*. In *The Challenge of Man's Future*, Brown envisioned a regime in which the "number of abortions and artificial inseminations permitted in a given year would be determined completely by the difference between the number of deaths and the number of births in the year previous."[3]

Brown exhorted readers to accept that "we must reconcile ourselves to the fact that artificial means must be applied to limit birth rates." If we don't, Brown warned, we will face a planet "with a writhing mass of human beings." He likened the global population to a "pulsating mass of maggots."[4]

Today Holdren characterizes researchers who doubt whether human activity is responsible for global warming, or that global warming even presents a serious threat, as people who "infest" the public discourse with "dangerous" ideas that pose "a menace" to humanity.

Holdren is a longtime anti-nuclear activist. From 1987 to 1997, he chaired the Executive Committee of the Pugwash Conferences on Science and World Affairs, an international group of scientists who promote arms control. In 1995, he delivered a Nobel Peace Prize acceptance lecture on behalf of the Pugwash Conferences. From 1993 to 2004, he chaired the Committee on International Security and Arms Control of the U.S. National Academy of Sciences. In 2005, he called on the United States to issue a "no first use" policy for nuclear weapons and to eliminate nuclear retaliation as a possible response to chemical or biological attacks.[5]

Holdren has already angered many members of Congress and the public with his involvement in the administration's "arrogant" actions. In January 2010, Obama and Holdren made the decision to cut NASA's Constellation program, angering Democrats and Republicans of Congress whose approval should have been sought before implementing a budget of this magnitude. Lawmakers just last year prohibited NASA from cancelling the program without Congressional approval. The Constellation program includes the expensive Ares I rocket that was meant to replace the space shuttle for human transportation in space and the Ares V that was supposed to launch fuel and supplies necessary to transport people to the moon.[6] The budget also cuts trips to the moon and NASA will be forced to outsource space travel to Russia to ride on the foreign nation's Soyuz vehicles that cost NASA $51 million for each seat.[7] Instead of space exploration, the National Aeronautics and Space Administration is to focus on Earth sciences, specifically (guess what?) climate change.

Holdren was also peripherally involved in the Climate-gate scandal that surfaced in November 2009 when a hacker posted private emails between climate researchers that suggested that they manipulated data to confirm the existence of global warming, deleted data to avoid inquiries under the Freedom of Information Act and conspired to keep conflicting research out of scientific journals. Holdren's contribution was the unethical disparagement of the credibility and mocking the work of Harvard-Smithsonian Center for Astrophysics in the Solar, Stellar, and Planetary Sciences Division astrophysicists Sallie Baliunas and Willie Soon who published a paper that runs counter to Holdren's apocalyptic images of global warming.[8]

What Will This Guy Control?

Congress established the Office of Science and Technology Policy in 1976. Under the law, "the primary function of the OSTP Director is to provide, within the Executive Office of the President, advice on the scientific, engineering, and technological aspects of issues that require attention at the highest level of Government." Further, the "Office shall serve as a source of scientific and technological analysis and judgment for the President with respect to major policies, plans, and programs of the Federal Government."

The OSTP director also manages the National Science and Technology Council, established by Executive Order 12881, which coordinates science and technology policy across the federal government, and co-chairs the President's Council of Advisers on Science and Technology, a council of external advisers that provides advice to the president, established by Executive Order 13226. In addition, the OSTP director plays a role in the communication of scientific and technical information by federal agency scientists and engineers.[9]

Since his inauguration, President Obama has issued executive orders, presidential directives, and executive memorandums regarding Holdren's positions as the OSTP director and the assistant to the president for science and technology, including appointing the OSTP director to the Domestic Policy Council, providing the OSTP director the ability to attend National Security Council meetings when science and technology issues are on the agenda, and requiring the OSTP director to develop recommendations for presidential action designed to guarantee scientific integrity throughout the executive branch.[10]

OSTP staff members manage activities of the National Science and Technology Council in conjunction with federal agency staff. The council has four primary committees: Science, Technology, Environment and Natural Resources, and Homeland and National Security. As shown on the following page, each committee has subcommittees, interagency working groups, or task forces focused on specialized topics. The members of these committees and subcommittees are generally not cabinet officials but lower-ranking staff.[11]

Dangerous Lack of Accountability

President Obama has decided to provide John Holdren, his administration's OSTP director, with the title of assistant to the president for science and technology as well as co-chair of the President's Council of Advisers on Science and Technology. This does not bode well for "transparency" or "openness" in government. The OSTP director can be required to testify before Congress, but assistants to the president may decline requests that they testify, citing separation of powers and/or executive privilege.[12]

In view of the span of control and influence Holdren has been given, as well as the unaccountable nature of his office, which can be sheltered from congressional oversight, it is not unreasonable to conclude that he is the most dangerous man in America today.

COMMITTEE ON ENVIRONMENT & NATURAL RESOURCES		
AIR QUALITY RESEARCH (SC)	GLOBAL CHANGE RESEARCH/ CLIMATE CHANGE SCIENCE (SC)	US GROUP ON EARTH OBSERVATIONS (SC)
DISASTER REDUCTION (SC)	OCEAN SCIENCE & TECHNOLOGY (SC)	WATER AVAILABILITY & QUALITY (SC)
ECOLOGICAL SYSTEMS (SC)	TOXICS AND RISK (SC)	

COMMITTEE ON HOMELAND & NATIONAL SECURITY		
DECONTAMINATION STANDARDS & TECHNOLOGY (SC)	FOREIGN ANIMAL DISEASE THREAT (SC)	NUCLEAR DEFENSE RESEARCH & DEVELOPMENT (SC)
DOMESTIC IMPROVISED EXPLOSIVE DEVICES (SC)	HUMAN FACTORS (SC)	STANDARDS (SC)
ELECTRIC GRID VULNERABILITY (IWG)	INFRASTRUCTURE (SC)	

COMMITTEE ON SCIENCE		
AQUACULTURE (SC)	HUMAN SUBJECTS RESEARCH (SC)	RESEARCH BUSINESS MODELS (SC)
BIOTECHNOLOGY (SC)	LARGE SCALE SCIENCE (SC)	SCIENCE TO SUPPORT FOOD & AGRICULTURAL RESEARCH (TF)
DIGITAL DATA (IWG)	PHYSICS OF THE UNIVERSE (IWG)	SCIENTIFIC COLLECTIONS (IWG)
DOMESTIC ANIMAL GENOMICS (IWG)	PLANT GENOMES (IWG)	SOCIAL, BEHAVIORAL, ECONOMIC SCIENCES (SC)
EDUCATION & WORKFORCE DEVELOPMENT (SC)	PRION SCIENCE (IWG)	TRANSBORDER MOVEMENT OF RESEARCH MATERIALS (IWG)

COMMITTEE ON TECHNOLOGY		
AERONAUTICS (SC)	HYDROGEN & FUEL CELLS (IWG)	NANOSCALE SCIENCE, ENGINEERING & TECH. (SC)
BIOMETRICS & IDENTITY MANAGEMENT (SC)	INNOVATION & COMPETITIVENESS (SC)	NETWORKING & INFORMATION TECHNOLOGY (SC)
BUILDINGS TECHNOLOGY RESEARCH & DEV. (SC)	MANUFACTURING RESEARCH & DEVELOPMENT (IWG)	QUANTUM INFORMATION SCIENCE (TF)

January 2009

Source: National Science and Technology Council, website, accessed June 2, 2009, at http://www.ostp.gov/cs/nstc/committees.

Note: SC = subcommittee; IWG = interagency working group; TF = task force.

[1] http://www.conspiracyarchive.com/Blog/?tag=club-of-rome

[2] Michelle Malkin, "Ghoulish Science Plus Obamacare Equals Health Hazard," Friday, July 24, 2009. http://townhall.com/columnists/MichelleMalkin/2009/07/24/ghoulish_science_plus_obamacare_equals_health_hazard

[3] Ibid.

[4] Ibid.

[5] http://conservativethoughts.us/2009/08/23/obamas-czars/

[6] Block, Robert and Mark K. Matthews. "Obama aims to ax moon mission." *Orlando Sentinel*. 27 Jan. 2010.

[7] "White House to Outsource Space Flight." FoxNews.com. 27 Jan. 2010 < http://www.foxnews.com/scitech/2010/01/27/white-house-outsource-space-flight/>.

[8] Ball, Dr. Tim and Judi McLeod. "Obama's Science Czar John Holdren Involved in Unwinding 'Climategate' Scandal." *Canada Free Press*. 24 Nov. 2009 < http://www.canadafreepress.com/index.php/article/17183>.

[9] Congressional Research Service. *The President's Office of Science and Technology Policy (OSTP): Issues for Congress*. RL34736, Deborah D. Stine, Specialist in Science and Technology Policy, June 3, 2009.

[10] Ibid.

[11] Ibid.

[12] Ibid.

Stimulus Accountability Czar — Earl Devaney

Official title:	Inspector General, U.S. Department of the Interior
Official responsibilities:	Chairman of the Recovery Accountability and Transparency (RAT) Board
Reports to:	Deputy Director of the Office of Management and Budget and Vice President Biden
Senate confirmation:	Yes, as Interior Department IG only
Salary:	Information unavailable
Ideology / political affiliation:	Non-ideological investigator

Who Is the Stimulus Accountability Czar?

Earl Devaney, the so-called stimulus accountability czar, has had a long and distinguished career as an honest cop, decorated Secret Service agent, and tough inspector general of the Department of the Interior. His latest career incarnation is as an executive with a new White House-controlled organization that is supposed to oversee Obama's $787 billion economic stimulus package, approved in February 2009. The Recovery Accountability and Transparency Board, also known as the RAT Board, has been given unprecedented authority over the powers of the cadre of supposedly independent inspectors general at each of the federal agencies.

Under the stimulus law, the RAT Board has the power to request "that an inspector general conduct or refrain from conducting an audit or investigation." The law goes on further to say that if IGs object to being told what to do and act independently—as we expect them to—they must submit a report to that board, the agency they oversee, and to Congress within 30 days.[1]

Senator Grassley: 'I Smell a Rat'

As Sen. Chuck Grassley recently stated, "Now, I don't know about everyone else around here, but that sounds to me like a lot of red tape for an independent watchdog to go about doing their job. In fact, it is fitting that the acronym for this board is RAT, because that is what I smell here." He went on to say: "But, most importantly, this provision strikes right at the heart of any inspectors' general independence. It appears to me that the majority that crafted this bill isn't all that interested in transparency and accountability. Let me say it loud and clear: I don't like this one bit, and from the chatter I hear, the IGs don't like it either — especially if it involves a criminal investigation."[2]

Grassley added:

> As to the argument about the make-up of the new board, it is true that inspectors general will make up the bulk of the board. However, it will be chaired by either: the Deputy Director of the Office of Management and Budget, a Presidential appointee confirmed by the Senate, or any other individual subject to Senate confirmation. So, based upon this model, you could have a situation where the President appoints a sitting Cabinet Secretary to oversee the board that oversees the inspectors general that oversee the agency run by the Secretary in charge of the board. I don't want to even try to imagine the scenario where the head of the board is a private sector corporate figurehead of a company that has a financial conflict stemming from the fact that the company receives stimulus money. The system this bill creates is not only unworkable; it is loaded with potential for conflicts of interest that are simply mind blowing.[3]

Redundancy and Duplication of Function: Why?

The senator went on to express his concern over the very existence of this organization.

> I also question the need for yet another board full of Government officials. Why do we need yet another Government entity? The inspectors general have worked cooperatively for years via the President's Council for

Integrity and Efficiency, PCIE, and the Executive Councils for Integrity and Efficiency, ECIE, which are made up of inspectors general. These entities were recently rolled into the Council of the Inspectors General on Integrity and Efficiency, CIGIE, by the Inspector General Reform Act of 2008. This new board created by the stimulus bill will simply duplicate already existing efforts in addition to hindering the independence of inspectors general.

It seems to me we all agreed independence was needed for IGs so long as it occurred when there was a Republican President. I hate to think that there is some conspiracy here, but when we have all backed the independence of IGs in the past, you have to question the change of direction buried deep within this bill.[4]

Devaney's Role: Figurehead or Honest Broker?

Will Earl Devaney and his fellow IGs have a truly independent role in overseeing the distribution and accountability of the billions of dollars in stimulus funds? When Obama announced that Vice President Joe Biden will be helping to distribute the funds, and, according to the provisions of the enabling legislation, the true leadership of the RAT will be the deputy director of the Office of Management and Budget — a presidential appointee and a direct employee of the White House — considerable doubt was raised as to the direction and integrity of this board.[5]

Placing Earl Devaney in a leadership post that despite its apparent grandiosity carries little real authority or power raises suspicions that he is being cynically used as a confidence builder to legitimize the stimulus program for the short term while creating a Potemkin Village, giving the president a free hand in spending the $787 billion appropriated in record time by Congress.

In November 2009, the Obama administration boasted what Devaney himself deems unreliable data on the number of jobs created by the stimulus. While Vice President Joe Biden claims that the massive spending was "responsible for over one million jobs so far," the Obama White House officially reported that 640,329 jobs had been created. But Devaney's watchdog group doubts the accuracy of these findings.

"I think it could be above or below 640,000. Missing reports might drive the number up, and misreporting might drive the number down," Devaney said in November of the failure of thousands of stimulus-receiving organizations to report what they have done with the money. California representative Darrell Issa, who serves as the top Republican on the House Oversight and Government Reform Committee, called the inflated numbers "propaganda." Even Democrat David Obey, one of the writers of the stimulus bill, called the mistakes "outrageous" and "ludicrous." Devaney was quoted by *The New York Times* as stating, ""My expectation is that any embarrassment suffered will encourage self-correcting behavior and lead to better reporting in the future."[6] If the current administration is going by the public shaming method of punishment, the stocks would probably be more effective.

At the same time that the inflated findings were publicized, *The Washington Times* reported the results of an audit performed by the Government Accountability Office that showed that $6 billion had been spent in 440 congressional districts that do not actually exist. *The Times* chief political correspondent Donald Lambro cited several fictitious districts in Ohio, Louisiana, Tennessee and North Dakota that received bailout money for job growth. According to the audit, liberal-leaning special interest groups (such as the AARP which received $18.2 million and subsequently endorsed Obama's health care plan) also received millions from the stimulus package.[7] Devaney and the rest of the Recovery Accountability and Transparency Board are charged with investigating misspent government funds among the recipients. But does the board also investigate where the funds are being allocated, like to Obama's political allies?

When his site Recovery.gov posted a figure of a little under 600,000 jobs created in the final quarter of 2009, Devaney acknowledged that he has detected no massive fraud yet, but "I've been around this town too long to not expect a train wreck at some point."[8]

At 61 years of age and previously looking forward to an early retirement, Devaney may serve a short-term need by the Obama administration to get the RAT off the ground with the appearance of legitimacy. The administration may soon replace him with a more politically compliant person. While time will reveal the true intentions, this post must be watched very carefully, particularly because of its extraordinary power to quash investigations throughout the government. This authority is certainly at odds with promises of increased openness and transparency in government that Obama promised in his election campaign.

---

[1] http://www.votesmart.org/speech_detail.php?sc_id=443025&keyword=&phrase=&contain
[2] Ibid.
[3] Ibid.
[4] Ibid.
[5] http://www.whorunsgov.com/Profiles/Earl_E._Devaney
[6] Cooper, Michael. "Stimulus Watchdog Says White House Jobs Numbers May Not Be Accurate." *The New York Times*. 20 Nov. 2009: A18.
[7] Lambro, Donald. "Money for phantom jobs; Audit indicates skullduggery." *The Washington Times*. 23 Nov. 2009: A15.
[8] O'Keefe, Ed. "Stimulus created 600,000 jobs at end of 2009; Count includes new hires only 'Created or saved' figure no longer tallied." *The Washington Post*. 1 Feb. 2010: A15.

Sudan Czar — J Scott Gration

Official title:	Special Envoy to Sudan
Salary / Direct cost to taxpayers:	Unknown
Responsibilities:	Will direct U.S. function in the aftermath of wartorn Darfur
Reports to:	Secretary of State Hillary Clinton
Senate confirmation:	No
Relation to Obama:	Close, personal friend;[1] met Obama in 2005 and served as a policy adviser for his 2008 campaign[2]
Ideology / political affiliation:	"Favors nuclear disarmament; believes there are too many nuclear weapons in America's arsenal and hopes to accelerate the 2002 Moscow Treaty that would reduce the operationally deployed strategic warheads to 2,000 by 2012; ...Supported Obama's plan during the presidential campaign to withdraw one brigade from Iraq each month over sixteen months."[3]

Being the Sudan Czar was J. Scott Gration's second choice, according to published sources. He wanted to head NASA - but his lack of space experience upset NASA advocates, causing Obama to get his friend and supporter another patronage position.[4] Many see this appointment as an indication that Obama's earlier strongly worded resolve to end the genocide in Darfur may have been little more than politically expedient lip service.

Who Is J. Scott Gration?

In 2006, retired Major General of the United States Air Force J. Scott Gration traveled to Africa on a five-nation, fifteen-day, fact-finding tour, accompanying Senator Barack Obama as an "African expert," and later endorsed Obama's presidential campaign. What makes Gration an "African expert"? Growing up in Congo in the family of American missionaries, in the early 1960s Gration and his parents were evacuated and became refugees during the Congo Crisis, which was yet another Cold War proxy battle between the United States and the Soviet Union. The Crisis that caused the death of some 100,000 people was fanned in part by communist intervention, including the personal presence of the murderous and virulently anti-American revolutionary Che Guevara, who came to Congo with a unit of Cuban fighters and spent six months training guerillas and leading rebellions.

Today, when many of Che Guevara's misguided admirers in America and abroad have flocked together in support of Barack Obama's policies and some of them have even joined his administration, it is rather odd to find in their ranks J. Scott Gration, who flew 274 combat missions over Iraq, was in Pentagon when it was struck on 9-11, and later commanded Joint Task Force-West during Operation Iraqi Freedom.

Apparently this respected and highly decorated Air Force veteran, while being a brave and loyal soldier, rather unfortunately happens to have a deaf ear to political and ideological tectonic shifts that are shaping today's geopolitical landscape. That causes reasonable doubts in his ability to lead a diplomatic effort that requires a deep comprehension of political causes and effects driving this and other international crises.

So far, Gration seems to be guided in his decisions by Obama's strategy of appeasement, which can only be described as rewarding bad behavior by bad actors. For example, he has already announced to the Senate his intention to remove Sudan from the list of state sponsors of terrorism, turning a blind eye to Khartoum's earlier appalling expulsion of humanitarian organizations from the suffering Darfur region.

Speak Softly And Carry A Large Carrot

Asked whether the U.S. would give up its biggest "stick" by easing the terrorism-related sanctions, Gration reportedly answered, "You know, carrots and sticks are great for leading donkeys. This is much more complicated." [5]

In March, *The New Republic* signaled that even liberals were upset with Gration's appointment: "[T]here are ... a few reasons for Darfur interventionists to worry. Significantly, Gration originally had his heart set on running NASA. Obama tried to put him there until defense lobbyists scotched the idea. This raises questions ... whether this new assignment is an afterthought for both Gration and the administration. If Obama sees the Darfur envoy simply as a patronage job for loyal supporters... then he may not be that ambitious about Darfur. That would certainly fit the widespread perception that Obama has so far been ineffectual about Sudan, only rushing to appoint Gration after an uproar from advocacy groups."[6]

Four months later Gration validated their concerns and drew fire from another liberal media outlet. In August, *The Washington Post* reported that "The Obama administration's Sudan envoy is facing growing resistance to a suggestion he made recently to civilians displaced from Darfur that they should start planning to go back to their villages. Darfurian civilians and U.N. relief agencies say it is still too dangerous to return to the region where a six-year-long conflict has led to the deaths of more than 300,000 people."

The comment came on the heels of Gration's announcement that Sudan would be taken off the State Department's list of state sponsors of terror, even after Sudan President Omar Bashir had just thrown out humanitarian aid groups attempting to help the oppressed citizens in the Darfur region.[7]

In an interview to NPR, the president of the Save Darfur Coalition, Jerry Fowler, stated that activists on Darfur are worried about Gration's softness on the issue and expressed his belief that the U.S. should not be manipulated by Sudan. "[The Sudanese] took this incredibly cruel and callous step of expelling humanitarian organizations in March and the process that we've mostly seen since then is them gradually easing up on that," said Fowler. "But it was a crisis they created themselves, and all we are doing is expending a lot of effort to get back to a status quo that was unacceptable and unsustainable in the first place."[8]

In March 4, 2009, Sudan's President Bashir was indicted by the International Criminal Court (ICC) for war crimes and crimes against humanity. The ICC warrant stated the following:

> Today, Pre-Trial Chamber I of the International Criminal Court (ICC) issued a warrant for the arrest of Omar Hassan Ahmad Al Bashir, President of Sudan, for war crimes and crimes against humanity. He is suspected of being criminally responsible, as an indirect (co-)perpetrator, for intentionally directing attacks against an important part of the civilian population of Darfur, Sudan, murdering, exterminating, raping, torturing and forcibly transferring large numbers of civilians, and pillaging their property. This is the first warrant of arrest ever issued for a sitting Head of State by the ICC.[9]

To anyone familiar with the situation, the lifting of sanctions four months following this indictment appears to be a rather odd move.

Broken Promises

During the presidential campaign, Obama made strong statements about his willingness to resolve the problem of Darfur. However, immediately after taking office that rhetoric wilted and his treatment of Sudan through Gration began to resemble the rest of Obama's foreign policy agenda, characterized in general by its unreasonable, almost irrational intent to accommodate Islamic extremism no matter how obdurate, murderous, or even genocidal it may be.

— *Angie Wheeler*

---

[1] Mahalo, "J. Scott Gration" -- http://www.mahalo.com/j-scott-gration
[2] Associated Press, "Obama to Name Envoy to Sudan", March 18, 2009.
[3] Conservative Thoughts, "Obama's Czars September Update", August 23, 2009 -- http://conservativethoughts.us/2009/08/23/obamas-czars/

[4] *The New Republic*, "Who is Scott Gration?" by Barron Young-Smith, March 20, 2009.
[5] NPR, "Does Envoy's Approach Hint At U.S. Shift On Sudan?" by Michele Kelemen, August 1, 2009 --
http://www.npr.org/templates/story/story.php?storyId=111422940
[6] *The New Republic*, "Who is Scott Gration?" by Barron YoungSmith, March 20, 2009.
[7] *Washington Post*, "Too Soon To Return Home, Say Darfurians" by Colum Lynch, August 6, 2009 -- http://www.washingtonpost.com/wp-dyn/content/article/2009/08/05/AR2009080503808_pf.html
[8] NPR, "Does Envoy's Approach Hint At U.S. Shift On Sudan?" by Michele Kelemen, August 1, 2009 --
http://www.npr.org/templates/story/story.php?storyId=111422940
[9] International Criminal Court, Press Release, "ICC Issues a Warrant of Arrest for Omar Al Bashir, President of Sudan", April 3, 2009 --
http://www.icc-cpi.int/NR/exeres/0EF62173-05ED-403A-80C8-F15EE1D25BB3.htm

TARP Czar — Herb Allison

Official title:	Assistant Secretary for Financial Stability
Official responsibilities:	Lead the federal bailout program
Reports to:	Treasury Secretary
Senate confirmation:	None
Salary:	Information unavailable
Ideology / political affiliation:	Donor to both political parties, hard to pin down on executive compensation, not averse to being a hatchet man and orchestrating massive layoffs

There are plenty of good things to say about Herb Allison. He is a Wall Street veteran with a wealth of experience, a Yale grad with an M.B.A. from Stanford, and a Vietnam War vet with the U.S. Navy.[1] He is an avid political donor, across party lines, and he has ties to several Republicans, including George W. Bush and John McCain, so he is clearly not a partisan appointment. As the head of the Troubled Asset Relief Program, he will have to work to keep all the banks receiving bailout money afloat.

Allison has a spotty reputation when it comes to the hot-button TARP issue of executive compensation. When he was asked to take over Fannie Mae, he refused to take any compensation at all, thinking of it as a "public-service" job. On the other hand, as the CEO of TIAA-Cref, he had an $8 million salary in 2003.[2] Allison was also a director of the New York Stock Exchange from 2002 to 2005 and was on the compensation committee when former NYSE Chairman Richard Grasso's $139.5 million retirement package was approved.[3]

He has also exhibited some rather cutthroat practices regarding his employees. He orchestrated two mass layoffs over the course of his career, one of which was a flagrant misplay in a time of recession. In 1998, he laid off 3,400 Merrill Lynch employees. He had overestimated the recession, and the move ended up hurting the company when the economy rebounded, as the company had to scramble to hire new analysts to replace the people he had cut. This may have been the mistake that ended up costing him the CEO position at the company. He also slashed jobs at TIAA-CREF, becoming the first person to do so. This move got him into a lot of trouble with the media, as he made the cutbacks to reduce costs at a time when he was being paid $8 million a year.[4]

— Rick Rush

---

[1] "Herbert M. Allison Jr.," Yale University, <http://mba.yale.edu/why/advisors/profiles/allisonh.shtml>

[2] "Herbert M. Allison Jr.," Who Runs GOV, <http://www.whorunsgov.com/Profiles/Herbert_M._Allison_Jr.>
[3] Avi Klein, "New TARP Chief Has Close Ties to Banking and Insurance Industries," 14 April 2009, Bailoutsleuth.com, < http://bailoutsleuth.com/09/04/218/new-tarp-chief-has-close-ties-to-banking-and-insurance-industries/>
[4] "Herbert M. Allison Jr.," Who Runs GOV, <http://www.whorunsgov.com/Profiles/Herbert_M._Allison_Jr.>

Technology Czar — Aneesh Chopra

Official title:	Chief Technology Officer
Salary / Direct cost to taxpayers:	Unknown
Responsibilities:	Promoting technology and computerizing medical records
Reports to:	President Obama, Vivek Kundra, Jeffrey Zients
Senate confirmation:	May 21, 2009
Relation to Obama:	Contributed $2,750 to his presidential campaign
Ideology / political affiliation:	Has given $23,000 since 1997 to Democrats, $1,000 to a sole Republican candidate

Who Is the Technology Czar?

Little is known about Aneesh Chopra. And little is known about the brand-new chief technology officer position that he has been appointed to fill. From what journalists in a variety of news media have reported, his assigned mission appears to be "to promote innovation, oversee the health IT initiative, and put technology to work for the nation's benefit"[i] and "to develop national strategies for using advanced technologies to transform the economy and society."[ii] How he hopes to accomplish this is shrouded in enigma, as is how technology will be harnessed to serve the immediate needs of the United States.

Though each report on the new czar describes his position differently, they all espouse the common notion that it is unclear. "It's not entirely clear what Chopra will actually do, and his first task may simply be to define his position inside the administration," wrote Amy Schatz in the *Wall Street Journal*[iii]. Science and technology policy specialist John Sargent authored a report for the Congressional Research Service in early 2010, warning that even after several months filling the role, Chopra's position has still not been clearly defined, nor has it been provided authorities or a dedicated budget.[iv]

What Is His Job? Does Anyone Know?

As Chopra will be the first person ever to occupy this post, it is necessary to define what exactly he will do to implement these changes, instead of mere spewing of the hope-and-change mantra that got Obama elected. "We will apply the most innovative technologies to our most important challenges — bending the healthcare cost curve, optimizing the energy grid to reduce our dependence on foreign oil, delivering an educational system focused on student excellence with special emphasis on science, technology, engineering, and mathematics, protecting our nation's critical infrastructure, and building the high-wage, high-growth jobs in all corners of our country," Chopra quipped during a Senate confirmation hearing.

Yet Another Bureaucrat to Fill a Contrived Position

Though his remark addressed many issues that should be resolved, adding yet another bureaucrat to fill an invented position may not be the most efficient manner of mending this country. The appointment appears to be redundant because Obama already has Vivek Kundra as the information czar and Jeffrey Zients as the performance czar. Chopra is to devise technology policy, Kundra will streamline the ideas to cut costs, and Zients will make sure that there is a positive outcome to these endeavors.

The tech czar position has been highly controversial since Obama introduced the idea during his campaign last fall. Political pundits have been concerned that the real issues will be lost in bureaucratic bickering over who should have power — those who traditionally controlled this field or the person assigned to the Obama-invented post. There have been concerns expressed by the Federal Communications Commission, which will possibly have to answer to the czar. Having a tech czar might create a turf war and politicize technology issues in the federal government.

"The idea of a federal tech czar is proving highly controversial, with critics raising concerns about the level of authority he or she would have and increased prospects for turf battles and gridlock that could undermine the overarching goal," wrote David Hatch in the *National Journal* last fall. "They emphasized that the White House Office of Science and Technology Policy already tackles some responsibilities the CTO would be tasked with."[v]

Glenn Beck notes on his website that the Commerce Department could have just as easily handled this issue internally.[vi] Many public policy experts have voiced the opinion that the creation of a tech czar is a misguided attempt of the federal government to control technological advances, a job that they say should be left in the private sector.

Government Choosing Winners and Losers

"Highlighting the importance of technology in public policy is probably not harmful," said Barbara Esbin, the director of the Center for Communications and Competition Policy at the Progress and Freedom Foundation. "But if creation of such a position did lead to the government choosing winners and losers in the fields of technology and communications, that certainly would not be a good thing."[vii]

The director of information policy studies at the CATO Institute, Jim Harper, wrote a scathing indictment of the idea to create the tech czar position. The CATO website boasts the mantra "Individual liberty, free markets, and peace."

"Technology, telecommunications, and information policy are important areas," Harper wrote, "but not everything that is important needs a lot of attention from the government. And as federal priorities go, tech is not even in the same league as national defense and fiscal order—issues that deserve a cabinet-level officer. Creating a cabinet-level 'tech czar' would be an odd joke, and it would stand out as a queer sop to some political constituencies. It's an unserious idea."[viii]

No Experience and Nothing to Add—Why Is He There?

And Obama's choice of Chopra, who served as Virginia's secretary of technology for four years, struck many as an odd choice. "Observers considered Chopra as a surprise pick for the Virginia technology job because he lacked practical policy and technological experience," wrote Ed O'Keefe in *The Washington Post*. "He conceded that he was no expert in technological systems."[ix]

One must question why, with the abundance of tech experts already in the federal government, someone who had little expertise in the field would be given the highest-ranking tech job in the White House. Chopra spent his first years out of college as an investment banker at Morgan Stanley. Chopra's education is not in technology or computer systems but in public health (bachelor's degree from Johns Hopkins University) and public policy (master's degree from Harvard). After receiving his graduate degree, he worked as a consultant for the Advisory Board, a healthcare research firm.[x] Because public medical care is one of Obama's major issues, Chopra's appointment could be looked at as a way to use technology and another bureaucrat to further the controversial universal care agenda.

Another Obama Donor Gets Promoted

And Chopra's connections to the party shed more light on why the president would choose such an obscure 37-year-old to be America's first chief technology officer. Prior to his appointment, Chopra worked for Virginia Democratic Gov. Tim Kaine and alongside Kundra, whom many reporters label as his friend. Chopra's time at the Advisory Board also overlapped with that of Zients, who worked for the firm from 1992 to 2004.

For the past 12 years, Chopra has been in the habit of donating thousands of dollars to Democrats' campaigns. With the exception of one $1,000 donation, all of the $24,000 he has spent in political contributions has gone to liberal candidates.

Worrisome Choice — Allegiance to Obama or to the Constitution?

Additionally, in 2007 and 2008, Chopra gave $2,750 to Obama's White House run. His obvious political allegiances make him a worrisome choice for conservatives as he may turn out to be yet another presidential puppet who will hijack technology to further a highly leftist agenda.

— Lucy Leitner

---

[i] "Federal CTO Chopra Completes Obama's Tech Triad." *Techweb* April 20, 2009.
[ii] Sternstein, Aliya. "Congress and the CTO." Weblog entry.
Nextgov.com. May 19, 2009. Aug. 27, 2009
<http://techinsider.nextgov.com/2009/09/congress_and_the_cto.php>.
[iii] Schatz, Amy. "Obama's CTO Nominee Offers Some Thoughts."
WSJ.com May 19, 2009. Aug. 27, 2009
<http://blogs.wsj.com/washwire/2009/05/19/obamas-cto-nominee-offers-some-thoughts/>.
[iv] Hoover, J. Nicholas. "Report: Fed CTO Role Needs Clarification."
Information Week. 15 Feb. 2010: 15.
[v] Hatch, David. "Tech Czar Might Rule Policy Under Obama." The
National Journal.com Sept. 10, 2008. Aug. 30, 2009
<http://www.nationaljournal.com/congressdaily/cda_20080910_6421.php>.
[vi] Beck, Glenn. "List of Obama's Czars." GlennBeck.com Aug. 21, 2009.
Premiere Radio Networks. Aug. 30, 2009
<http://www.glennbeck.com/content/articles/article/198/29391/>.

[vii] Britt, Phil. "Role, Value of Technology Czar Under Debate." Heartland.org, Feb. 1, 2009. The Heartland Institute. Aug. 30, 2009 <http://www.heartland.org/publications/infotech%20telecom/article/24572/Role_Value_of_Technology_Czar_Under_Debate.html>.

[viii] Harper, Jim. "A 'Tech Czar'? No Thanks." CatoAtLiberty.org. Weblog post. Cato at Liberty. Sept. 10, 2008. Aug. 30, 2009 <http://www.cato-at-liberty.org/2008/09/10/a-tech-czar-no-thanks/>.

[ix] O'Keefe, Ed. "Who Are Jeffrey Zients and Aneesh Chopra?" *The Washington Post,* April 18, 2009.

[x] "Aneesh Chopra." WhoRunsGov.com. Aug. 30, 2009 <http://www.whorunsgov.com/Profiles/Aneesh_Chopra>.

Terrorism Czar — John Brennan

Official title:	Assistant to the President for Homeland Security and Counterterrorism
Official responsibilities:	Coordinate U.S. antiterrorism policy
Reports to:	National Security Adviser James L. Jones
Senate confirmation:	None[1]
Salary:	$172,200
Ideology / political affiliation:	Appears to swing with the wind depending upon who the President is[1]

Sycophant-in-Chief

John Brennan's debut as Obama's terrorism czar was a display of sycophantic behavior that immediately raised questions about his suitability for such a critical national security post. In his address to the Center for Strategic and International Studies in Washington, Brennan 90 times in 5,000 words invokes "President Obama," "he," "his," or "the president."[2] Disturbingly, Brennan ascribes virtually every thought or policy in his speech to the wisdom of the One. This cringe-inducing lecture brings to mind a North Korean functionary paying homage to the Dear Leader.[3]

Specifics are no better. Most fundamentally, Brennan calls for appeasing terrorists: "Even as we condemn and oppose the illegitimate tactics used by terrorists, we need to acknowledge and address the legitimate needs and grievances of ordinary people those terrorists claim to represent." Which legitimate needs and grievances, one wonders, does he think al Qaeda represents? Brennan carefully delineates a two-fold threat, one being "al Qaeda and its allies" and the other "violent extremism." But the former, self-evidently, is a subset of the latter. This elementary mistake undermines his entire analysis. He also rejects any connection between "violent extremism" and Islam: "Using the legitimate term *jihad*, which means to purify oneself or to wage a holy struggle for a moral goal, risks giving these murderers the religious legitimacy they desperately seek but in no way deserve.

Worse, it risks reinforcing the idea that the United States is somehow at war with Islam itself."[4]

Brennan revealed his intellectual shortcomings — as well as a severe logic handicap reminiscent of the Clinton administration's analytical and decision-making failures that led to the 9/11 attacks on the United States when he stated:

"Poverty does not cause violence and terrorism. Lack of education does not cause terrorism. But just as there is no excuse for the wanton slaughter of innocents, there is no denying that when children have no hope for an education, when young people have no hope for a job and feel disconnected from the modern world, when governments fail to provide for the basic needs of their people, then people become more susceptible to ideologies of violence and death."[5]

Brennan stated that poverty and a lack of education do not *cause* terrorism, but a lack of education and a job *make people more susceptible* to the ideas leading to terrorism. What is the distinction? Woe on us when the White House accepts illogic as analysis. Further, let's focus on the statement, "When governments fail to provide for the basic needs of their people, then people become more susceptible to ideologies of violence and death," for it contains two stunning errors. First, it assumes the socialist fiction that governments provide basic needs. No. Other than in a few commodity-rich states, governments protect and offer legal structures, while the market provides. Second, every study on the subject finds no connection between personal stress (poverty, lack of education, unemployment) and attraction to radical Islam. If anything, massive transfers of wealth to the Middle East since 1970 contributed to the rise of radical Islam. The administration is basing its policy on a falsehood.[6]

Self-Deception and Propaganda

Brennan was deeply involved in the Obama administration's word games whereby it embraced a sanitized lexicon of acceptable terminology that will be used to describe the terrorist threat. This represents the nexus between complete politically correct propaganda and an extreme degree of self-deception that will make the United States more vulnerable to terrorist attacks in the future. One would have thought that one of the principal lessons of 9/11 — that ignoring or unilaterally defining a threat as insignificant does not make it so — could not be so quickly forgotten or intentionally suppressed.

Brennan amazingly announced that the United States is no longer engaged in a "war on terrorism," nor is it any longer battling "jihadists" or engaged in a "global war." The only terminology Brennan said the administration is now using is that the United States is "at war with al Qaeda ... We are at war with al Qaeda. We are at war with its violent extremist allies who seek to carry on al Qaeda's murderous agenda."

"Nor does President Obama see this challenge as a fight against 'jihadists,' " Brennan explained in defining the administration's new terminology for the Islamist terrorist threat. He noted, "And this is why President Obama has confronted this perception directly and forcefully in his speeches to Muslim audiences, declaring that America is not and never will be at war with Islam."[7]

This distorted mind-set stands in direct conflict with a more reasoned analysis: the U.S. Central Command Red Team report, *Freedom of Speech in Jihad Analysis: Debunking the Myth of Offensive Words*. This report concluded, "While there is concern that we not label all Muslims as Islamist terrorists, it is proper to address certain aspects of violence as uniquely Islamic ... The fact is our enemies cite the sources of Islam as the foundation of their global jihad. We are left with the responsibility of portraying our enemies in an honest and accurate fashion."[8]

The positions regarding how to describe terrorists — Muslim terrorists in particular — by both the Bush and the Obama administrations, "are evidence to strategic mistakes being made now by the administration at the heart of U.S. defense and national security," Walid Phares told HSToday.us.[9]

An adjunct professor at the National Defense University School for National Security Executive Education and director of the Future of Terrorism Project at the Foundation for Defense of Democracies, Phares is the author of *Future Jihad: Terrorist Strategies against the West*, and *The War of Ideas: Jihadism Against Democracy*.

Phares said, "As we read [Brennan's speech], we realize that the administration is going backward in understanding the threat and explaining it to the public. They say the doctrine is 'to safeguard the American people from the transnational challenge that poses one of the greatest threats to our national security — the scourge of violent extremists who would use terrorism to slaughter Americans abroad and at home.' What does that mean?" Phares continued, "Nothing. It is as if they speak in abstract. Which 'transnational challenge is posing the greatest threat to U.S. national security?' It is the global jihadist threat, with its two networks, the Salafists and the Khomeinists, not the Nazis, the Soviet Communists, or militaristic regimes. Why is the Obama administration regressing into a level way below what most educated Americans understand?" [10]

Phares added:

> The administration criticizes the narrative of its predecessor and we do as well, but instead they propose something weaker and in some aspects dangerous to U.S. national security. After eight years of confrontation with a world web of jihadists, both Salafists and Khomeinists, on two major battlefields in Iraq and in Afghanistan, and in various regions of the world such as Pakistan, Somalia, Indonesia, the Levant, the Maghreb, and as the threat penetrates the West with homegrown cells, the administration's doctrine on the threat understanding is entirely disconnected from reality. In short, the new doctrine asserts that the U.S. is no

longer engaged in a 'war on terrorism.' They disengage from the conflict as if in a wishful, thinking that they can redesign world realities in different colors and names. As if one party in a conflict can decide on the ideology and the strategies of the foe."[11]

Charles Faddis, a former career CIA counterterrorist in the Middle East and head of the NCTC's WMD terrorism branch when he retired last year, told HSToday.us that "as with most things, I think the real test will be in what the administration actually does versus what it says . . . What would bother me," Faddis added, "is if this turned out to be the first step in a return to Bill Clinton's approach, which was to try to handle this threat exclusively through law enforcement channels. I don't have any problem with indicting and trying al Qaeda members when we have the means to do so, but the scope of this threat is such that we are going to have to continue to employ armed forces for many years to come. In short, we can debate the characterization of the threat and exactly what tools we should be using, but at the end of the day we are still at war."[12]

Several seasoned active-duty intelligence-community counterterrorists who've focused on Islamic jihadists and who frequently talk to HSToday.us on background said they do not agree with the Obama administration's new policy on how to characterize America's battle against Muslim jihadists as outlined by Brennan. They noted in recent interviews that they objected to the strategy when it was first broached by the Bush administration. The counterterrorists said they agree with Phares and other experts about why the new "terminology" policy is off the mark and misses the point with regard to the inherent nature and religious ideology of Muslim jihadists.[13]

Maybe the sterilized vernacular was one of the reasons that Nigerian terrorist Umar Farouk Abdulmutallab was allowed to board and nearly blow up a plane headed from Amsterdam to Detroit on Christmas Day 2009. The information was there, but Brennan claimed that "It was a failure to connect and integrate and understand the intelligence we had" that allowed an aspiring suicide bomber to board a plane. On November 18, 2009, the 23-year-old's father, wealthy banker Alhaji Umaru Mutallab, met with CIA agents in Nigeria and expressed his concerns over his son's increasingly extremist views. His name was added to a 550,000-name list of potential threats, yet not to the more specific lists, nor was his U.S. visa revoked. Thus, Abdulmutallab boarded the plane in Amsterdam and when approaching Detroit, lit his pants on fire and was tackled by the other passengers. A few weeks after the incident, Brennan admitted his failure at a White House press conference, garnering praise for taking the fall for what was almost a tragic oversight.

Then, in January, it was discovered by the press that authorities only initially interrogated the terror suspect for 50 minutes. Abdulmutallab was then Mirandized and stopped talking, denying authories vital information about al-Qaeda in Yemen. The second interview was even shorter. A column in the Wall Street Journal with the subtitle "The more we learn about his 'interrogation,' the worse White House policy looks" read,

> This is awful. This talky terrorist should have been questioned for 50 hours, not 50 minutes. More pointedly, Abdulmutallab should not have been questioned by local G-men concerned principally with getting a conviction in court. He should have been interrogated by agents who know enough about the current state of al Qaeda to know what to ask, what names or locations to listen for, and what answers to follow up. The urgent matter is deterring future plots, not getting Abdulmutallab behind bars.[14]

In late January, a commission that investigated U.S. failures related to 9/11 said that the administration mishandled the interrogation by not contacting U.S. intelligence agencies before reading Abdulmutallab his Miranda rights.[15] The treatment of the Christmas terrorist reinforces a heated argument about Obama's commitment to try terrorists in civilian criminal court, instead of military courts, leading many opponents to believe that he values the rights of terrorists over those of American soldiers. In response to Obama's decision to try 9/11 mastermind Khalid Sheikh Mohammed in New York City civilian court, Debbie Lee, spokeswoman for the pro-troop organization, issued the following statement;

> The clear implication is that the United States military courts are not good enough to try these terrorists. This is a horrible affront to our military, which comes as no surprise given the extreme left-wing political leanings of Obama appointees in the U.S. Justice Department. They are more concerned with the well-being and rights of the terrorists than those that are currently on the frontlines defending our country from these evil men.[16]

American citizens object to the public platform that will be given to Mohammed in his trial, allowing a means for him to spew his anti-American rhetoric. Oddly enough, there have been three terror-related attacks in the United States since Obama has been in office, but the government has spent federal resources setting up a sting operation in Switzerland that led to the extradition and trial of Roman Polanski.

Two Republican congressmen (Lindsey Graham and Peter King) are already calling for Brennan's resignation after another incident that came in the form of a comment. In February 2010, the terror czar said that a twenty percent recidivism rate for terrorists imprisoned at Guantanamo Bay "not that bad." "He has lost my confidence," Sen. Graham, R- S.C., said.

Amidst all the criticism of the administration's mishandling of the Abdulmutallab case, Brennan lashed out at Republicans for using the SNAFU to further their own politics. He even accused his critics of "unfounded fear-mongering" that "will only serve the goals of al-Qaeda." But the opponents fired back, bringing up the valid argument that the Obama administration is trapped in a political hole that promised civil liberties (albeit undeserved) to terrorists and keeping Americans safe.[17] These two promises are mutually exclusive.

In a *Washington Times* editorial penned by Senators Mitch McConnell (R-Ken.) and Kit Bond (R-Missouri), they write,

> The Obama administration's latest decision is to require the Department of Justice and FBI to consult with the intelligence community - something that should have been routine - before deciding whether to read terrorists Miranda warnings. The failure to consider the Christmas Day bomber suspect's intelligence value, consult our intelligence chiefs or even contemplate an alternative to immediate criminal charges suggests that, after only one year, the administration has managed to undo eight years of post-Sept. 11 progress in moving the FBI away from a "law enforcement only" mentality. It also suggests that, more than one year after issuing executive orders that gutted the intelligence community's detention and interrogation policies, this administration still has no comprehensive plan or policies in place to deal with the full range of capture and detention issues it inevitably will face in this war.[18]

Terrorism Knowledge That Never Went to His Head

Barry Rubin, editor of the *Middle East Review of International Affairs*, puts it this way:

> Brennan on Hezbollah: "Hezbollah started out as purely a terrorist organization back in the early 1980s and has evolved significantly over time. And now it has members of parliament, in the cabinet; there are lawyers, doctors, others who are part of the Hezbollah organization. However, within Hezbollah, there's still a terrorist core. And hopefully those elements within the Shia community in Lebanon and within Hezbollah at large—they're going to continue to look at that extremist terrorist core as being something that is anathema to what, in fact, they're trying to accomplish in terms of their aspirations about being part of the political process in Lebanon. And so, quite frankly, I'm pleased to see that a lot of Hezbollah individuals are in fact renouncing that type of terrorism and violence and are trying to participate in the political process in a very legitimate fashion." So in other words, it cannot be terrorist because it

has parliamentarians, doctors, and even lawyers. Sticking with doctors for the moment, I can think of terrorist doctors who led some of the most terrorist PLO and Palestinian groups, the number two leader of al Qaeda, and several of Hamas's top leaders.[19]

A Very Bad Choice

Unfortunately, despite Brennan's distinguished career within the intelligence community, it appears very clear that he is an extraordinarily poor choice for such an influential position. His lack of intellectual independence as demonstrated in his CSIS speech discussed earlier and his inability to absorb history and effectively understand the nature of various murderous terrorist organizations should have disqualified him for this post. However, this is the Obama administration, where faulty judgment, kowtowing to Islamist enemies of the United States, and bowing before the barbarian king of Saudi Arabia are the order of the day.

---

[1] "John O. Brennan." Who Runs Gov?. *The Washington Post*. 2009. Apr. 13, 2010 <http://www.whorunsgov.com/Profiles/John_O._Brennan>.
[2] http://www.whitehouse.gov/the_press_office/Remarks-by-John-Brennan-at-the-Center-for-Strategic-and-International-Studies/
[3] Daniel Pipes, "Counterterrorism in Obama's Washington," *FrontPageMagazine.com,* August 18, 2009
http://www.danielpipes.org/7525/counterterrorism-in-obamas-washington

[4] Ibid.
[5] http://www.whitehouse.gov/the_press_office/Remarks-by-John-Brennan-at-the-Center-for-Strategic-and-International-Studies/
[6] Daniel Pipes, "Counterterrorism in Obama's Washington," *FrontPageMagazine.com,* August 18, 2009
http://www.danielpipes.org/7525/counterterrorism-in-obamas-washington

[7] Anthony Kimery, "Rejection of 'Jihadist,' 'War on Terrorism' Terms Draws Fire, Debate," Homeland Security Today, (13 August 2009) http://www.hstoday.us/content/view/9760/150/

[8] Ibid.

[9] Ibid.

[10] Ibid.

[11] Ibid.

[12] http://www.investigativeproject.org/blog/2009/08/the-war-of-the-words

[13] Ibid.

[14] "Abdulmutallab in 50 Minutes." *The Wall Street Journal*. 26 Jan. 2010.

[15] Lake, Eli. "9/11 panel chiefs fault handling of bomb suspect; Say intel agencies should have been consulted." *The Washington Times.* 27 Jan. 2010: A1.

[16] Kouri, Jim. "Obama gives terrorists preferential treatment over US soldiers, say critics." *The Washington Examiner*. 13 Nov. 2009.

[17] Kuchner, Jeffrey T. "Duplicity, delivered; The White House is playing politics with national security." *The Washington Times*. 12 Feb. 2010: B3.

[18] McConnell, Mitch and Kit Bond. "Two steps forward, one step back; Detainee intelligence-gathering needs wartime strategy." *The Washington Times*. 25 Feb. 2010: B1.

[19] Barry Rubin, Brennan on Hezbollah: "They Can't Be Terrorists! They Have Lawyers!" (10 August 2009) http://www.rightsidenews.com/200908115906/editorial/brennan-on-hizballah-they-cant-be-terrorists-they-have-lawyers.html

Tobacco Czar–Lawrence Deyton

Official title:	Director, FDA's Center for Tobacco Products
Official responsibilities:	To enforce Obama's new tobacco legislation
Reports to:	FDA Commissioner Margaret Hamburg[1]
Senate confirmation:	None
Salary:	Information unavailable
Ideology / political affiliation:	Background working with veterans, more public health minded than outwardly political, some anti-tobacco leanings

Who is the Tobacco czar?

The Food and Drug Administration has named Dr. Lawrence R. Deyton their tobacco czar, heading up the new Center for Tobacco Products. A graduate of the University of Kansas, the Harvard School of Public Health and the George Washington University School of Medicine, Deyton is an expert on veterans' health issues and public health, and a clinical professor of medicine and health policy at George Washington University School of Medicine and Health Sciences.[2] Deyton is a physician, and until recently was the chief public health and environmental hazards officer at the Veterans Health Administration. He had been working in various capacities in veterans' health since 1998. He has a long history in the medical field and was a congressional aide in the 1970s.[3]

Deyton does have some experience with tobacco, in his words:

> My public health career actually started out in tobacco control. I was the first full-time staff member assigned to help set up the federal Office on Smoking and Health in 1978.
> And my public health career has taken me into fascinating areas spanning broad public health policy issues facing Congress, HIV/AIDS

research and treatment, and then into veteran's
health and environmental exposure issues as
well as bioterrorism, emergency preparedness,
influenza, and pandemic flu.

The honor of being asked to help set up FDA's
new Center for Tobacco Products feels like
coming home to an issue that galvanized my
interest in public health. I am thrilled to join my
colleagues at FDA to address the public health
consequences of tobacco use.[4]

Deyton also claims to have reduced smoking among
veterans enrolled in a cessation program from 33 percent
in 1999 to 20 percent in 2007.[5]

Why is there a tobacco czar?

The need for a Tobacco czar arises from the Family
Smoking Prevention and Tobacco Control Act Obama
signed on June 22, 2009, which gave the FDA jurisdictional
authority to regulate tobacco products. The concept of the
bill was to form a compromise between the fact that 43
million Americans are addicted to the nicotine in tobacco,
most of whom say they wish they could quit, and the fact
that taxes on tobacco sales provide a great deal of revenue
for states.[6]

Some of the major points of the law:

- The FDA has to approve new tobacco products before
  they are marketed in the U.S., will have access to
  companies' health studies, and can deny approval for
  new products if the company cannot prove that they will
  market the product in a manner that "would be
  appropriate for the protection of the public health."
  Basically, this means that companies can only introduce
  new tobacco products if they are less addictive or
  harmful than previous products.

- The FDA cannot simply ban an entire class (cigarettes, snuff, cigars, chew, etc.) of tobacco products.
- The FDA can demand the amount of nicotine in products to be reduced, but cannot stipulate that nicotine be totally eliminated.
- Tobacco companies can only advertise in black-and-white text when ads will be seen outdoors, in and near stores where tobacco is sold, or in publications that have "significant teen readership."
- The FDA will decide what future tobacco packaging will look like: be it new warning labels covering half of the package, pictures of diseased lungs on cigarette packs, or whatever else they choose.
- The FDA can reduce or remove ingredients from tobacco products. This is mostly aimed at harmful ingredients, but is also being used to ban certain flavorings deemed to appeal to children and teens.
- The FDA can force tobacco companies to divulge their research regarding the health effects and contents of their present and future products to them. And then the FDA can release the information to the public.[7]

Reaction

While the legislation has immediately set off a firestorm of legal action, there seems to be little or no resistance to Deyton himself heading the campaign. He has been met with approval from both sides of the tracks. The American Lung Association issued a statement applauding his appointment.[8] The president of the Campaign for Tobacco-Free Kids, who was an important in instigating the legislation, spoke highly of him as well. Altria, the company that owns Marlboro, was pleased with the choice, too. The tobacco analyst at Morgan Stanley was also pleased, saying the industry was pleased that the FDA went with someone with a health background instead of an antismoking zealot.[9] Overall, Deyton seems as good a choice as any. His job is more problematic.

Job description

The Center for Tobacco Products is charged with carrying out the new legislation. The FDA says the center "will use the best available science to guide the development and implementation of effective public health strategies to reduce the burden of illness and death caused by tobacco products."[10] Deyton has to deal with the lawsuit brought by tobacco companies alleging that the new legislation violates the First Amendment. He is supposed to have his center work with the Centers for Disease Control and Prevention, the National Institutes of Health, and other public health leaders to work against tobacco.[11] He has also established a 12 member scientific advisory committee consisting of 7 representing science and medical disciplines, 3 (who cannot vote) from the tobacco industry, 1 from government, and 1 from the general public.[12]

His plan

Deyton has stated that his priorities are to:

- prevent youth from using tobacco;
- help adults who use tobacco to quit;
- provide accurate information on the contents of tobacco and consequences of tobacco use to the public; and
- use regulatory tools, including tobacco product standards, to reduce the public health burden of tobacco in the United States.[13]

He said the FDA is taking a different approach to tobacco than they do with anything else under their jurisdiction. Instead of evaluating the safety and effectiveness of tobacco, as they do when evaluating pharmaceuticals, the FDA is judging tobacco products on their overall effect on the public health of the entire country. As he says:

When we get an application for a new tobacco product, the law tells us we have to consider whether permitting the product's marketing protects the public health and we have to evaluate the effects of the product on the population as a whole. We're directed to consider both users and nonusers, and whether our action might encourage people who don't use tobacco products to begin using them, or encourage people who might otherwise quit to continue using them.[14]

Problems with the law

There are a lot of issues to prevent this little plan from swiftly solving youth smoking and the greater public health problem caused by tobacco products in America. Certain provisions restricting ways in which the tobacco companies can advertise are likely to be repealed as First Amendment violations according to the Association of National Advertisers. The lawsuits, some of which have already been filed, could delay the law's implementation. The advertising lobby feels that the precedent set by this law is important to industries aside from tobacco and that the upcoming court case "is extremely significant."[15]

Giving this responsibility to the FDA may also be a mistake. The FDA has already been straining to carry out its traditional responsibilities, and this is a pretty hefty new project to dump on the organization. Also, there is the issue of the FDA essentially endorsing some tobacco products over others. Some consumers could interpret this as the new products that the FDA allows to market actually being safe, rather than simply less harmful than the alternative tobacco products.[16]

And like many of the other instances of Obama's use of czars to expand the government, the new legislation may be needlessly affecting the business world. Altria supported the legislation while fellow tobacco giants such as R.J. Reynolds and Lorillard fought against it. These companies believe that the legislation and its affect on tobacco advertising will help protect Altria's market.[17] The lawsuit filed by Reynolds, Lorillard and others alleges that the new law infringes on their right to advertise their products to adult tobacco users. They also object to the FDA having control of the size and placement of warning labels, which may end up taking up the entire top half of cigarette packs, leaving the tobacco companies only a small area beneath to print their logos and messages, which is often not even visible in a traditional store cigarette display. Also in question is the restriction on ability of companies to advertise the relative health risks of tobacco products, such as comparing chewing tobacco to cigarettes, if these statements are not beneficial to the greater American public health. Also being contested is the provision that if a tobacco company sponsor a sporting event, concert, or similar event they can only mention the corporate name of the company, for example Altria can be listed as a sponsor but Marlboro cannot.[18]

The bill has drawn fire from all sides. Scott Ramminger, president of the American Wholesale Marketers Association, which represents distributors who supply tobacco products to convenience stores, believes that the best-case scenario is that the regulations do not "accomplish anything except cost the taxpayers a lot more money." But it could end up much worse. "In Canada and other places where draconian regulations have gone in effect, it has basically driven up the cost of the product. . . . What it does is create a great opportunity for organized crime and people interested in subverting the system to bring in bootleg products on the black market. Cigarettes are very easy to make. . . . In California, you've already had a problem with counterfeit cigarettes from China." Meanwhile, Stanton Glantz, a professor of Medicine and director of the Center for Tobacco Control Research and Education at UC San Francisco, believes "the bill is a huge missed opportunity for public health. The FDA's scientific advisory committee will have three tobacco industry representatives on it. They are non-voting, but I don't think that will matter. The fact that they are there at all is a problem. I think people have grossly underestimated how much trouble that will cause."[19]

Final Thoughts

So, all in all, Lawrence Deyton seems like a decent enough guy. But that does not change the fact that he is tasked with an impossible mission, that is largely unconstitutional, and could very easily backfire and create greater problems that do not exist at this time. It could eventually lead to a Prohibition type of situation where criminals control the cigarette industry, or it could function as a sort of reverse scenario to the marijuana legalization issue. A central leftist argument in support of legalization is that by making marijuana accessible without encountering drug dealers will prevent users from escalating to harder drugs. By making cigarettes harder to acquire and potentially sold on the black market, the government may eventually create a new gateway drug. And above all, allowing the government near total control of how tobacco companies advertise not only defeats the entire purpose of allowing them to advertise at all, but sets a dangerous precedent of governmental interference in the business world.

-Rick Rush

---

[1] Duncan, David Ewing. "FDA Chief: Regaining Your Trust." CNN Money. Oct. 14, 2009. Apr. 8, 2010 <http://money.cnn.com/2009/10/13/news/economy/fda_ha mburg_interview.fortune/index.htm?section=money_latest&ut

m_source=feedburner&utm_medium=feed&utm_campaign=Fee
d%3A+rss%2Fmoney_latest+%28Latest+News%29>.
[2] "Regulating Tobacco: Q&A with Lawrence Deyton, M.S.P.H.,
M.D." Sep. 28, 2009. U.S. Food and Drug Administration,"
<**http://www.fda.gov/ForConsumers/ConsumerUpdates/ucm18
3919.htm**>
[3] Duff Wilson, "Veterans' Doctor to Lead F.D.A. Tobacco
Division" Aug. 19, 2009. New York Times
<http://www.nytimes.com/2009/08/20/health/policy/20toba
cco.html>
[4] "Regulating Tobacco: Q&A with Lawrence Deyton, M.S.P.H.,
M.D." Sep. 28, 2009. U.S. Food and Drug Administration,"
<**http://www.fda.gov/ForConsumers/ConsumerUpdates/ucm18
3919.htm**>
[5] Duff Wilson, "Veterans' Doctor to Lead F.D.A. Tobacco
Division" Aug. 19, 2009. New York Times
<http://www.nytimes.com/2009/08/20/health/policy/20toba
cco.html>
[6] Melissa Healy, "The tobacco law: What the FDA can and can't
do," Jun. 29, 2009, Los Angeles Times,
<http://articles.latimes.com/2009/jun/29/health/he-
tobacco29>
[7] Ibid.
[8] Rosie Mestel, "FDA opens new Center for Tobacco Products,"
Aug. 19, 2009. Los Angeles Times Blogs
<http://latimesblogs.latimes.com/booster_shots/2009/08/fda-
opens-new-center-for-tobacco-
products.html?utm_source=feedburner&utm_medium=feed&ut
m_campaign=Feed%3A+BoosterShots+%28Booster+Shots%29>
[9] Duff Wilson, "Veterans' Doctor to Lead F.D.A. Tobacco
Division" Aug. 19, 2009. New York Times
<http://www.nytimes.com/2009/08/20/health/policy/20toba
cco.html>
[10] Rosie Mestel, "FDA opens new Center for Tobacco Products,"
Aug. 19, 2009. Los Angeles Times Blogs
<http://latimesblogs.latimes.com/booster_shots/2009/08/fda-
opens-new-center-for-tobacco-
products.html?utm_source=feedburner&utm_medium=feed&ut
m_campaign=Feed%3A+BoosterShots+%28Booster+Shots%29>

[11] Duff Wilson, "Veterans' Doctor to Lead F.D.A. Tobacco Division" Aug. 19, 2009. New York Times <http://www.nytimes.com/2009/08/20/health/policy/20tobacco.html>

[12] "Regulating Tobacco: Q&A with Lawrence Deyton, M.S.P.H., M.D." Sep. 28, 2009. U.S. Food and Drug Administration," **<http://www.fda.gov/ForConsumers/ConsumerUpdates/ucm183919.htm>**

[13] Ibid.

[14] Ibid.

[15] David Kesmodel et al. "Tobacco Giants Challenge Law," Sep. 2, 2009, Wall Street Journal <http://online.wsj.com/article/SB125174788118073575.html>

[16] Melissa Healy, "The tobacco law: What the FDA can and can't do," Jun. 29, 2009, Los Angeles Times, <http://articles.latimes.com/2009/jun/29/health/he-tobacco29>

[17] Duff Wilson, "Veterans' Doctor to Lead F.D.A. Tobacco Division" Aug. 19, 2009. New York Times <http://www.nytimes.com/2009/08/20/health/policy/20tobacco.html>

[18] David Kesmodel et al. "Tobacco Giants Challenge Law," Sep. 2, 2009, Wall Street Journal <http://online.wsj.com/article/SB125174788118073575.html>

[19] Shari Roan and Shara Yurkiewicz "Tobacco industry experts weigh in on the new law," Jun. 29, 2009, Los Angeles Times <http://articles.latimes.com/2009/jun/29/health/he-tobacco-viewpoints29>

Urban Czar — Adolfo Carrión

Official title:	White House Director of Urban Affairs
Appointed:	February 19, 2009
Official responsibilities:	Coordinating transportation and housing initiatives, as well as serving as a conduit for federal aid to economically hard-hit cities
Reports to:	President Obama
Senate confirmation:	None
Relation to Obama:	Active campaigner for Obama, traveling across the country to speak on his behalf. He focused particularly on states with large Hispanic populations.
Direct cost to taxpayers:	$158,500 annually
Ideology / political affiliation:	A populist Democrat with a history of taking bribes and putting the interests of his donors above those of the community

"If Adolfo does for the U.S.A. what he has done for The Bronx, then we are in for a very tough time," wrote *Gotham Gazette*[1] about Adolfo Carrión's nomination as White House Director of Urban Affairs - a newly created position in which he will oversee federal investment in urban areas. Many have expressed concern over Carrión's history of corruption, yet others have doubts he can cope with the many problems faced by American cities, given his lack of experience at the federal level.

So far, Carrión seems to have been able to make up for his lack of ethics and aptitude with populist rhetoric and shrewd political instinct. After a few years of working with local Puerto Rican communities in the Bronx, in 1998 he was elected to the City Council, moving on to Bronx Borough President in 2001. Since running against the wishes of top Democrats in the Bronx political machine had cost him useful connections, he compensated that by aligning himself with Mayor Bloomberg and became re-elected in 2005.

His propensity to fan the flames of Puerto Rican nationalism couldn't hurt either. In May 2001, playing to the emotions of his voting base, Adolfo Carrión joined Rev. Al Sharpton and three other well-known Puerto Rican grandstanders in a political stunt of protesting near the U.S. Navy bombing site on Vieques, Puerto Rico. The extensive national TV coverage and a spell of lionizing media stories cost the five of them forty days in jail - a harmless adventure but a strong calculated boost in votes from the less law-abiding sector of Carrión's constituents.[2]

Having initially endorsed Hillary Clinton early in the 2008 presidential contest, Carrión quickly jumped on Barack Obama's bandwagon once his chances became stronger. Carrión campaigned for Obama across the country, with the focus on identity politics in states with large Hispanic populations. At a fundraiser in Chicago he met some people whom he described as Obama's "friends and supporters, very intimate people with Senator Obama." They must have detected a kindred spirit because then and there Adolfo Carrión was tapped into Obama's network.[3]

Skillful networking and political instinct may have helped Carrión to advance his career while avoiding charges of corruption and ethical violations in the past, but to perform his new set of duties may also require a different set of skills - unless, of course, the White House has chosen him precisely for the skills he already had.

Along with many other appointed Czars, Carrión was lucky that his appointment did not require Senate confirmation.

Who Is Adolfo Carrión?

Adolfo Carrión was born in 1961 in Manhattan, in the family of a Protestant minister of Puerto Rican descent, and grew up in the Bronx. He started his career as an associate pastor at a Bronx Church, later acquiring a master's degree in urban planning from Hunter College and getting a job at the Bronx office of the NYC Department of City Planning. His networking in various Latino community organizations allowed him to make a quick political career, and although Carrión's tenure as Bronx Borough President (2001-2009) was marred with corruption scandals, many reporters predicted his run for New York City mayor in the next ten years.

In 2007 Carrión was elected president of National Association of Latino Elected and Appointed Officials (NALEO), the nonpartisan leadership organization of the nation's 6,000 Latino elected and appointed officials. As President, he announced an increase in efforts to help file naturalization papers for eligible legal permanent residents before impending fee increases take effect as part of NALEO's "ya es hora" campaign.

A Preference For Personal Gain Over Impartiality and Legality

Surely the recent controversy surrounding the newly appointed Urban Czar may have caused the legislative branch to voice objections. The New York Daily News has been publishing its investigations into Carrión's tenure as Bronx Borough President since March, delving into the numerous campaign contributions he accepted from local developers that he consistently followed by approving his donors' projects. As the law forbids city officials from taking gifts from anyone requesting their approval, Carrión's actions clearly indicate a preference for personal gain over impartiality and legality.

The most staggering and written about tale of corruption involves the borough president's suspicious inability to pay an architect's bill for a personal project while repeatedly approving the man's subsequent substantial Bronx projects. In the fall of 2006, Carrión hired Hugo Subotovsky to design a new porch and balcony for his City Island $925,000 home. Though Subotovsky had finished the job over two years ago, his $3,627.50 for 51.5 hours of work[4] was unpaid until the Daily News articles put pressure on the White House to urge Carrión to pay off his debt[5]. The total job cost was estimated at $32,000 in 2006 when the borough president's records showed that he owed at least $15,000 in credit card debt and was paying off more than $500,000 for his two mortgages.[6]

A few months after Subotovsky finished his work on Carrión's two-family Victorian abode, the borough president approved the zoning changes needed for his architect's new $7.5-million project of Boricua Village; 679 housing units and a 14-story college tower. Atlantic Development Company, the publicly funded project's developer, sought Carrión's approval to rescind height restrictions for the tower. The initial application was filed in March 2006 and was followed less than a month later by $52,400 in contributions from

Atlantic employees and owners Peter Fine and Marc Altheim to Carrión's campaign funds and another $17,512 from Boricua College administrators. In March 2007, the borough president approved the project.

In late April 2009 the New York Police Department and the Department of Investigation raided Atlantic's Manhattan offices to find out whether the company illegally influenced Carrión with its substantial donations. The government watchdog group Citizens for Responsibility and Ethics in Washington (CREW) had been calling for an investigation since the Daily News broke the story a month prior.

"If the era of pay-to-play politics is over, Adolfo Carrión did not get the message," said Melanie Sloan, executive director of CREW.

Indeed, the Boricua College scandal was not an isolated incident. In 2008, Jonathan Coren, a first-time fundraiser, raised $2,577 from several donors in a matter of a few weeks. On March 26, Carrión approved Coren's company Idle LLC's plan to build 166 affordable housing units in the Parkchester area. After a few weeks, he raised an additional $1,255 and a month later the Planning Commission approved the project. Total donations from the 43 donors that Coren solicited exceed $6,500.

Jackson Development Group was working to build affordable housing on the site of an old brewery when the project stalled. Three years later, company employees made 41 donations to Carrión that totaled $35,650 in November 2007. The following spring, the project was granted approval and the borough president announced that he would sponsor $3 million in public funds. Around the same time, Ader Group owner Israel Neiman donated $4,950 to Carrión and received $1 million in taxpayer funds to finance 177 low-income rentals. BTM Development Partners, a subsidiary of Related Companies, sought zoning changes, permit approval, and height restriction modifications for the Gateway mall project, so Related executives sent $5,000 in donations. They quickly gained the necessary approvals.

Yet the most generous donor is Tri-Line Contracting, Inc. owner Jose Velazquez who has raised $83,700 for Carrión and in turn worked on two of the largest projects that Carrión advocated. Along with his company's work on a Staples store at Gateway, Velazquez also has his hands in the new Yankee Stadium[7], a Carrión cause that is controversial in its own right.

In 2006, A Bronx community board voted against the billion-dollar construction of the new stadium because of the loss of the two neighborhood parks it was built on. Shortly after, Carrión replaced or demoted several members of the board[8].

"The needs of the (Yankee) organization was put ahead of the needs of the people, notwithstanding the Bronx businesses that may or may not have a shot at Yankee money," said City Councilwoman Helen Foster.

The Gateway project has also angered Bronx residents due to increased traffic and the displacement of over twenty ethnic food merchants and produce wholesalers who occupied the former Bronx Terminal Market.

"Carrión acted in such a perverse manner to really go out of his way to thwart community and small-business concerns," said Richard Lipsky, a city planner who lobbied for the ousted merchants[9].

Carrión critics also note the former borough president's failure to deliver on planned projects to better the neighborhood. In 2003, he promised to build three ice rinks that never materialized. Though job creation in urban areas will be one of his chief concerns in his new czar position, Carrión's job-hunting website has shut down and the Bronx's unemployment rate is the highest in New York City. Last year, the borough also boasted the second highest number of homicides, although it has the second smallest population. At best, Carrión could be called ineffectual. But his tendency to allot taxpayer money to finance his generous supporters' projects is disconcerting as his new post will have him overseeing how federal money is spent on urban areas.

In fact, the five presidents of the New York City boroughs have spent over $450 million in taxpayer funds in the past two years. Of the $466 million that the presidents controlled, $406 was spent on pet projects. Carrión employed an architect for $64,000 per year and a full-time chauffeur[10]. Michelle Malkin calls him a "lavish spender - squandering nearly $20,000 on a teleprompter, junkets to San Juan, and $50,000 on a going away party for himself."[11]

The party was in celebration of Carrión's appointment to the Urban Czar position and financed by campaign funds raised while he was running for city comptroller, a race from which he dropped out upon receiving his presidential assignment[12].

The Power To Shower Federal Dollars

Substantial news accounts of Carrión's rather shady political dealings render him a bit of a pariah of the New York media, yet he was still appointed without the approval of congress to this powerful new position in the United States government. As Malkin writes, "Obama gave Carrión the unprecedented power to shower federal dollars on urban areas and coordinate urban policy across several bureaucracies. In practice, the job empowers Carrión to carry out the kind of pay-to-play schemes that sullied his tenure in the Bronx on a nationwide scale."

This appointment affords a great deal of authority to someone who is known for abusing taxpayer dollars and getting arrested during a protest against U.S. government policies alongside Rev. Al Sharpton[13].

— *Lucy Leitner*

---

[1] Carrion off the Washington? Some Hope Not," *Gotham Gazette*, Dec. 11, 2008
[2] *Sharpton and 3 From Bronx Are Jailed in Vieques Protest* by Eric Lipton, *New York Times*, May 24, 2001
[3] *Carrion Says He's Tapping Into Obama's Network* by Azi Paybarah, New York Observer, June 9, 2008
[4] Buettner, Russ. "Bronx Prosecutors Checking on Work Done for Ex-Borough President." The New York Times, March 12, 2009: p. 23.

[5] Smith, Greg B. "Watchdog Group Calls for Investigation of Adolfo Carrión, Bronx Pres. Tapped as Obama's Urban Czar." New York Daily News, March 12, 2009:

[6] Gearty, Robert and Greg B. Smith. "Carrion Home Repairs Eyed. Ex-Beep's Architect Had Business With the Borough." New York Daily News, March 10, 2009: 10.

[7] Lesser, Benjamin and Greg B. Smith. "Buildings Sprang Up as Donations Rained Down on Bronx Pres. Adolfo Carrión, Obama's New Urban Czar, Got Campaign Cash From Developers He Helped." New York Daily News, March 1, 2009: p. 8.

[8] Fitzgerald, Jim. "Obama's Pick for Urban Affairs Has Fans, Foes." The Associated Press, August 25, 2009.

[9] Goldsmith, Samuel and Bill Hutchinson. "White House Mum as Foes Rip Carrión." New York Daily News, March 2, 2009: p. 15.

[10] Moore, Tina, Erin Einhorn, and Benjamin Lesser. "What the Beep? Pols Dish Out 450M! Borough Presidents Spend Our Tax Bucks But We Get Little Back." New York Daily News

[11] Malkin, Michelle. Culture of Corruption: Czars of the Obama Underworld [Internet]. Michelle Malkin LLC. July 26, 2009 [cited August 26, 2009]. Available from: http://michellemalkin.com/2009/07/26/culture-of-corruption-czars-of-the-obama-underworld/.

[12] Seifman, David. "Carrión Spent Campaign $$ for 'Parting' Party." NY Post.com. April 5, 2009: August 25, 2009 <http://www.nypost.com/seven/04052009/news/regionalnews/carrion_spent_campaign_for_parting_part_162971.htm>.

Violence Against Women Czar — Lynn Rosenthal

Official title:	White House Advisor on Violence Against Women
Salary / Direct cost to taxpayers:	Unknown
Responsibilities:	advise the President and Vice President on domestic violence and sexual assault issues
Reports to:	President Obama and Vice President Biden
Senate confirmation:	No
Relation to Obama:	Unknown; association primarily with Vice President Biden through Violence Against Women Act and other Domestic Violence legislation
Ideology / political affiliation:	Ultra-Feminist

On June 26, 2009 Vice President Biden announced that Lynn Rosenthal was appointed to a newly created position at the White House as the Advisor on Violence Against Women. The White House describes the position as being "dedicated specifically to advising the President and Vice President on domestic violence and sexual assault issues."[1] *However, many question yet another government expansion, as well as the usefulness, and given Rosenthals background and public statements, the politicization of the policy and programs from which the position was created.* Even *US News and World Report* criticized the new position citing Obama's czar list as "endless."[2]

Ultra Left Anti-Father's Rights Hardliner

Though Rosenthal is technically qualified for the position, serving as the Executive Director of the National Network to End Domestic Violence (NNEDV) from 2000-2006, and is thus considered an expert in the area of domestic violence policy, *the fact that Rosenthal is praised most by ultra left, feminist organizations and is anti-father's rights (and thus children's rights) is alarming.*

The Obama Administration's clear quest for power is seen time and time again with the vast number of czars he has appointed, and has yet to appoint. With regard to the Violence Against Women Czar, one can ask why the need for this position now? The Senate passed the Violence Against Women Act in 1994, and President George W. Bush signed an extension to the act in 2006. According to Fox News "the extension included new provisions on health care, early intervention and outreach to American Indian women."[3] But the Obama Administration apparently didn't see this as enough government control, so they created the new czar position.

The Violence Against Women Act (VAWA), however, in and of itself is very contentious. One questionable component to the VAWA is the fact that it was authored by then-Senator Joe Biden, and radical feminist group, Feminist Majority, "played a major role in the passage of VAWA and its reauthorization."[4] According to the Feminist Majority's website, their platform is in lockstep with the Obama Administration's far-left agenda. The stated platform of the organization, also citing their alignment with the Obama Administration is further evidence of just how radical the Obama Administration is.

Glenn Sacks, the Executive Director of Fathers & Families, says the VAWA and general government domestic violence policies have been shaped in part by Rosenthal's group, the NNEDV, and represents state domestic violence coalitions & allied organizations. Sacks said there are many problems with these policies in terms of violating civil liberties, victimizing innocent men, and--worst of all--forcibly separating decent, loving fathers from their children. Sacks says he has received thousands of letters from men in these situations. In his article in the *New York Daily News*, Sacks and co-author Mike McCormick, the Executive Director of the American Coalition for Fathers and Children write, "[The] VAWA has helped provide an easy avenue for disgruntled women to kick decent, loving fathers out of their homes and exclude them from their children's lives via restraining (aka "protection") orders. In the wake of VAWA, there has been an explosion of such orders. When a restraining order is issued, the man is booted out of his own home and can be jailed if he tries to contact his own children, even though he has never been afforded the opportunity to defend himself in court. The hearings held two weeks later to make the orders permanent are often just a formality for which no more than 15 minutes are generally allotted."[5] Overall, Rosenthal's agenda which is demonstrated in VAWA "has greatly weakened the institution of fatherhood, and has harmed fathers and the children who love them and need them."[6] More evidence is found displaying Rosenthal's anti-father's rights, divisive ideology. In an article dated April 7, 2002 from the leftist group "The American Prospect", Cara Feinberg wrote with regard to an interview with Rosenthal "...Rosenthal remains worried about the potential for an 'unholy merger' between social conservatives and the growing movement for fathers' rights. Though she respects much of the work that fathers' rights groups have done in calling for more paternal responsibility and accountability, she fears that some men will latch on to the claims of right-wingers who resent gains by the battered-women's movement -- and by the feminist movement generally -- and will seek to cripple these movements' effectiveness by demanding their defunding."[7] Per her own remarks, Rosenthal's feminist agenda aims solely to aid in the façade of helping abused women while leaving the real problems unresolved and disregarding real victims.

There is also a sex-discrimination factor to Rosenthal's new czar position, as well as to the VAWA. Why does the position and the policy only aim to help abused women when there is also a significant problem for abused men? In an article entitled "Biden Selection is Bad News for America's Fathers", Glenn Sacks and co-author Mike McCormick implicate the need for men to be included in the domestic violence policy: "Greg Schmidt, who created the Seattle Police Department's domestic violence investigation unit in 1994, says that mandatory/presumptive arrest laws force police officers to make arrests 'in petty incidents, often where the abuse is mutual or it is unclear who the aggressor was.' When mandatory arrest laws were first passed, they led to a

sharp increase in the number of women arrested. This reflects
what DV [domestic violence] research has long showed: women
are as likely to initiate and engage in DV against their male
partners as vice versa, and women use weapons and the element
of surprise to partially balance the scales. In response, the VAWA-
funded DV establishment promoted the primary aggressor
doctrine. Under this doctrine, when police officers respond to a
domestic disturbance call, they are instructed not to focus on who
attacked whom and who inflicted the injuries. Instead, they are
compelled to employ factors such as comparable size and
strength, which will almost always weigh against men."[8]

Domestic Violence Committed by Women is Ignored

In another of Sack's articles, "No One Believed Me," which
appeared on MSN.com, Sacks notes, "Domestic violence
committed by women against men is generally ignored or
minimized, yet more than 200 studies have found that women
initiate at least as much domestic violence (DV) against their male
partners as males initiate against their female partners. Research
shows that men comprise about a third of DV injuries and deaths.
Women often compensate for their lack of physical strength by
employing weapons and the element of surprise... just as recently
murdered former NFL star Steve McNair's girlfriend allegedly
did." The article continues, "Many of the world's leading
authorities on domestic violence recently gathered at the 'From
Ideology to Inclusion 2009' conference in Los Angeles and
detailed new research contradicting this view and offering
solutions that will benefit all. Researchers emphasized their
findings that ignoring female-perpetrated DV puts children, men,
and also women in harm's way. The conference was presented by
the California Alliance for Families & Children and co-sponsored
by the Family Violence Treatment & Education Association. DV
researcher Deborah Capaldi, Ph.D., a social scientist at the Oregon
Social Learning Center, told the conference that the most
dangerous DV scenario for women is that of reciprocal violence,
particularly if that violence is initiated by women. The best way

for many women to be safe is to not initiate violence against their male partners. 'The question of initiation of violence is a crucial one ... much DV is [reciprocated], and initiations -- even that seem minor -- may lead to escalation,' she explained. Dr. Capaldi's research shows that whereas men are often thought of as the only abusers and also as serial abusers, a young woman's DV is just as predictive of her male partner's future DV as the man's own past DV. While Rosenthal and numerous others have created many programs and services to help abused women, there are very few services available to abused men. Those who seek help often face hostility or indifference from domestic violence hotlines, service providers, and law enforcement."[9]

Denise Hines, Ph.D., of Clark University in Worcester, Massachusetts, has studied the abuse of men in traditional relationships. Sack's article cites, "In Hines's study of male victims of domestic violence, 64 percent of the men who called a DV hotline were told that they 'only helped women,' and over half were referred to programs for male perpetrators. Overall, only 8 percent of the men who called hotlines classified them as 'very helpful,' whereas 69 percent found them to be 'not at all helpful.' Worse, when an abused man called the police, the police were more likely to arrest him than to arrest his abusive female partner."[10]

False Statistics Justify An Unnecessary Position

Rosenthal's new position is also considered dubious by domestic violence writer Trudy Schuett. In an article in *The Examiner*, Schuett implies that the position is unnecessary as there is "no evidence" to back up their statistics and that the claims are made to "keep funding rolling into existing programs."[11] Schuett states that Rosenthal is "no advocate for women, rather she is only an advocate for the feminist political viewpoint regarding the issue."[12] Schuett says Rosenthal's background confirms this statement as she supported Biden's creation of the Violence Against Women Act which established "an incorrect perception of a human problem, and codifying it into law as a political and gender issue, while also establishing a special victim class in society… Had the needs of women been considered at the time, rather than the goals of the feminist political lobby, a far more equitable and effective law may have been the result; if in fact government intervention would have been recognized as advantageous at all." Schuett says that improvement is certainly needed, but that "there can be little hope of that with a feminist political operative at the helm."[13]

– Angie Wheeler

[1]Press Release, Office of the Vice President, June 26, 2009 - http://www.whitehouse.gov/the_press_office/Vice-President-Biden-Announces-Appointment-of-White-House-Advisor-on-Violence-Against-Women/
[2]*US News and World Report,* "Obama's Endless Czar List Now Includes a Domestic Violence Aide" by Bonnie Erbe, June 29, 2009 - http://www.usnews.com/blogs/erbe/2009/06/29/obamas-endless-czar-list-now-includes-a-domestic-violence-aide.html
[3]Fox News, "Obama Appoints Adviser on Domestic Violence", June 26, 2009 - http://www.foxnews.com/politics/2009/06/26/obama-appoints-adviser-domestic-violence/
[4]Feminist Daily News Wire, "White House Advisor on Violence Against Women Appointed", June 29, 2009 - http://feministmajority.org/news/index.asp?id=11783
[5]*New York Daily News,* "Biden Selection is Bad News for America's Fathers" by Glenn Sacks and Mike McCormick, August 27, 2008.
[6]*New York Daily News,* "Biden Selection is Bad News for America's Fathers" by Glenn Sacks and Mike McCormick, August 27, 2008.
[7]The American Prospect, "Hitting Home" by Cara Feinberg, April 7, 2002 - http://www.prospect.org/cs/articles?article=hitting_home
[8]*New York Daily News,* "Biden Selection is Bad News for America's Fathers" by Glenn Sacks and Mike McCormick, August 27, 2008.
[9]MSN.com, "No One Believed Me," by Glenn Sacks and Ned Holstein, August 1, 2009 -- http://lifestyle.msn.com/your-life/bigger-picture/article.aspx?cp-documentid=20968901&page=0

[10]MSN.com, "No One Believed Me," by Glenn Sacks and Ned Holstein, August 1, 2009 -- http://lifestyle.msn.com/your-life/bigger-picture/article.aspx?cp-documentid=20968901&page=0

[11]*Examiner*, "Lynn Rosenthal Is No Advocate For Women" by Trudy Schuett, July 4, 2009 - http://www.examiner.com/examiner/x-12866-Domestic-Violence-Examiner~y2009m7d4-Lynn-Rosenthal-is-no-advocate-for-women

[12]*Examiner*, "Lynn Rosenthal Is No Advocate For Women" by Trudy Schuett, July 4, 2009 - http://www.examiner.com/examiner/x-12866-Domestic-Violence-Examiner~y2009m7d4-Lynn-Rosenthal-is-no-advocate-for-women

[13]*Examiner*, "Lynn Rosenthal Is No Advocate For Women" by Trudy Schuett, July 4, 2009 - http://www.examiner.com/examiner/x-12866-Domestic-Violence-Examiner~y2009m7d4-Lynn-Rosenthal-is-no-advocate-for-women

War Czar -- Douglas Lute

Official title:	Deputy National Security Adviser for Iraq and Afghanistan
Official responsibilities:	Oversee war policy and implementation in Iraq and Afghanistan
Reports to:	National Security Adviser
Senate confirmation:	Yes
Salary:	Information unavailable
Ideology / political affiliation:	Bush appointee, retained by Obama

Amid the sea of new czars, Lieutenant General Douglas Lute is a rare holdover from the Bush administration. Bush created the position of war czar to oversee the wars in Iraq and Afghanistan, giving Lute the ability to direct the Pentagon, the State Department, and any other agencies that may find themselves involved with the situation. When the job was created, many Democrats took issue, saying that the National Security Advisor should be handling such tasks, but that was before Obama arrived to kickoff the czar craze in the Democratic Party.[1] Lute is widely respected, but was not a very big name when he was appointed, and was only given the job after several higher profile retired generals turned it down.[2] There was some worry that a relatively unknown three-star general would be able to be successful as the coordinator of a war effort given all the four-star generals and cabinet members that were already involved.[3] Some commentators doubted he would even last through the end of the Bush administration.[4] Yet he has weathered the storm and Obama has kept him on in his czar capacity.

Said to focus on "policy and implementation," the position was created in an attempt to make stronger connections between the military and other government agencies. Lute is intended to deal with all the Washington bureaucracy so other key players in the region like ambassadors and General David Petraeus do not have to.[5] He essentially functions as an intermediary, someone with a military background who is working in Washington that can focus all his efforts on making sure the military and the other agencies are on the same page.

General James L. Jones, Obama's National Security Advisor, and Lute's immediate supervisor, elected to keep Lute at his post because he felt that it would be advantageous to maintain a level of continuity in military policy and leadership despite the change in administration. Jones also said that elements of Lute's recent review of Afghanistan policy for President Bush, may be retained and used in this administration.[6] Additionally, Obama recently named Lute's wife, Jane, as a new Deputy Secretary of Homeland Security.[7]

---

[1] Helene Cooper, "War Czar for Bush to Keep His Job," 13 January 2009, The Caucus: The Politics and Government Blog of The Times, <http://thecaucus.blogs.nytimes.com/2009/01/13/war-czar-for-bush-to-keep-his-job/>

[2] Martha Raddatz, "Bush Taps New 'War Car,'" 15 May 2007, ABCnews.com, <http://abcnews.go.com/US/story?id=3176644&page=1>

[3] Jim Mannion, "Bush picks general as war czar,'" 16 May 2007, News.com.au, <http://www.news.com.au/story/0,23599,21740520-1702,00.html>

[4] "Douglas Lute," Source Watch, <http://www.sourcewatch.org/index.php?title=Douglas_Lute#Question_of_effectiveness>

[5] Jim Mannion, "Bush picks general as war czar,'" 16 May 2007, News.com.au, <http://www.news.com.au/story/0,23599,21740520-1702,00.html>

[6] Helene Cooper, "War Czar for Bush to Keep His Job," 13 January 2009, The Caucus: The Politics and Government Blog of The Times, <http://thecaucus.blogs.nytimes.com/2009/01/13/war-czar-for-bush-to-keep-his-job/>

[7] "Jane Lute," Who Runs GOV, <http://www.whorunsgov.com/Profiles/Jane_Lute>

California Water Czar–David J. Hayes

Official title:	Deputy Secretary of the Interior
Official responsibilities:	Coordinate federal agencies to alleviate California's water shortage[1]
Reports to:	Secretary of the Interior Ken Salazar
Senate confirmation:	Yes
Salary:	Information Unavailable
Ideology / political affiliation:	Convenient environmentalist, partisan Democrat

Who Is the California Water Czar?

Like so many other appointees in the administration of change, Deputy Secretary of the Interior David J. Hayes will launch America into the future by doing the same job he did more than a decade ago in the Clinton administration. Most of his non-government is related to the environment, as he is a senior fellow at the World Wildlife Federation, and recently taught at Stanford University's Woods Institute for the Environment.[2] He was also a lawyer and lobbyist, and worked on Obama's transition team. Secretary of the Interior Ken Salazar has tasked Hayes to "bring all of the key agencies to the table" to solve the California water shortage.[3]

A Conflict of Interest

Hayes has a long and questionable history when it comes to California water. During Hayes' confirmation, Senator John McCain questioned him regarding his time as a lobbyist, during which he represented the Southern California Metropolitan Water District after negotiating an agreement with them during his first stint as deputy secretary of the Interior.[4] This certainly seems to suggest a conflict of interest already existing back in 2001, and put up a red flag about him even returning to his general job in the department of the Interior. Naturally, it did not dissuade the Obama administration from putting him in charge of the same exact issue, which he has both regulated and lobbied for, as if his previous conflict of interest somehow makes him the most qualified expert on the subject.[5]

Shifty Environmentalism

While almost all of his private sector work has "environment" or "wildlife" in the title, his record is far from pristine. From 2005-2007 he represented the Ford Motor Company in a case stemming from Ford's dumping of toxic waste in a largely Native American community in Ringwood, New Jersey. Hayes pushed for the Ringwood community to pay for the clean up.[6] For an environmentalist, this seems to be a questionable side to take. And it is not the only instance of such behavior from Hayes. During his confirmation hearing, Senator Robert Bennett grilled Hayes about 77 oil and gas lease sales in Utah, which Hayes said Interior Department agencies had not coordinated. Bennett produced evidence against this, and while Hayes sent a letter to Bennett attempting to explain, Bennett was never satisfied, and did not believe Hayes was giving him straight answers.[7] In 1989, he represented the Chemical Manufacturer's Union to oppose President George H. W. Bush's list of carcinogens, attempting to cripple the report by causing the list to be drastically abbreviated, once again siding with big business over the health of humans.[8]

Attacks on Republicans

While at the Progressive Policy institute in 2006, Hayes wrote an article in which he stated that "Like Ronald Reagan before him, President [George W.] Bush has embraced the Western stereotype to the point of adopting some of its affectations — the boots, brush-clearing, and get-the-government-off-our-backs bravado." When John McCain made him answer for this statement during his confirmation hearing, Hayes admitted that his comments were inappropriate, yet never suggested that he did not believe in them.[9] He has also accused Bush of leaving a "damaging legacy" regarding the management of natural resources.[10] He claimed that the administration ignored alternative-energy development and took backward steps in the field from the Clinton administration. This all in spite of the fact that as part of the Clinton administration he supported oil and gas exploration on U.S. Public lands. Yet he continues to attack Conservatives. He even criticized Bush for using a Washington-based governing system, which he called "out of step" with other Western leaders.[11]

---

[1] "List of Obama's Czars." Premiere Radio Networks, Inc. Aug. 21, 2009. Apr. 8, 2010
<http://www.glennbeck.com/content/articles/article/198/29391/>.
[2] "Working Group Members," Change.gov The Office of The President-Elect,
<http://change.gov/learn/working_group_members>
[3] "Ken Salazar Assigns Deputy As Calif. Water Czar," Jun. 28, 2009. CBS 2 KCAL 9,
<http://cbs2.com/local/Ken.Salazar.Deputy.2.1063489.html>
[4] "David Hayes," Who Runs GOV,
<http://www.whorunsgov.com/Profiles/David_Hayes>
[5] "Recommending Himself? David Hayes as Secretary of the Interior?" Dec. 13, 2008. Daily Kos,
<http://www.dailykos.com/story/2008/12/14/22835/880>
[6] Ibid.
[7] "David Hayes," Who Runs GOV,
<http://www.whorunsgov.com/Profiles/David_Hayes>
[8] "Recommending Himself? David Hayes as Secretary of the Interior?" Dec. 13, 2008. Daily Kos,
<http://www.dailykos.com/story/2008/12/14/22835/880>
[9] "David Hayes," Who Runs GOV,
<http://www.whorunsgov.com/Profiles/David_Hayes>
[10] "List of Obama's Czars," 21 August 2009. Glenn Beck.com,
<http://www.glennbeck.com/content/articles/article/198/29391/>
[11] 11 "David Hayes," Who Runs GOV,
<http://www.whorunsgov.com/Profiles/David_Hayes>

Weapons Czar — Ashton Carter

Official title:	Under Secretary of Defense for Acquisition, Technology, and Logistics
Official responsibilities:	Work to ensure that the communications field is competitive and generates widespread opportunities for women, minorities
Reports to:	Defense Secretary Robert Gates
Senate confirmation:	Yes
Salary:	$
Ideology / political affiliation:	Left-wing academic dilettante

Who Is He?

Ashton Carter is a physicist by training and an academic who was chair of Harvard's International Relations, Science, and Security program. He served as assistant secretary of defense for international security policy (1993 to 1996), and he has donated primarily to Democratic politicians since 2000. He donated $6,900 in 2007 and 2008 to then New York Democratic Sen. Hillary Rodham Clinton. He gave the same amount to then Sen. Barack Obama, Democrat from Illinois, during that same span. President Obama appointed him to the extraordinarily powerful post of under secretary of defense for acquisition, technology, and logistics.

Carter graduated from Yale University and then went to Oxford University as a Rhodes scholar and earned a doctorate in theoretical physics. He has been closely associated with former Defense Secretary William Perry throughout most of his career and played an instrumental role in managing the evisceration of dual-use export controls while facilitating advanced militarily useful technology to the People's Republic of China and other potential adversaries.

Appointment That Is Ironic to Say the Least

Ashton Carter is a charter member of a long-running cabal that for years worked tirelessly to undermine and neutralize the U.S. and international export control system that was designed to protect our military's technological superiority against a range of potential foreign adversaries. Obama has now appointed this guy to a position responsible for determining what weapons systems the U.S. military should procure in anticipating an uncertain future—an uncertain future that he had a hand in creating.

Some might say that he is the incarnation of the dark side of the military/industrial complex that President Dwight Eisenhower warned us about so many years ago. After all, by subverting the export control systems that served the United States so well for decades, Carter greatly advanced the military capabilities of scores of nations that are current or likely future military rivals/adversaries of the United States. Now this Clinton administration retread, like a snake oil salesman, is in a position to sell us the cure for a disease that he was instrumental in spreading. He recently held a lucrative job as a consultant to Goldman, Sachs, an investment house that bankrolls much of the defense contracting sector. These folks are more influential than your run-of-the-mill lobbyists. In addition, his academic and public careers to date in no way qualify him to sit in judgment on issues of weapons system development, tactical and strategic requirements, or weapons prioritization or procurement. During his previous political appointment by Clinton as assistant secretary of defense for international security policy, he managed to alienate and earn the enmity of many military and civilian officials in the Pentagon while building a reputation for being shallow, arrogant, untrustworthy, and anti-military and for answering to an external community ideologically opposed to many aspects of the Defense Department's mission.

The arrogance and untrustworthiness surfaced shortly after Carter was appointed by Clinton and awaiting confirmation by the Senate. In taking up the Pentagon post prior to confirmation, he promised Congress that he would not involve himself in decision-making or the appearance of decision-making and was only to begin to receive background briefings for his future job. Instead, Carter was accused of signing or initialing off on two procurement actions in violation of his promises, government ethics codes, and the law. Others similarly caught acting in this manner were forced to resign and forgo public service — such as Harvard's Graham Allison — but it was said that Perry was able to protect Carter from a similar fate.

Carter's Ideological and Intellectual Cabal

The political wagon that Carter is associated with is driven by Perry. In addition to being a former defense secretary, Perry is long-term friend of the People's Republic of China and one of the leading architects of the proliferation of advanced conventional and nonconventional military technology through the successful evisceration of governmental safeguards for preventing the reckless transfer of militarily sensitive dual-use technologies around the world. This group of people also forced the Defense Department to abandon a large part of its Milspec (Military Specification) standards in manufacturing and procurement and instead buy Commercial Off The Shelf (COTS) technology on the commercial market, citing cost savings as the primary driver of this massive policy change. The most tragic impact has been on U.S. technological superiority and survivability as these moves destroyed much of the uniqueness that went into our weapons systems and created a situation where many of our key parts and components are purchased from manufacturers in such quality-free Meccas as Red China. Many in the Pentagon during the dark days of Jimmy Carter were shocked when Perry narrowly escaped indictment after many of his direct subordinates were arrested in a bribery/gratuity-taking scandal involving some large Pentagon contractors and free trips to hunting cabins in the Carolinas. What a role model!

Sometimes Government Conspiracies Actually Exist

The author had the unique experience of having the export decontrol operation explained to him by one of the principal participants. The key players in this tragedy were William Perry, Ashton Carter, Mitchell Wallerstein, and Lawrence E. McCray —

all of whom were associated with the National Academy of Sciences, MIT, and Harvard. The NAS ran a years-long propaganda effort entitled Finding Common Ground, an amusing cover name for a program to eliminate export controls. The arrival of the Clinton administration created the perfect opportunity for the anti-export-control crowd to infiltrate the Pentagon with the express purpose of using political appointments to neutralize the Defense Department's role in the interagency and international process.

At his own confirmation hearing for the position of deputy secretary of defense, William Perry, who would, of course, later become secretary of defense, declared that controlling dual-use technology was a "hopeless task." Control, he said, "only interferes with a company's ability to succeed internationally." This put Perry, a former electronics executive, in direct conflict with the U.N. inspectors then in Iraq who were reporting that without strict maintenance of export controls, Saddam Hussein would soon reconstitute his mass-destruction war machine.[1]

Whether Perry realized it or not, virtually every part of a nuclear weapon is made with dual-use equipment. Iraq, in fact, had already imported dual-use "isostatic" presses to shape nuclear-bomb parts, dual-use mass spectrometers to sample bomb fuel, and dual-use electron-beam welders to increase the range of its Scud missiles. During the Gulf War, one of these increased-range Iraqi Scuds had killed a group of U.S. soldiers in their barracks in Saudi Arabia, prompting a Pentagon official to remark that "when you talk about export controls, you're not talking about politics; you're talking about body bags."

Unbeknownst to voters, or even to most policy experts, the new administration came to Washington in January 1993 with a coherent plan for gutting the entire export-control system, which it called a "wasting asset" left over from the Cold War. The plan was devised by Perry, Carter, and Wallerstein and published with little fanfare in 1992 by the National Academy of Sciences. Perry, Carter, and Wallerstein were appointed to the

Defense Department during the first weeks of the new Clinton administration and given responsibility for putting the plan into action.[2]

Key to their plan was the placement of Wallerstein into the role of deputy assistant secretary for counterproliferation. Wallerstein was the secretary of the Common Ground exercise and was very reluctant to take the Defense Department position because he felt threatened to be near the military. McCray and Carter twisted his arm sufficiently to persuade him to take the job, explaining to him that it was vital to their plan to neutralize the Pentagon as the Defense Technology Security Administration—the Defense Department's primary export controllers—would be directly under his control. Wallerstein managed to earn even more contempt from Pentagon staff than Carter, and he resigned after a couple of years in office.

Export control is a hoary topic, dating from the years immediately following World War II. In our efforts to rebuild Europe and fashion NATO as a barrier to Soviet expansionism, it became obvious that the West would inflict serious harm on itself if American goods and equipment were sold to the Soviets or the Chinese. There had to be a fence around the United States and its allies, one inside which trade could flourish but that would be strong enough to keep useful technology—especially of the military sort—away from rivals outside. The fence was COCOM, the Coordinating Committee for Multilateral Export Controls, born in 1949.[3]

COCOM was a phenomenal success. It did not stop everything from getting out, any more than the best police force can stop all crime. But by systematically helping to deprive the East of the West's technology, it left Russia and its allies in the dust. After the end of the Cold War, COCOM officials toured the former Warsaw Pact to measure the historical impact of controls. What they learned from former East-bloc officials was that equipment had sometimes been smuggled in, but spare parts and service had been impossible to obtain. This made it risky to build manufacturing operations around such equipment. Even today, more than a decade after the end of the Cold War, the dilapidated industrial infrastructure of Russia and Eastern Europe offers lingering testimony not only to the abysmal failures of socialist planning but to the power of export controls.[4]

Back in the '80s and early '90s, under the Reagan and (first) Bush administrations, the Defense Department had successfully battled attempts by the industry-friendly Commerce Department to dilute controls. Under Clinton and Perry, this institutional counterweight disappeared. As one disillusioned Pentagon staffer complained, "We now have four layers of bosses who don't believe in export controls." The bosses included Ashton Carter, Perry's assistant secretary, who actually proposed giving Pakistan the special electronic locks that make nuclear warheads safer, as well as supplying nuclear fuel to India, and Carter's own deputy, Wallerstein, who had directed studies decrying export controls for the National Academy of Sciences.[5]

With the Pentagon thus neutered, the Commerce Department was able to give exporters what they wanted. The two greatest beneficiaries were the American computer industry and the People's Republic of China. Before 1996, China had been denied virtually all access to high-performance computers. These computers can simulate the conditions inside an exploding nuclear warhead or the forces acting on a missile from launch to impact; they enable a country to build not only better missiles but also smaller, more powerful nuclear weapons without explosive testing. Between 1996 and the end of 1998, China succeeded in acquiring over 600 such high-performance computers from American companies, all with the approval of the Commerce Department.[6]

Carter: A Wholly Inappropriate Choice

Defense Secretary Robert Gates announced a fiscal 2010 budget plan that would drastically alter Pentagon priorities, shifting money away from expensive, elaborate weapons programs to ones better suited to today's unconventional warfare. Ashton Carter has virtually no experience in these matters, no demonstrable evidence of any inkling of either conventional or unconventional warfare material requirements or of weapons systems procurement issues. What he does possess is a long history of undermining our national defense and helping to create the military threats of tomorrow. One the other hand, who is better qualified to decide what weapons are needed to defend ourselves from our enemies than one of the guys most responsible for helping to arm them?

---

[1] Gary Milhollin, "Trading With the Enemy," *Commentary Magazine* (May 2002) http://www.iranwatch.org/ourpubs/articles/wponac-tradingwiththeenemy-0502.htm.

[2] Kenneth R. Timmerman, "Insight Symposium: Has Clinton's China Policy Put U.S. National Security at Risk?" (Nov. 6, 2000) http://www.freetrade.org/node/215.

[3] Gary Milhollin, "Trading With the Enemy," *Commentary Magazine* (May 2002) http://www.iranwatch.org/ourpubs/articles/wponac-tradingwiththeenemy-0502.htm.

[4] Ibid.

[5] Ibid.

[6] Ibid.

WMD Czar — Gary Samore

Official title:	Special Assistant to the President and White House Coordinator for Arms Control and Weapons of Mass Destruction, Proliferation, and Terrorism
Official responsibilities:	Oversees efforts to reduce existing nuclear arsenals, stop proliferation to additional countries and prevent terrorists and other non-state actors from acquiring nuclear weapons
Reports to:	Secretary of State
Senate confirmation:	None
Salary:	Information unavailable
Ideology / political affiliation:	Non-ideological pragmatist, generally works under Democrats

Obama Appoints Another Clinton Retread

Once again, Obama has appointed a new czar to address the same issues he already addressed in a more traditional position. WMD czar Gary Samore has a long history in the field as a State Department official, adviser to President Bill Clinton, and an expert at several top foreign policy think tanks. He has spent years as a nonproliferation treaty negotiator and is known to some in arms-control circles as a "non-ideological pragmatist."[1] However, to others he is forever tainted by the role he played in defending the Clinton administration's China policy. And as usual, he is being placed in a situation where there is no clear way to define short-term success. "The first thing the Obama administration needs to do is a very forceful statement of policy that nuclear disarmament remains the ultimate U.S. objective, even though it's not going to be achieved anytime soon."[2]

Samore Was Clinton's 'Designated Liar' on China

For someone who is being tasked to keep WMDs out of enemy hands, Samore has a major question mark on his résumé, and it concerns his pivotal role in assisting the Clinton administration cover up Chinese nuclear espionage and technology theft from the

United States. While serving as a key staffer on Clinton's National Security Council, Samore worked directly with the notorious Sandy Berger in attempting to downplay the importance of Wen Ho Lee's theft of U.S. nuclear secrets from Los Alamos National Laboratory. In fact, while Samore, senior director for nonproliferation on Clinton's National Security Council, didn't object to additional security at the labs, he emphasized that U.S.-Chinese scientific exchanges — where some of the espionage took place — would continue because that was administration policy.

Samore used the timeless methods of bureaucratic obfuscation, passing the buck, tasking endless agency reviews, denigrating security officials who uncovered the espionage, and whatever other delaying tactic he could possibly find to defuse the political danger to the White House. Samore proved that he is fully qualified to play the Washington role of "designated liar." When Samore testified before Congress and gave misleading information in the form of Washington doublespeak, he was fulfilling that role on behalf of Clinton and Berger. Unfortunately, this is a form of behavior played out in Washington on a daily basis and usually by officials bearing the title of press secretary, briefer, or sometimes president.

Even the *New York Times* Thought Samore Was a Liar

At the time, many U.S. officials asserted that the White House sought to minimize the espionage issue for policy reasons. "This conflicted with their China policy," said a U.S. official. "It undercut the administration's efforts to have a strategic partnership with the Chinese." The White House denied the assertions. "The idea that we tried to cover up or downplay these allegations to limit the damage to United States-Chinese relations is absolutely wrong," said Samore, who was then the senior National Security Council official who handled the issue.[3]

Yet a reconstruction by the *New York Times* revealed that throughout the government, the response to the nuclear theft was marked by delays, inaction, and skepticism — even though senior intelligence officials regarded it as one of the most damaging spy cases in recent history.[4]

Welcome to Samore's World

Samore has thrived in an atmosphere where fact and fiction are blurred; where individuals can no longer differentiate between where their own wisdom begins and where it ends; where analysts have difficulty discerning what is theirs, what they read, and what they believe; and where qualified judgments, unattributed sources, anonymous reports, and rampant plagiarism make one analyst's view just as valid as the next one's, and where arrogant, paternalistic attitudes develop. A belief that one's own "informed" views are right (despite the above limitations) in turn leads to the familiar litany for justifying official lies, such as "The average person is too unsophisticated to understand these issues." "The public doesn't want to know the truth; it can't handle it." "No one really cares about this obscure issue, so I have wide latitude to act." "I am an unsung hero." "It is for the greater good that I do this."[5] Most of these rationales are lurking in the various pronouncements and testimonies of Samore but are less unique to him than they are common to the atmosphere and culture of national security decision-making.

Korea

Another potential issue with Samore is that, like so many of Obama's czars, he seems to have been chosen for the job based largely on the fact that he handled similar duties under Bill Clinton. Of course, given that he has done this job before, many of the current problems can be traced back to his prior work. Samore helped negotiate the original U.S. nonproliferation agreement with North Korea, in which even he seems to have lost all faith.[6] He seems resigned to the fact that it will take a very long time to disarm North Korea. He is not willing to force the issue there, as he said, "I don't think we need to run the risk of precipitating a crisis with North Korea by threatening them. I think the North

Koreans are willing to play ball in exchange for food and heavy fuel oil and fertilizer and so forth but in a process that's going to be torturous .... We can't ignore North Korea because they'll make mischief. We can't coerce them and force them to give up their nuclear weapons. And the only alternative, I think, is a long-term disarmament process which will involve very painful, slow, incremental progress." In fact, he has such a lack of confidence in our ability to disarm North Korea that he seems to think the fastest way to do so would be to sit back and wait for the country to implode. In his words, "At some point, I think, the North Korean regime is likely to fade and collapse. So our game is to sort of manage this process until it eventually disappears."[7]

Iran

The other country that Samore will have to focus on, Iran, is a different story. Samore says that the Iran situation is very delicate and that the policy he wants to employ in North Korea would not work there. "A sweeter offer that isn't accompanied by a bigger threat will be seen in Iran as vindication of its current confrontational policies," Samore said at a 2007 talk. He believes Iran could be influenced with methods such as an arms embargo or a ban on investing in Iran's gas and oil industries.[8] While he hopes to avoid violence, he believes a firm stance must be taken. As he says, "We also want the Iranians to believe that if they actually try to make nuclear weapons, or if they build secret facilities that we detect, they run the risk of being attacked."[9]

— *Rick Rush*

---

[1] "Gary Samore," Who Runs GOV,
<http://www.whorunsgov.com/Profiles/Gary_Samore>
[2] "Nonpro Positions of WMD Coordinator Gary Samore," Nukes of Hazard,

<http://nukesofhazard.blogspot.com/2009/02/nonpro-positions-of-wmd-coordinator.html>

[3] James Risen & Jeff Gerth. "China Stole Nuclear Secrets From Los Alamos, U.S. Officials Say" *The New York Times* (March 6, 1999)

[4] Ibid.

[5] Peter M. Leitner and Ronald J. Stupak, "Ethical Dynamics and the National Security Process: Professionalism, Power, and Perversion" *Journal of Power and Ethics: An Interdisciplinary Review*, 1(1), 2000: pp. 2-22.

[6] "Gary Samore," Who Runs GOV, <http://www.whorunsgov.com/Profiles/Gary_Samore>

[7] "Nonpro Positions of WMD Coordinator Gary Samore," Nukes of Hazard, <http://nukesofhazard.blogspot.com/2009/02/nonpro-positions-of-wmd-coordinator.html>

[8] "Gary Samore," Who Runs GOV, <http://www.whorunsgov.com/Profiles/Gary_Samore>

[9]9 "Nonpro Positions of WMD Coordinator Gary Samore," Nukes of Hazard, <http://nukesofhazard.blogspot.com/2009/02/nonpro-positions-of-wmd-coordinator.html>

About the Editors

Scott Wheeler

Scott Wheeler, the Executive Director of the National Republican Trust PAC, is a former television producer and investigative journalist. As a writer he has focused on domestic and international security issues. Mr. Wheeler has produced seventeen television documentaries and consulted on more than a dozen others. For the past eight years Mr. Wheeler has been on the forefront of the most crucial issues facing national security – from the war zones in Yugoslavia, to the drug fields of South America and following the trails of international arms smugglers to Canada, Europe and the Middle East. Mr. Wheeler is a veteran of the U.S. Army infantry.

Peter Leitner

Dr. Leitner, former Treasurer of the National Republican Trust, previously worked in the Office of the Secretary of Defense starting with Casper Weinberger up until his retirement under current secretary Robert Gates. He was also a founding professor at the National Center for Bio-defense at George Mason University in Fairfax, Va. Dr. Leitner brings 31 years of experience as a high ranking federal official in a number of national security positions, particularly in the field of technology controls, nonproliferation, bio-defense and counterterrorism. He has testified before the U.S. Congress numerous times and holds a doctorate from the University of Southern California and four master's degrees.